NEW HISTORICAL PERSPECTIVES ON MIGRATION

Series Editors

Crispin Bates and Marina Carter

Voices from Indenture

Voices from Indenture

Experiences of Indian Migrants in the British Empire

MARINA CARTER

LEICESTER UNIVERSITY PRESS
London and New York

DT
469
.M445
E2734
1996

First published 1996 by
Leicester University Press, *A Cassell imprint*
Wellington House, 125 Strand, London WC2R 0BB, England
127 West 24th Street, New York, New York 10011, USA

© Marina Carter 1996

All rights reserved. No part of this publication may be reproduced or transmitted in any form or by any means, electronic or mechanical, including photocopy, recording or any information storage or retrieval system, without permisssion in writing from the Publishers or their appointed agents.

British Library Cataloguing in Publication Data
Carter, Marina
  Voices from indenture : experiences of Indian migrants in
  the British Empire. – (New historical perspectives on
  migration)
  1. Indentured servants – Great Britain – Colonies 2. India –
  Emigration and immigration 3. Great Britain – Colonies –
  Emigration and immigration 4. Great Britain – Colonies –
  Asia
  I. Title
  325.2'54

Library of Congress Cataloging-in-Publication Data
Carter, Marina.
  Voices from indenture : experiences of Indian migrants in the
  British empire / Marina Carter.
      p.   cm.—(New historical perspectives on migration)
  Includes bibliographical references (p.   ) and index.
  ISBN 0-7185-0031-8
    1. East Indians—Mauritius—History—19th century. 2. Indentured
  servants—Mauritius—History—19th century. 3. Mauritius—
  Emigration and immigration—History—19th century. 4. India—
  Emigration and immigration—History—19th century. I. Title.
  II. Series.
  DT469.M445E2734 1996
  306.3'63'0899141106982—dc20   95–43296
                                                          CIP

Printed and bound in Great Britain by Biddles Limited, Guildford and King's Lynn

33 94 8741

For Luce and Lalita,
who helped me a lot.

Contents

Foreword

The intention of this series is to address the unprecedented mass migrations of the nineteenth and early twentieth centuries that followed in the wake of European imperialism and the globalization of the world economy. The volumes to be published in the series will all assume novel approaches – looking at new types of source or less well-known or previously unresearched labour movements, or adopting new perspectives and methodologies which, for example, cut across the interpretative divide that has often separated white and non-white forms of labour migration. Whilst being rooted in historical problematics, the series will further seek to encourage methods of interpretation which are cross-disciplinary, and which help break down the barriers between historical, sociological, literary and political modes of analysis.

Research into European migrations, and migrations to the New World, has of course long been well established. Global diasporas have impacted hugely upon the making of modern European and American societies, and it is these movements and these societies that have inevitably attracted the most attention. Voluntary and involuntary diasporas elsewhere in the world have by comparison been relatively understudied. In the United States a particular concern has been the slave migrations of the eighteenth and nineteenth centuries, but reference is made to this phenomenon largely in the context of early American social history or Afro-American studies. The lack of a wider comparative literature on non-European migrations has often been lamented. At the same time, interest in non-European labour migrations and diasporas as a field of studies in its own right has been growing for several years, in recognition of the fact that the movements of peoples within Asia, within Africa, or between Asia and Africa were a product of the same global forces and had an important impact on just as many people's lives as the movements of peoples that helped populate Europe and North America.

The emphasis in this series is thus on movements of people that have been little researched and written about in the past. This means that by preference and of necessity the emphasis will be primarily on the non-western, non-European world and on those who have been described as 'the people without history', or in terms of empowerment (and their lack of it) the 'subaltern classes' of the colonial world. Consequently the focus will be primarily on Africa, South Asia, the Indian Ocean, South-East Asia, East Asia, the Pacific rim and also the Caribbean and Latin America. It is worth recollecting of course that not all subalterns are necessarily African or Asian by descent, and that peoples such as the white convict population of Australia were also at one time a subordinated group, whose history was for long neglected, as were the migrant European populations that helped constitute the present-day societies of Latin America. We do not propose to adopt divisive racist practices in the development of this series. We do, however, intend that all of its volumes should both address neglected fields and offer a non-traditional approach to their subject, and hence represent a departure from the currently available historiography. Above all, it is intended that contributions to the series will describe not only the structure and conditions of these migrations, but the genius of individual migrants, and the variety of ways in which migrants reproduced or reinvented their cultures, adapted and resisted, or otherwise turned their new-found circumstances to their advantage. The emphasis in this endeavour will thus be on primary sources and wherever possible on making use of articulations of those experiences issuing from the migrants themselves.

We hope that the series will have a broad impact and application, and will be of interest not only to scholars of African and Asian history but also to historians and social scientists who teach courses on migrations and diasporas in Europe and the United States. As well as being of interest to those studying labour history, migration, ethnicity and colonial topics generally, it is further hoped that the series will inform the lives of the descendants of migrant men and women, and empower them with a new knowledge about who they are and where they come from. By looking afresh at issues such as slavery, indentured labour, plantation economies, rural–urban and rural–rural migrations, and by addressing comparative issues, such as gender, from an original and wider perspective, it is hoped that the series will ultimately cross-fertilize and re-invigorate debate about the nature of the great variety of voluntary and involuntary diasporas which have occurred around the globe in modern times, and which have played such a crucial part in shaping the world in which we now live.

                                                    Crispin Bates and
                                                    Marina Carter

Preface

The idea for this book emerged from a particularly fruitful research trip to Mauritius in the early 1990s, when I discovered a number of letters written by indentured labourers and their relatives in the nineteenth century. Since then, I have incorporated other types of verbatim source, and extended my search to include material from the Caribbean, Fiji, Natal and Reunion. Some use has already been made of folk songs and oral depositions – notably in Lal (1980) and Mahabir (1985) – and I have preferred to give more space to previously unpublished material from the nineteenth century, which can help to provide new insights into the Indian indenture experience. The vast majority of the material is the work of indentured or time-expired labourers and their families. In one or two cases I include letters from Indians whose origin is uncertain, but whose activities (including commerce) illustrate the position of the overseas Indian in the British Empire. All verbatim sources used in the text are presented in italics. A comprehensive glossary is provided, although caste names are not included. For further information on these, please refer to J.H. Hutton (1963) *Caste in India, Its Nature, Function and Origins*, Oxford University Press, Delhi. Letters requiring clarifications are annotated in the footnotes.

I would like to express my gratitude to the following for the help I received during the preparation of this study:

The Director, Mr Sooprayen, and staff of the Mauritian Archives for their charm, co-operation and tolerance of their harassed overseas visitor!

Mr Bissoondoyal of the Mahatma Gandhi Institute for his encouragement, and for allowing me to use the Immigration Archives; Saloni Deerpalsing, the Curator of the Folk Museum; and Mr Govinden, who was indispensable in helping me to trace individual migrant data from these records

Mahendra Koreemun who took the photographs

Christian Cuniah who acted as my research assistant, and painstakingly wrote out many of the petitions collected here

Pieter Emmer for his comments on an earlier draft of the manuscript

Crispin Bates for his careful reading, suggestions and comments on the text, and help with the glossary

Sudhir Patel for his help with preparation of the typescript

Lara Burns for her encouragement of the project

and finally my friends and family in Mauritius and England for providing their help and support.

Responsibility for any errors remains, of course, my own.

Marina Carter
London 1995

Glossary

adivasi/hill coolie	'tribal'
anna	unit of currency
arkati	local recruiter
ayah	wet nurse
baboo/babu	an educated man, or clerk
batta	daily ration
begari	forced labour
bhajan	devotional song
bhojpuri	language and culture of the inhabitants of the Hindi heartlands, northern India
bhunja	parched grain
bigha	a measure of land, $\frac{5}{8}$ of an acre
biraderi	brotherhood, fraternity, community
burkendauz/ticca	guard
burrah	bird
bustee/basti	settlement, colony, slum
cambu	working implement, prob. scythe
chait	a season of the year (March), the time of the year when the *rabi* wheat crop is harvested
chalan	group/band
chaprasi/chupprassee	office bearer, messenger
chittack	a unit of measurement
comptoir	French territory in India
coolie	generic term for field labourer
creole	colonial-born person, also lingua franca
dagga	alcohol (prob. slang for rum)
daroga	local chief of police or head constable
dhobi/y	washerman
dholl/dal/doll	a type of pulse
dhoti	loin cloth
doodies	a small unit of currency

duffadar	local recruiters, or non-commissioned officers
dustooree	agent's commission, customary payment (food)
fakir	mendicant
ghee	clarified butter
girmit	labour contract (indenture)
gooloomor/gooloomol	evil, confusion
gram	a type of pulse (chickpea)
hoqqah	pipe
hundi	bill of exchange, draft
jehaji bhai	shipmates
jemadar	a native officer of the army, head of a body of men
juar	a kind of millet
kala pani/blackwater	the sea
kamia/kamiati	bonded labour/bonded labourer
kamira/kamera	a workman's assistant
kangani	labour foreman/recruiter used in Malaya and Ceylon (present-day Sri Lanka)
khorakee	food
khorpee	small implement used for digging
kist	revenue instalment, a charge paid on land-holding to government
kos	a measure of length, approx. $\frac{3}{4}$ of a mile
lakh	a hundred thousand
lota/h	small brass waterpot
mahajan	a great person, money lender, landlord
mahitee	prob. magistrate
maidan	a plain of field
maistry	a recruiter (south India), a foreman
malabar	a term for Indian (derogatory, Mauritius)
manahee	prob. employer
mantra	incantation, charm or spell, a Vedic hymn
mochi	a shoemaker, cobbler
moonsiff	officer employed to superintend measurement of land, also a native civil judge
mufassil	country stations and districts
namaskar	greeting
narak	Hell, the infernal regions
old immigrant	time-expired indentured labourer (in Mauritius)
pagoda	generic term for place of worship (such as a temple)
pagri	a turban or a head tax (by extension)
palki	a palanquin

pandit	a priest
pargana/pergunah	a sub-division of a district (zillah)
pattadar/patidar	owner of a share in a village, plot-holder, share-holder
peon/pion	(from Portuguese *peo*) messenger
pice/paise	a small copper coin ($\frac{1}{4}$ of an anna)
rattan	Asiatic climbing palm tree, stick (Mauritius)
ryot	a peasant
sagaie	tool used for cutting sugar cane (in Mauritius), sickle
saheb/sahib	master, lord, boss, gentleman, a European
sawat/saut	co-wife or rival wife
sepoy/sepahi	native infantryman
serang	recruiter/foreman of lascars and ship crews
sirdar/sircar	a leader or commander, or a foreman
tahsil	an administrative sub-division of a district
tahsildar	official in charge of a tahsil
taluq	as tahsil (south and west India)
tambura	musical instrument
thanah	a police station
topas	member of the ship's crew (menial, sweeper)
up-country	the interior of India, away from the coast
valy	a unit of land
wallah (as in depot wallah)	a person
zamindar	landowner
zilla/h	a district, as defined for administrative and revenue purposes by both Mughals and British

Introduction

The actions and reactions of subordinate social groups in history rarely reach the researcher except through the medium of official reports or observers' accounts; in both cases the transcribers of testimonies or the interpreters of responses would have been distanced from the migrant's situation. Yet where recruits were allowed to express in their own idiom the issues and dilemmas of the indenture process, the results are extraordinarily revealing, and the range and complexity of experiences are apparent.

The purpose of this work is to reappraise existing views of the characteristics of the nineteenth-century Indian indentured migrations through the utilization of a hitherto neglected resource: the letters, petitions and depositions of the migrants themselves. These documents belie many of the accepted notions of the post-slavery Indian diaspora in the British Empire by shifting the focus of historical attention from the macro to the micro level; in other words, away from official perceptions and the administrative concerns of contemporaries, and the appraisal of causes and functions of migration schemes by historians, towards closer analysis of the preoccupations and problems articulated by indentured and ex-indentured Indians in those few of their writings and statements which have been left to us.

Naturally, the opinions of Indian migrants rarely emerge uncontaminated by the translations and biases of European mediators. Depositions were solicited and their contents to some extent dictated by local enquirers; petitions depended on the skill and often reflected the particular style and background of individual writers; even some letters of migrants survive only in translated form. Unobjective questioning and less than faithful transcription are a continuing problem with the use of these sources. Nevertheless, the essential value of these documents, albeit diluted by the intervention of European intermediaries, lies in the opportunity they offer to discover and assess features of the nineteenth-century Indian diaspora insufficiently covered by the official sources which are the historian's first and principal resource. In fact, taken as an ensemble, the oral and written testimonies of migrants can effectively challenge existing stereotypes in the historical literature. In this work, therefore, an attempt has

1

been made to highlight those features of the indenture experience about which these documents are particularly revealing, rather than to offer a general history of migration through them. Because of the character of these sources and their relative neglect in previous studies of indenture, the format which has been adopted in this work is to reproduce a selection of the writings and depositions which constitute direct or indirect (transcribed and translated) statements of migrants, and to group them thematically alongside a narrative which situates the experiences described within the wider context of the indenture system, and provides a commentary on specific texts. Spellings are retained as they appear in the original documents, but some minimal punctuation has been introduced to increase readability.

The Migration Literature

This collection of statements and letters of Indian labour migrants, dealing with individuals' perceptions of migration and contacts with home, is the first of its kind. Due to the nature of the material, it offers insights into the indenture experience which seem at times more consonant with our understanding of the parallel streams of European migrants to America and Australia than the slave diaspora with which indenture is more commonly associated. This contrasts with the current division of the literature, and of the theoretical models offered, into two distinct circuits or flows, of non-white labour (largely towards planta- tion economies) and white 'contract' or 'settler' migration. The logic of a separate treatment of European and non-European labour migrants is based on a number of perceived factors principally comprising differentials in risk and choice. Thus, Indian indentured migration has been stereotyped as involving a higher degree of coercion in recruitment and a consequently inferior knowledge of receiving societies, a greater emphasis on single male migrants as opposed to families, harsher living and working conditions at the point of production, a negligible and uncertain remuneration for work undertaken, the application of harsh physical and judicial methods of disciplining labour and consequently a more limited means, for Indians, of achieving mobility and establishing family and kin-based settlements or a semi-independent economic sector in the new setting.[1] The argument for a distinctive – and disadvantaged – role of Indian migrants within the Empire has been most forcefully articulated by Hugh Tinker in his widely quoted work *A New System of Slavery* (1974). Scholars have been influenced by this depiction of indenture as a neo-slave migration to argue that conditions of transfer and transplantation were essentially coercive and acted, as with slaves, to alienate migrants from family, kin and nation permanently.[2]

Few subsequent studies have pointed to the great gulf between slaves, who were effectively chattels for life with no opportunity to return to their birth- place, and Indian migrants whose terms of service, although often extended, were legally finite and who returned home in large numbers (*c.* 30 per cent of migrants).[3] On the other hand, attempts have been made to drop the conventional distinction between 'colonization' to the white settlement colonies and 'labour migration' to the tropics. As Newbury has pointed out: 'most of Europe's fifty million emigrants were labour recruits ... On the other hand, many of the indentured labourers became small farmers and leaseholders in the sugar colonies'.[4]

The differences between the European and Indian diasporas have been accentuated by the treatment offered to these migration streams by historians. The usual perspective adopted in indenture studies has been that offered by government sources, whether these are critical or supportive of the system.[5] In the European literature, by contrast, much use has been made of letters written by migrants. As Charlotte Erickson writes:

> Manuscripts of emigrant letters constitute a unique historical source material. The act of emigration led many ordinary working people to record their actions and attitudes. From such letters we can gain some knowledge of the inner social history of the nineteenth century, of the motives and ways of looking at their world of people who did not lead armies or governments or business firms, but who participated in the greatest movement of people the world has ever known, journeying overseas as individuals and families with little or no outside assistance in taking this great step.[6]

Migrants wrote home for a number of reasons: to encourage others to follow them, for financial support, or merely to combat loneliness. It has been pointed out that the emigrant who did so was often also the unassimilated individual, and for all these reasons the information contained in them may not be less biased than that in the more typical historical sources.[7] On the other hand, such documents provide not only important details about prospects, wages and conditions in the regions of settlement, but also information about the societies from which the migrants came. Thus Thomas and Znaniecki's work shed much light on the operation of Polish peasant society at the turn of the century.[8] In both the European and Indian migrations, letters home were an important source of knowledge about the overseas colonies. Despite or even because of high rates of illiteracy, letters reached large numbers of people, since they were read to gatherings in the home villages.[9] When a letter was being composed, others would often ask for greetings to be passed on to their own families, and thus a private communication could transmit information about a large number of individuals.

To date, comparable material concerning Indian migrants has been neither published nor even much discussed in the available studies. This work presents a selection of the writings and statements of migrants in an attempt to fill this lacuna. Naturally, the source material available for collections such as those of Erickson and of Thomas and Znaniecki is much larger than that so far discovered concerning Indian migrants. In the European context, many letters from migrants were published for propaganda purposes, whilst private correspondence series have been donated to a number of American libraries and archives. As regards the Indian diaspora, there has to date been no sustained effort to collect and catalogue such material. Consequently the documents selected for this volume include, alongside the few letters written by migrants and their relatives which I have been able to obtain, the petitions of labourers or their families and the depositions of indentured workers before Committees of Enquiry and before the courts.

The Sources

The voice of the indentured labourer reaches us only at certain flashpoints of history: emerging from a moment of crisis, a scandal or an enquiry, simply as the result of an accident or coincidence, or out of an individual exercise of effort born of desperation. In almost every case, the communication of the migrant is necessarily mediated by outsiders, whether professional writers or European officials.

Depositions taken from migrants are the source most directly associated with administrators, because they emerge from enquiries conducted by the state. Thus, following accusations of coercion in the recruitment of 'coolies' to Mauritius and British Guiana in the 1830s, committees were set up in the Indian Presidencies to investigate. They generated a number of interviews with returning migrants.[10] The principal enquiry at this time, the Calcutta Commission, debated the value of the evidence provided by the first wave of return migrants from Mauritius. Dowson, a merchant who argued in favour of indenture, claimed that returning Indians were unreliable in giving evidence. J.P. Grant, on the other hand, considered that they made good witnesses because they were unaffected by the debate then raging between the Anti Slavery Society supporters and their mercantile adversaries.[11] In his verdict, W.W. Bird recognized that the lack of credibility was not always the fault of those who gave the statements:

> I do not place much reliance on the testimony of the Coolies who have lately returned from the Mauritius. It is fortunate for the exporters that these persons should have arrived at this particular juncture, whilst the subject is under consideration, to give so favourable an account of the treatment which they have met with; but I am not satisfied with the summary manner in which their examinations have been taken by the chief magistrate, who appears throughout in the character of a partizan arguing in favour of the Cooly trade.[12]

Later enquiries were concerned with more specific problems associated with perceived inadequacies in the working of emigration establishments or the personnel involved in the mobilization of labour, but also include interviews with migrants which are a rich source for the 'subaltern' historian.[13] Most of these enquiries took place in India, where the solicitude of humanitarians, the interests of local capitalists, and the preoccupations of colonial governments seeking to streamline their recruiting operations combined to create a collective scepticism about the efficacy of existing strategies of labour mobilization.

By the mid-1860s, however, the focus had shifted to the principal employing colonies, where suspicions as to the use – or abuse – of Indian labour incited the appointment of Royal Commissions in Mauritius and British Guiana to investigate the conditions and treatment of indentured workers. Prior to the arrival of the external investigators, officials in Mauritius were taking part in a local enquiry to investigate the conduct of the police in Mauritius towards old immigrants in 1867. J. Fraser, one of the officials who was asked to participate, commented more sensitively than most on the difficulties encountered in dealing with verbal evidence presented by Indian complainants:

> I believe it to be one of the most difficult things to get from the general mass of Indian immigrants a plain ungarnished statement of any complaints they may have to make, however well founded, and the more simple the tale, the more highly they are apt to overlay it with fiction ... it happens perhaps not unfrequently in consequence that, because part of a complaint is untrue, on the face of it, the other portion which is well founded is disbelieved also.[14]

In British Guiana the Royal Commissioners declined to hear evidence from Indians under indenture, noting that there had already been 'a sudden increase in numbers going to the Immigration Department to complain'.[15] The Guiana Royal Commission was succeeded by that which arrived in Mauritius in April 1872, and spent several months on the island, producing a report in 1875.[16] The Commissioners interviewed a wide range of individuals associated with Indian labour as employers, administrators or spokesmen. Representatives of the Indian community itself were again not called as witnesses in the voluminous Minutes of Evidence produced by the enquiry.

The Commissioners, however, also perused a large number of documents which revealed attitudes and actions towards Indians in Mauritius, including court cases and individual petitions, and undertook inspections of plantations, camps and other institutions employing or holding Indian labour.[17] Their investigations created within the Indian community, as in British Guiana, an expectation or realization that an opportunity had arisen for particular grievances to be aired and, more importantly, action taken. The Commission itself had, in part, been instigated by the presentation of the 'Petition of Old Immigrants' (Appendix C), which was a list of individual grievances collected largely by a planter, Adolphe de Plevitz, aided by V. Rajarethnum, who wished to draw attention to the constraints placed upon time-expired labourers.[18] Once the Commissioners had arrived in Mauritius, and opened their enquiry, Indians were encouraged to believe that their plaints would be listened to, and a trickle of petitions addressed to the Commissioners rapidly grew into a flood, and were diverted to the Protector's office, giving rise to a second invaluable source for this collection.[19]

Some idea of the excitement aroused amongst the Indians during the time the Commissioners were in Mauritius is given by a later Governor of the island, Sir Charles Bruce, writing in 1910:

> The consequences [of appointing the Royal Commission] were unfortunate in the extreme ... It must be borne in mind that the immigrant coolie in Mauritius is not confined, as is often supposed in this country, to the area of agricultural industry. He is employed in every department of public and private activity; he is engaged in every household. In the excitement and exasperation that followed the appointment of the Commission it was conceived that an inquisition was to be held not only into the administration of a system, but into the confidential concerns of every business and every household. The colony was at once divided into two camps, the Governor and his friends holding one, the planters and their friends the other ... The routine of public and private life was dislocated ... while the Heads of Departments were on their trial, there were not wanting subordinate officials ready to give away their superiors ... Informers, acknowledged or anonymous, abounded everywhere; espionage, gossip and scandal were the environment of society. Distinctions of class, colour, and creed excited animosities that had slumbered.[20]

The Royal Commissions acted, then, as a catalyst for the expression of Indian grievances, and in so doing witnessed a flowering of a lengthy tradition of petition writing amongst the overseas Indians. Such documents, invariably addressed to the Protector or to the Governor, except during the visit of the Commissions, date back to the first batches of indentured arrivals. Early petitions, such as that of Dassin Nakir in 1843, prayed for assistance following accidents which had left the petitioners crippled, or for return passages.[21] Even the Indian convicts who had preceded the indentured labourers to Mauritius adopted this form of seeking redress. Hurry Bappoo began his by commenting

> It appears very odd indeed; that I am a prisoner; and I have got a Girl about 5 years and four months old; her name is Luckchemee; as I am condemned until death to remain here, I wish to send the said Girl Luckchemee, to Bombay near my family, where she would be better off than here.[22]

The Protector reported that the girl was Bappoo's child by an Indian woman who had immigrated in 1843. His petition to allow the girl to return free of charge with her mother was granted.[23]

The granting of such favours and acts of clemency persuaded increasing numbers of Indians to have recourse to the Protector's office, despite the general recognition that he was an administrator of the system rather than a spokesman of the Indians. His office, set up first in Mauritius by Act XV of 1842, was initially concerned principally with the reception of arriving Indians and their allocation to employers.[24] Other Indian-importing colonies set up similar offices. By the middle of the century, the department's duties had expanded to include the reception of vagrants, the distribution of tickets and passes, and the supervision of returning migrants.[25] Individuals presenting petitions to the Immigration Office in the various colonies did so largely in the knowledge that decisions about specific issues, such as the provision of return passages and distribution of new immigrants, particularly women, were made by him. Most petitions therefore were limited to such pleas as those for a free return passage or a wife from the depot. At the same time, because the Protector controlled the certificates which determined the Indian's legal status overseas, he occupied a unique position of authority. His co-operation could restore to a man his deserted wife, remove an Indian from prison, or send him back to India. This could only be effected, however, if the Immigration Office could find the relevant records. Many petitioners were disappointed because the registers of immigrants were inaccurate and uninformative. The Royal Commissioners commented on 'the difficulty petitioners have in proving their relationships' and 'the inutility of the Immigration Office as at present administered in any attempt to discover the relationship of Indian immigrants'.[26]

The Immigration Office nevertheless came to occupy a unique place in the minds of indentured immigrants, and a tradition grew up whereby the incumbent would be formally solicited to intervene in a range of domestic and employment issues involving Indians. Of course, he was not the only European whose help was enlisted by indentured labourers. Colonel Pike, who wrote one of the best travellers' accounts of Mauritius in this period, included in his appendix a petition he had received from one Surwurrah, a Mauritian-born Indian, which he described as 'about the best begging letter I ever received'.[27] The large number of petitions available in the archives provides the amplest source from which to recreate the experience of Indian labour settlement overseas.

For Indians who could not afford the expense of drawing up a petition, the most direct means of being heard was at the magistrate's court, as either a complainant or a defendant. There was an almost universal lack of confidence on the part of European officials in verbal depositions made by Indians. Captain Ogilvie, a stipendiary magistrate in Mauritius, had this to say of their court statements:

> I despair of ever being able to put a stop to perjury. False swearing is part and parcel of the Indian character . . . In India perjury is even more prevalent than in this Island; sometimes an Indian witness speaks the truth but in India in ninety nine cases out of a hundred, the witnesses, though perhaps deposing to facts which have really occurred, are false witnesses. In most, indeed I may say in all Courts in the interior of India, giving evidence is as much a trade, as exercising the profession of a pleader before the Courts.[28]

Not everyone blamed the Indians. In 1868 the Colonial Office questioned the competency of the interpreters who translated the depositions of Indians before the colonial courts. In British Guiana it had been proved by Desvoeux that interpreters were not above taking bribes to alter a man's plea. In Mauritius the Procuror General reported that:

> all translations of documents in the Indian languages required by this Department are entrusted to Mr John Joachim of the Immigration Department, a Deacon of the Church of England for the Indians, and a gentleman who is a perfect master of the Tamul, Teloogoo, Hindustanee and Nagree dialects.

He pointed out none the less that:

> in judicial enquiries carried on through the medium of interpretation, the judge and the parties are entirely at the mercy of the interpreter. A misinterpretation by him may irretrievably compromise the character and fortunes of individuals. It becomes therefore of the utmost importance that the interpreter selected should not only be, as far as possible, beyond the reach of corrupt influences, but also that he should be a person of education and intelligence.[29]

The problem of appointing interpreters with an adequate knowledge of all the Indian languages spoken was recognized by the Governor; for in Mauritius, only one interpreter was allowed per court, and hence had to be proficient in all the necessary languages. It was also proposed:

> to empower these translators to draw up, for the Indians, on payment of a small fee, all minor agreements, purchases and sales, and other small transactions; and they will, I have every reason to believe, be a great boon to the petty Indian traders, as their little transactions are often now drawn up by illiterate and unprincipled persons, frequently far from the intention of the parties, and not seldom verging closely upon fraud.

Court depositions gave the Indians a chance to air their grievances and, as Kelly explains in the case of Fiji, were 'the one documentary source . . . in which the intrusion of white overseers in the sexual and social lives of the indentured labourers is repeatedly and provocatively discussed – almost always by the Indian defendants and their witnesses'.[30] Given the daily injustices and insults to which they were exposed, Indians in diaspora welcomed such opportunities to describe their abuse. They developed strategies of dealing with colonial adjudicators which earned them the tag of being 'proverbially litigious'. Where possible they made collective complaints, and made the most of the only evidence they had: their own wounds. As one of the stipendiary magistrates in Mauritius commented:

> An Indian who has received a blow which has made his nose bleed, invariably brings as a 'piece de conviction' the handkerchief or cloth which he has used to stop the bleeding. And I have more than once seen an Indian who has received a scratch on his face which has bled a little come into the Court five or six days after the commission of the Assault with the clotted blood still on him, having evidently not washed his face since he was beaten.[31]

A rarer source material, but perhaps the most revealing in this collection for the light it throws upon the migration process, is the correspondence sent between overseas Indians and their relatives at home. The extent of this correspondence cannot be estimated because there are as yet no collections of such letters. Despite estimated high illiteracy rates amongst overseas Indians, letters were being despatched between Mauritius and India almost as soon as indentured immigration began, from the 1830s. As early as December 1837, the Chief Commissary of Police at Mauritius, John Finniss, forwarded a letter to the Superintendent of Police at Calcutta, 'from the Indian Sittoo in the service of Mr St Felix of this colony, who is very desirous it should reach his family'. Finniss stressed:

> it is very desirable that these people should have every facility of communicating with their friends, and some of them may occasionally wish to remit to them a portion of their earnings; I shall therefore feel obliged by your informing me if any arrangement could be made by which that could be effected.[32]

The British Indian official, W.W. Bird, nevertheless noticed, and deprecated the fact, that most of the return emigrants interviewed by the Calcutta Commission in 1840 had maintained no contact with their families, which he regarded as tantamount to 'desertion'.[33] An enquiry conducted in Mauritius itself into the conditions of the Indian labourers in 1838 also sought to determine the frequency of communications by letter between migrants and their families.[34] However, the questions were put to the plantation owners rather than to the labourers, and the replies were vague. The owners of the Reunion and Bellevue estates in the districts of Pamplemousses asserted that their Tamil labourers sent letters home through 'their friends at the port', perhaps a reference to the large free Tamil community established in the Mauritian capital. At D'Arifat's estate in Flacq, the owner asserted that his labourers did write and receive letters, but the magistrate who visited evidently spoke Hindi, for he added that this was denied by the workers, who told him 'we do not like the island and more particularly our master'! In the southern district of Grand Port, sirdars were reported to write or to forward letters and to send money to India through friends. The Indian cook on the Sauveterre estate had reportedly written to his family to come and join him, and at the Mare d'Albert estate, a named individual, Ram Chunder, had apparently received a letter from India. At the Plaisance estate, the labourers remarked to the visiting magistrate that 'if their letters contained a remittance, they would be welcome, if not, they would not be worth the postage which their friends would have to pay in India, and they would not thank them for writing'. From our knowledge of the most frequent topic in letters sent home by migrants, this statement has a ring of authenticity and underscores the fact that, for the participants in this diaspora, the great issue was the acquisition of the means to a livelihood.

In 1838, the Governor of Mauritius requested the Indian Government to consider 'the expediency of the letters from the emigrants to their relations in India being allowed to pass free of postage'. In Mauritius itself the Chief

Commissary of Police was authorized to receive and deliver, free of charge, all such letters, and since, in his view:

> a free intercourse by letter between Indians in the island and their families in Bengal would be a certain and effectual means of making known to that class of the natives most concerned the real and true condition of the labourers in Mauritius,

he hoped the Bengal government would give instructions for the exemption from postage of all the letters of the emigrant Indians.[35]

However, in 1841 the Postmaster General in Madras reported a problem which was to persist throughout the period: that many addresses given by immigrants in Mauritius were 'written so unintelligibly that I am apprehensive great difficulty will be experienced on discovering the party for whom it is designed'. He suggested that addresses on letters be written in English as well as the vernacular languages of the emigrants. Following this rule, the next communication of the Mauritian Colonial Secretary gave the names and addresses of the parties for whom fifteen letters had been sent by a group of labourers employed on the estate of a Savanne sugar planter. Thus we know the names of some of the earliest recipients of letters from the plantations: Appavan Padiachy of Combaconum, Lingapillay of Tanjore and Pettiperoumal Chettyar at Pattancoully were among the number.[36]

By the mid-nineteenth century a number of measures had been put in place to facilitate the flow of correspondence between migrants and their families. In 1867, the Governor of Mauritius suggested:

> the levying of a lower rate of postage on letters from Indian labourers in this colony to their friends in India, in somewhat the same way as the letters of soldiers and sailors are treated throughout the British Empire. It is proposed to reduce the current rate of 11d per half ounce to 3d.[37]

Mangru suggests that there was 'a perceptible increase in correspondence between immigrants and their families and friends in India' between 1871 and 1881, but notes, in the case of British Guiana, that migrants complained of 'heavy postal charges and the alleged dishonesty of creole postmen'.[38] By the time Grierson was touring the Bengal Presidency in 1883 he found 'in every village to which I went, three or four letters, which were shown to me, had been received during the past year or two, from one colony or another'.[39]

The letters of Indian migrants used in this volume have been gleaned principally from the files of the Immigration Office and Emigration Agents held at the National Archives of Mauritius (PA and PB series), in one case from a private family collection, and in another from a published source. In general such letters only reached the archives when relatives could not be traced or difficulties of communication arose, necessitating the intervention of the authorities. In spite of the present paucity of this material – until such time as further letters in private hands may be traced and reproduced – the very existence of this correspondence confirms the extent of contact between Indians at home and abroad. The letters themselves point to regular channels of communication between certain families, describe kin and village networks overseas and the means and frequency of remittances, and express prosaic concerns about family events and the local agrarian cycle in ways which are highly reminiscent of the contemporaneous correspondence of European rural migrants. Of course, in some respects these documents, which one might expect to be of the most intimate nature, rarely offer more than glimpses into the inner worlds of migrants, because they were not generally private documents, in the sense of being written and read by intermediaries, and were composed by persons not well versed in description and elaborate prose. Thus Major Pitcher, shown a specimen of a migrant's letter in the 1880s, commented:

> Ajudhia Kurmi of Nagraon left his wife and children 15 years ago and went to Mauritius. He has sent two remittances, one of which had been received, but the other for Rs 50 had not come to hand. A brother to whom the letter was sent came along and showed me the letter, a most commonplace affair for an absentee of 15 years. His only enquiry was as to how the rice crops of a certain field were this year.[40]

The fact that migrants were in regular contact with relatives in India also helped the authorities to settle the claims of heirs when labourers died. When the new immigrant Latchmana Reddi, No. 425, 784, died on the Estate Bel Air in the district of Savanne, Mauritius, belonging to A.J. Wilson, two letters found in the possession of the deceased revealed that his father, Moorgapen Reddi, was still living, and resided at Konethoor in Madras. Latchamana had a deposit book showing that he had in the Savings Bank the sum of a hundred rupees, and was further entitled to a sum of Rs 5.65 due to him for wages by the Estate Bel Air. It was thus a relatively simple matter for the authorities to establish the father's claim to his son's estate.[41]

The value of letters between migrants and their families lies also in their relative originality and honesty as historical documents. Some of the correspondence detailed in this collection is purely and simply the work of the letter writer conserved in its original form. Others, still in vernacular form, have been written by Bengali, Tamil or Hindi scribes on behalf of migrants in India, for example Saeed ul Nisa Begum's letter to her husband (Figure 4.7). In some cases British Indian magistrates were called upon to pen, in English, a translation of a verbal plea for help. Letters written by labourers overseas also took one or other of these forms, although the number of signatures rather than crosses on petitions and other documents reveals a surprising degree of literacy amongst the indentured population.

Mediators and Petitioners

The intervention of mediators in the fabrication, translation and transcription of documents progressively distances the originator of the statement from his or her plaint. The intermediaries who transcribed the voice of migrants range from Indian petition writers and court interpreters to European lawyers, magistrates and sympathizers. They wrote, translated, recorded or simply forwarded the statements, views and opinions of migrants. Their motives, and skills, were highly varied.

Many of the documents betray the style and learning of the writer rather than the voice of the originator. Latin terms are used and legal references cited. Vencatachellum Appoo's petition called on 'the international law passed between England and France' for the extradition of his wife from Reunion (see p. 144). The carefully and elegantly worded petitions of Pandoo and Mootoo-samy are the work of the Advocate General, W.W. Kerr (see p. 122). De Plevitz's hand crafted the 'Petition of Old Immigrants' (see Appendix C). Professional petition writers like Edmund Edwards sometimes signed their handiwork (see p. 159). Occasionally employers helped with those petitions which did not affect their interests adversely. On the other hand, an excess of humility, for example, Hurry Bappoo's 'Honored Sir, I prostrate myself at Your clemency to show an eye of sympathy', would not have seemed at all out of place to petitioners at that time.[42] Beeharry begged 'ten times ten' for a favour (see p. 158). European officials are addressed as 'Most respected and honored Sir' (see p. 156) or 'you are my father and mother for us' (see p. 109) and even 'Cherisher of the Poor' (see p. 198). Saeed ul Nisa Begum addresses her own husband as 'Respected Sir' (see p. 177).

The intervention of the translator, as in the case of Ganesh's letter, is at times jarring (see p. 184), and the most gripping documents are often those whose language is more simple and direct. Murdemootoo and his friends, who addressed a letter to the Protector to solve a murder case, are painfully honest: 'We came from Industan to work in this Mauritius for get some monies' (see p. 109). Goordyal's deposition comes straight from the heart: 'My life is miserable ... I am very unhappy' (see p. 117). Rungen's account of 'my poor Distress' resulting from the loss of his land is compelling (see p. 126). Boodoo simply asserted that if his request was not heeded 'your poor servant will be in trouble' (see p. 156). The petition of Govinden, a sirdar, on the other hand, is far from humble, conveying instead a sense of hauteur and self-pride (see p. 123). Many of the petitions and even letters are written in the third person, referring by name to the supposed author (see for example p. 78).

Those petitions and letters whose language betrays an unlearned hand may not necessarily have been the work of the signatory. Yet the very fact that the tone and style are not mellifluous lends an urgency and a directness to them, for such writers rarely do more than transcribe the message of the signatory, and there is no artistry to obscure the request. Perhaps the document which best expresses the world view of the Indian outside the intervention of a European author, and away from his principles, is the petition of the Telegus (see p. 138). The letter sent to Dwarika with its salaams to family members and references to the gods (see p. 186) is also, by this token, a far more revealing social record than the petitions crafted by Kerr and de Plevitz, which yet tell us so much more about the injustices committed against Indians in Mauritius.

De Plevitz and W.W. Kerr were motivated by a sense of humanitarianism to take a stand on behalf of the indentured Indians. For their actions they were rewarded with the general opprobrium of the planting community. Another individual who took it upon himself to defend injustices perpetrated against Indians in Mauritius was the British official Draper Bolton. He adopted the case of two Indians, Pemchand and Gannoo, who had been falsely accused of theft by another Indian. They were condemned to twelve months' imprisonment, and their witnesses to six months'. Draper Bolton appealed on their behalf, on the grounds that the chief witness against them had perjured himself too. The official also drafted a petition for them to the Governor. Despite all his efforts, and having amassed evidence which proved the convictions to have been unjust, the government declined to interfere. Draper concluded that 'weeks, months passed away, and these poor men suffered on as criminals' despite the authorities knowing full well that they were innocent.[43]

Other Europeans, like Edmund Edwards and Duval, wrote out petitions because they received a fee for the task. Edwards was the creole-born son of an English merchant and a French Mauritian mother. He was a qualified attorney at law in the district of Plaines Wilhems, but, probably on account of his youth, wrote petitions to supplement his income. His career was brief: he died at the age of 27 in 1874.[44] Potun's petition (pp. 130–1) gave his address as care of a Mr Marceau of the Police Court, Moka, and it is likely that this latter was a member of the legal profession and probably the petition writer for Potun.

In some cases the fees taken by such professional writers were condemned by magistrates as extortionate. Duval persuaded Chavreemootoo to petition the Protector when the latter failed to have his complaint heard at the District Court because he only had three shillings. His fee was, naturally, the three shillings the Indian possessed. The District Magistrate complained that Duval's conduct was 'disgraceful', and since it was not the first instance, moved to have his licence as a general agent withdrawn.[45] Although Chavreemootoo's case was lost, one is tempted to see dislike of potential spokesmen for the Indians in the Magistrate's words.

It is difficult therefore to judge whether petitioners were in fact being cheated of their money, as officials often lamented, by professional writers who encouraged them to pay for the drawing up of complicated documents, or whether magistrates and immigration clerks were simply irritated with the activities of those who overburdened them with written requests on behalf of Indians. Certainly, the quality and clarity of the work produced by petition writers were highly variable. In 1848 the Protector received a second petition on behalf of Veerasamy and Amamade praying for an answer to their previous petition. Apparently this requested free return passages for them both, and had been dated three months earlier. On investigation the Protector reported:

> The Petitioners having never appeared at this office to explain the object of their petition which was unintelligible, no report has been made, they ought to have ascertained previous to petitioning whether there was any difficulty at all, or the nature of any that might exist – they are grossly imposed upon by the parties they pay to draw up these useless petitions and are told of difficulties where none exist.[46]

The practice of having a petition drawn up was thus not always the best means of achieving a desired end. It was sometimes simpler just to turn up at the Immigration Office and have one's request taken down by a clerk, when it could be dealt with by the Protector. This, however, would have done the writers out of a job, and the Protector's irritation when presented with unnecessary and costly petitions is demonstrated by his remarks on the case of Veerasamy and Amamade.

When a government employee, Mr Madge, became involved in this lucrative work, the reprimand was swift. Madge explained that two Indians, Ramchurn and Dabeedeen, had come to his house and asked him to draw up a petition to help Ramchurn obtain a situation of peon in the Police Department. They offered him six dollars, with a promise of more to come, presumably if his intervention was successful in securing Ramchurn the job. When the Governor's attention was drawn to Madge's handiwork, he called for a report on his misconduct. Madge hastily returned the money, and the Protector ended the affair with a letter to the Colonial Secretary:

> The conduct of Mr Madge, in this case, can in no way be excused, but in consideration of his having been attentive to his duties, and of his having a family to support, I hope his conduct will for this time, have no more serious consequences for him, than a severe admonition. As to his future conduct, although this transaction is in no ways connected with the department, or his duties, he should understand, that government servants, however modest their position, are expected to keep up respectability of character.[47]

The position of Vellyvoil Rajarethnum Moodeliar was more complex. He was undoubtedly a champion of his countrymen in Mauritius, leading delegations, holding meetings and assisting de Plevitz in the formulation of the 'Petition of Old Immigrants'.[48] At the same time he had to earn his living, and was appointed a government translator and teacher. He evidently also worked as a petition writer. Ramalingum and six other old immigrants paid Mr Rajarethnum 25 rupees to write their petition in April 1873.[49] But his role can hardly be described simply in commercial terms. Instead one begins to understand why some magistrates viewed petition writers as a thorn in their sides, in considering his correspondence concerning the Indian Chellun. Rajarethnum took up his case directly with Lapeyre, a District Magistrate who had retained Chellun's ticket after the latter declined to be employed by him. Vellyvoil first wrote directly to Lapeyre from his address in Church Street, Port Louis:

> I have the honor to inform you that the Indian Chellen no. 20398, who works as dhoby rents a room in my court. He states that he had thought of working with you and gave you his ticket, but afterwards changed his mind, preferring to work as dhoby. He has a pass from the Depot, but he has requested me to ask you to return his ticket as otherwise he will have to pay for a duplicate one.[50]

When Lapeyre declined to co-operate, Rajarethnum wrote a second letter to the Protector, arguing that Chellen should not have to pay for a duplicate simply because Lapeyre would not hand over the old one. He added that the Magistrate had threatened Chellen with prison if the Indian would not work for him. The Immigration Department cordially replied to Rajarethnum, informing him that Chellen would obtain his ticket and police pass on application to the office.[51]

Sadly, two champions of the Indian immigrants became involved in a dispute over another such case. Adolphe de Plevitz had also taken up the grievances of individual Indians after authoring the notorious petition. In one letter, he accused Mr Lafond of ill-treating his labourers, saying he had personally seen the man beating an Indian boy and ducking him in a pond. In another letter to the Protector, he informed him that a band of twenty-seven men had come to complain about an illegal transfer from one estate to another.[52] In 1873 he tangled with Rajarethnum over the case of Appavoo. De Plevitz informed the Protector that Appavoo had been impersonated before M. Barrie, a notary of Port Louis, with the view of extorting goods and chattels. It appeared that another Indian, Chinnapen, had demanded a cart, an ass, a cow and a calf from Appavoo. Vellyvoil Rajarethnum, described as a 'translator of Indian languages', had supposedly acted as umpire between them and declared that it was the property of Chinnapen. By this judgement, said de Plevitz, Appavoo had been ruined, adding 'I am informed that Mr Rajarethnum's doings have been confirmed by a judgement of the District Magistrate of Pamplemousses'.[53] What lay behind these criticisms, and the validity of them, remain for now a mystery. What is clear is that in the wake of the Royal Commission both men had become, for Indians, independent arbiters to whom they could take their grievances in the face of a partial administration. They were the early spokesmen for a community which slowly but surely was beginning to create its own leaders.

Letter writers were sometimes drawn from the most prominent of their communities. They were also vital to the maintenance of contacts between overseas Indians and their families. Unlike the petition writers they were not necessarily professionals, and perhaps took on the task for no remuneration, simply because they were more literate. In British Guiana one Babu Lal Behari, from the village of Dumraon in Bihar, 'became very popular in his district because of years of free letter-writing performed for his compatriots'.[54]

Whilst there were some slaves, like Equiano, who wrote accounts of their lives, the indentured Indians in most colonies did not have spokesmen from their own communities. However, in Fiji, which was one of the last colonies to turn to Indian labour, some oral evidence has been collected, and one ex-indentured migrant wrote several treatises in Hindi. Gillion describes his life:

> Totaram Sanadhya of Rewa became an important leader in Fiji and critic of the indenture system in India. Totaram went to Fiji as an indentured labourer in 1893 from Firozabad, Agra, and like many Brahmins had been registered as a Thakur. He served his term of indenture at Nausori and afterwards settled at Wainibokasi, marrying the daughter of a rich Indian farmer. Although not well-educated when he left India, he studied in Fiji and became accepted as a pandit.[55]

Amongst his writings he has left a manuscript on 'The Religious and Social Condition of the Indians in Fiji', and, with Chaturvedi, authored the polemic 'My Twenty One Years in the Fiji Islands'. However, like the works of the abolitionists before him, his writings may be said to have been constructed to convince an audience rather than present the bare facts of the case.

The problems of recapturing the voices of indentured Indians are many. Their stories appear as fragments in official files, often without sequels or endings. In order to discover the origin or end of a particular incident, several sources may need to be tapped (as in the saga of Chennapah, told in Chapter 4). Fortunately some of the archives of the Indian diaspora are complete enough for us to succeed in this quest, and the documentary, statistical and pictorial evidence in the Mahatma Gandhi Institute Immigration Archive must rank as one of the best repositories of data and photographs concerning nineteenth-century Indian villagers. The material which I have collected in the present volume is largely derived from the Mauritian archives where I have done most work, but where possible examples of letters, petitions and statements have been added from the other colonies which imported Indian labour.

The issues raised in this work are by and large those that have been neglected in previous studies of the nineteenth-century Indian diaspora, which have tended to stress either the opportunities or the cruelties of indenture. In this volume, I am attempting instead to depict the migration as it was experienced by those who signed indenture contracts, and, through their appraisals of recruitment, working conditions and domestic problems, to deconstruct the official version of events, which has hitherto been the primary resource of historical accounts. By focusing the point of enquiry at the subaltern level, I hope to begin the task of providing for the Indian diaspora some elements of the detail of daily lives, aspirations and disappointments, as encountered and expressed by migrant families, which has for long been available to analysts of European migration.

Notes

1. Eltis, 1983; Emmer, 1986c: 5–7.
2. Tinker, 1974; Emmer, 1984.
3. Hu-De Hart, 1993; Omvedt, 1980: 189. Grierson estimated that of 232,802 migrants leaving for Mauritius from Northern India between 1842 and 1882, around 80,000 returned: G. Grierson, *Report on Colonial Emigration from the Bengal Presidency*, 1883, p. 10.
4. Newbury, 1975: 235; Marks and Richardson, 1984: 2. For a discussion of the conditions of European indentured servants see Clark and Souden, 1987; Salinger, 1987.
5. Jan Breman's *Taming the Coolie Beast* (1989) is a recent example of a study of labour in Sumatra based on a single government report.
6. Erickson, 1971: 1.
7. Reynolds, 1935: 211; Baines, 1991: 37.
8. Thomas and Znaniecki, 1920/1984.
9. Schrier, 1959: 41; Semmingsen, 1978: 166.
10. Parliamentary Papers 1841 XVI (45) Calcutta Commission of Enquiry Report; Bombay General Proceedings, Bombay Committee Report, 20 Sep. 1838; Madras Public Proceedings Range 247, vols 60, 67–8.
11. Parliamentary Papers 1841 (427) Minute of J.P. Grant, p. 15.
12. Parliamentary Papers 1841 (43) Minute of W.W. Bird, 6 May 1841.
13. MA B Series, Beyts Report 1859; Parliamentary Papers 1846 (691–II) R. Neave and R. Brenan Reports, June 1845.
14. Report of J. Fraser to Major General Selby Smyth, President, Police Commission, 7 Mar. 1872.
15. Mangru, 1987a: 189.
16. Parliamentary Papers 1875, XXXIV (c.1115) Report of the Royal Commission.
17. Parliamentary Papers 1875, XXXIV (c. 1115–I) Appendices to the Report of the Royal Commissioners, B, G and H.
18. CO 167/529 Gordon to Kimberley, 17 Nov. 1871.
19. See especially PA 14 for numerous petitions addressed to the Protector or the Royal Commissioners at this time.
20. Bruce, 1910: 336–7.
21. PL 57 Colonial Secretary to D. Nakir, 23 Mar. 1843.
22. PA 6 Hurry Bappoo to Governor, 29 Dec. 1857.
23. PA 6 Immigration Department Note, 14 Jan. 1858.
24. Parliamentary Papers 1844 XXXV (530) Act XV of 1842, pp. 177–83.
25. Royal Commissioners' Report pp. 180–94, 208–39.
26. *Ibid.*, p. 480.
27. Pike, 1873: Appendix.
28. CO 167/427 Stevenson to Secretary of State, Mar. 1861, encl. Report of Captain Ogilvie.
29. CO 167/506 Barkly to Duke of Buckingham and Chandos, 3 Mar. 1868 (Conf.), encl. Procuror General to Private Secretary, 25 Jan. 1868.
30. Kelly, 1992: 262.
31. CO 167/427 Stevenson to Secretary of State, Mar. 1861, encl. Report of Captain Ogilvie.

32. Parliamentary Papers 1841 (45) Appendix to Calcutta Commission Report, letter from Finniss to Birch, 13 Dec. 1837.

33. Parliamentary Papers 1841 (43) Minute of W.W. Bird, 6 May 1841.

34. Parliamentary Papers 1840 (58) Nicolay to Glenelg, 21 May 1839, encl. Report of Mauritius Committee of Enquiry.

35. CO 167/210 Dick to Secretary, Government of Bengal, 31 Oct. 1838.

36. Madras Public Proceedings 247/63 Colonial Secretary to the Government of Madras, 20 July 1841, encl. details of the recipients of fifteen letters sent by labourers employed on a Savanne sugar estate.

37. CO 167/497 Barkly to the Earl of Carnarvon, 29 May 1867.

38. Mangru, 1987a: 67.

39. Grierson Report, 1883, p. 18.

40. Pitcher Report, 1882, p. 76.

41. PL 31 Curator of Vacant Estates to Protector of Immigrants, 25 Nov. 1908.

42. PA 6 Bappoo to Governor, 29 Dec. 1857.

43. CO 167/493 Draper Bolton to the Editor of the *Commercial Gazette*.

44. Registrar General's Department, Port Louis, Death Certificate of Edmund Edwards, 23 Aug. 1874.

45. PA 12 District Magistrate, Pamplemousses, to Protector, 17 Nov. 1871.

46. PL 32 Protector's Report, 18 Oct. 1848.

47. PL 32 Protector to Colonial Secretary, 7 Apr. 1849.

48. See Reddi, 1986: 34–56, for further information about this man.

49. PA 14 Petition of Ramalingum *et al.* to Protector, Apr. 1873.

50. PA 14 Rajarethnum to Lapeyre, 15 July 1873.

51. PA 14 Immigration Department Note for Mr Rajarethnum, n.d.

52. PA 22 A. de Plevitz to Protector, 19 June 1872 and 11 Nov. 1874.

53. PA 14 A. de Plevitz to Protector, 9 May 1873.

54. Samaroo, 1987a: 44.

55. Gillion, 1962: 147.

CHAPTER ONE

The Indian labour diaspora: an overview

Indian indentured labour migration was brought into being to offset the consequences of terminating the slave trade, and it was constantly compared to another great diaspora – the settlement of the British Dominions. The commencement of government-regulated indentured migration to Mauritius, followed by the West Indies, the French colonies, Natal and Fiji, was in fact a rescue package for sugar plantations, but took place at a time when the much larger diaspora was under way of Europeans to America and Australia. The decade from 1840 to 1850 has been described as 'a period of colonization mania', when schemes to relieve distress and unemployment at home and populate the colonies flooded the Colonial Office in Britain and were taken up by Parliament.[1] At the beginning of the decade, two Colonial Land and Emigration Commissioners were appointed to supervise the recruitment of migrant labourers and their management on the ships which transported them to the colonies.[2] In their first report, the new Commissioners made specific reference to post-abolition immigration schemes for Britain's sugar colonies:

> it is needless to say how leading a question it has become in the present state of society in those colonies. We are deeply impressed with its importance. From the day on which sugar raised by free labour could be brought to market cheaper, and of better quality, than sugar produced by slaves, would date the fall of negro slavery throughout the world. Every consideration of humanity, therefore, must concur with a due regard for the interests of property, and we may add, for the general welfare of these communities, in recommending that no obstruction be unnecessarily offered to the procurement of an adequate supply of labour. But on the other hand, it must no less be admitted that the labourers introduced should be confined to people of suitable constitutions and habits (for which purpose we doubt whether it will not be necessary at last to limit also to race), and that being of a suitable description, they should be brought in under adequate conditions for their protection in a strange land.

Mauritius was offered the opportunity to become the site for this 'great experiment' in the use of free labour to harvest sugar because of its previous experience with Indian workers, its large expanse of virgin land and its proximity to the source of supply (Figure 1.1). It was to be the model for other

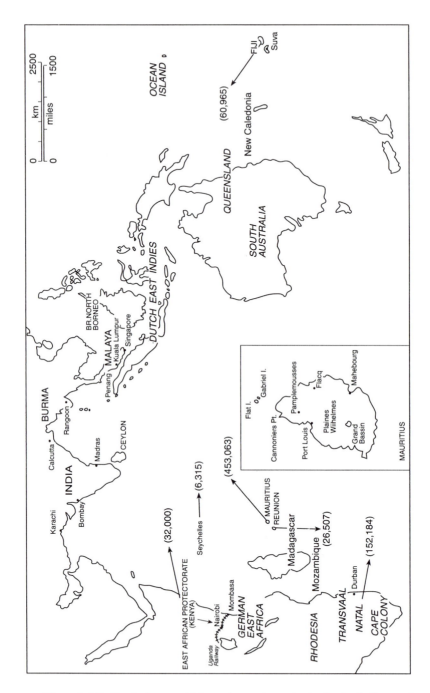

Figure 1.1 Indian indentured labour-importing colonies in the Indian and Pacific Oceans. Numbers of Indians received are given in parentheses.
Source: Tinker, 1974: 62; Lal, 1983: 13.

British sugar colonies to follow. In this field, the island had been leading the way since 1834, when the importation of indentured Indian workers really began. Almost immediately the scheme became a subject of interest to capitalists elsewhere in the British Empire.

Thus in 1836 we find the Mauritius-based English firm of Blythe & Sons writing to Messrs Bettington & Co. of Sydney, Australia, in the following terms:

> The planters having introduced free Indians, apprenticed generally for five years, keeps our cultivation in as healthy a state as we have ever seen it. The experiment of free labour has been entirely successful; we have 50 free Indians on our own estate . . . they are quiet, docile and industrious. The total cost, including passage here and back, at the end of their apprenticeship, which is generally five years, together with food, clothing, etc. . . . is no more than 5 shillings per week, which you will allow is cheap labour in any country . . . It seems to us, that in New South Wales the deficiency of agricultural labour might be beneficially supplied from Bengal.[3]

Accordingly, sixty-one male labourers were shipped to Sydney on 22 August 1837 and a further twenty-eight in December of that year. Around four hundred men and a handful of women and children also embarked for Demerara and Berbice on the ships *Whitby* and *Hesperus* in January 1838. During the years 1837 and 1838, Mauritius, for its part, imported more than five thousand male labourers, but only around a hundred women.[4]

Around this time, however, the emigration of so-called 'coolies' was brought to the attention of the British Parliament by the Anti-Slavery Society and its sympathizers. A series of debates between them brought the whole issue into the public domain and led to the suspension of migration, until it was resumed to Mauritius alone and under government control in 1842. The exportation of Indian labour was first raised in the House by Buxton on 10 July 1837, when he queried the status of the emigrants. He was assured that the labourers concerned were 'perfectly free'. In February 1838, however, Lord Brougham denounced the system, and while his views were not immediately accepted, in July of that year he called for prohibition, and was informed that, pending enquiries, the trade would be stopped. In the meantime a Natives of India Protection Bill to regulate the migration was being put through the usual procedures. In 1840, Lord John Russell took advantage of a Bill to extend the operation of the Passengers Act to intercolonial migrations, in order to propose that the prohibition should be lifted in the case of Mauritius, but this did not pass. It was not until two years later that the question was decided in favour of reopening migration to Mauritius, with the passing of Act XV of 1842.

The Scale and Operation of Regulated Migration

The 1842 law provided the basic foundations from which government-run indenture was to be maintained and expanded over the course of the nineteenth century. The legislation initially established an Emigration Agent for Mauritius at each of the principal ports in India, and migrants began to arrive from 1843. After a huge influx of more than thirty thousand immigrants to Mauritius from the three Presidencies in that year, emigration was restricted to Calcutta for subsequent years.[5]

In 1844, migration to the West Indies recommenced, and the agents at Calcutta and Madras were authorized to send 5000 emigrants each to British Guiana and Jamaica and 2500 to Trinidad (Figure 1.2). However, as the Land and Emigration Commissioners explained, 'owing to different reasons (of which the scarcity of shipping in India was one)', the numbers actually sent in that year were only 250 for Jamaica, 56 for British Guiana, and 226 to Trinidad. In the succeeding years, the numbers of immigrants shown in Table 1.1 were requisitioned for and despatched.

Between 1845 and 1846 Jamaica had thus received 4,250 immigrants, British Guiana 7,617, and Trinidad 4,159. In 1847 and 1848 no further emigration took place for Jamaica when the House of Assembly intimated their wish that it should be discontinued, whilst 5000 more immigrants were authorized to be despatched to British Guiana and 1000 to Trinidad. Half were to be sent from Calcutta, and the other half from Madras. Once again, however, scarcity of shipping meant that the agents were only able to engage three vessels. In any case, the West India Committee reported that the West Indian Colonies were unable to provide funds for further immigration, and the Indian agents were temporarily relieved of their duties.[6] Following this suspension, Mauritius, which had been continuing to receive a steady inflow of 6000 immigrants per year, was poised to increase its contingent.

At this stage, the West Indies began to cast envious glances at the volume of the Mauritius emigration and the apparent popularity of the island amongst recruits. In 1850, their agent took a close look at the working of the Mauritius emigration depot and reported to the Governor of British Guiana as follows:

> All the emigrants intended for the Mauritius present in the yard, about 500 in number, were brought up for my inspection. I examined them carefully, and I am of opinion that they present the same average appearance of health, strength and physical ability for labour as the last few cargoes which arrived in Demerara from the presidency.
>
> I found that a considerable number of them were returned emigrants, men who had previously been to Mauritius and who had returned from there at the expiration of the five years, or who had anticipated that period by paying themselves a portion of the return passage money. In physical appearance and muscular development, and perhaps also in intelligent expression, these men

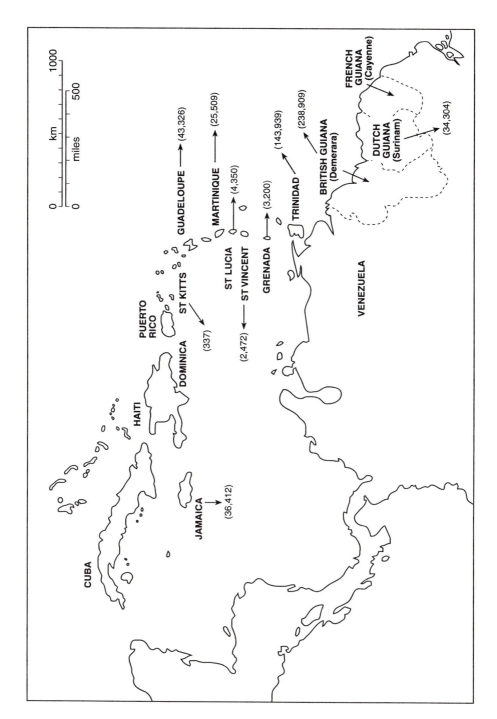

Figure 1.2 Indian indentured labour-importing colonies in the Caribbean. Numbers of Indians received for the period 1846–1914 are given in parentheses.

Source: Tinker, 1974: 114; Lal, 1983: 13; Clarke *et al.*, 1990: 76.

Table 1.1 Number of immigrants requisitioned and despatched, 1845–6

Year and place	Authorized to be sent	Actually despatched	Balance not sent
1845:			
Jamaica	1,750	1,735	15
British Guiana	9,500	3,497	6,003
Trinidad	4,750	2,083	2,667
Total	*16,000*	*7,315*	*8,685*
1846:			
Jamaica	5,000	2,515	2,485
British Guiana	6,000	4,120	1,880
Trinidad	4,000	2,076	1,924
Total	*15,000*	*8,711*	*6,289*

appeared to me somewhat superior to the others, and were evidently returning to Mauritius with the conviction that their situation there would be preferable to their situation in India.

Of these returned emigrants a few were men who, having acquired the confidence of the proprietors or managers of the plantations on which they had been located in Mauritius, were now employed by them as agents for the collection of fresh emigrants in India. These men having all their expenses paid, and the prospect of remuneration proportioned to the number and quality of the emigrants they should bring back with them to Mauritius, had procured labourers in the villages and districts of the country to which they belonged. Mr. Caird has therefore little or no difficulty in obtaining labourers, and has no occasion to employ agents of his own. Emigrants come to the yard of their own accord, or are brought there by the collecting agents acting on behalf of the Mauritius planters.

... Emigration to Mauritius commenced at an early period, and has been continued since 1842 without interruption, regularly and systematically. There is a constant intercourse with the island, as emigration continues throughout the year, and emigrants are going and returning by almost every vessel ... The length of the voyage is well known to the emigrants. Their position on their arrival there is equally well known, and they know also, that if they should be dissatisfied with their position, they can secure a return passage for the sum of 8 or 10 rupees. All these circumstances combine to make the Mauritius emigration attractive to the natives of India, and to inspire them with confidence, and as now conducted it may be considered as being on a permanent and satisfactory footing. While it continues open I apprehend the natives will give a preference to it over all other emigration.[7]

The pertinent observations of the West India agent, notably the knowledge disseminated about the island by its large group of returnee recruiters, was to constitute a special feature of the indenture system in Mauritius throughout its operation, and one which other islands tried with varying degrees of success to emulate.

The envy of the West India labour exporters was very soon to turn to open rivalry when emigration was reopened to British Guiana and Trinidad at the start of the 1850s. The Colonial Land and Emigration Commissioners described the difficulties of:

> suddenly reviving an emigration of this kind. The rival emigration to Mauritius was on foot and was proceeding rapidly. The natives of India are described as excessively attached to the place of their birth, and clinging tenaciously to the joint property which they inherit in the land transmitted to them from their fathers. They will not consent to take with them, and consequently must make up their minds to be separated from, their wives and families; the country to which they are to proceed is only to be reached by a long sea voyage, which they greatly dread, and by which, if Hindoos, they lose their caste. That country is only known to them (if at all) from the fact that, when this emigration recommenced, some thousands of their countrymen had proceeded thither who had not then returned to India, or from the representation of those interested in the rival emigration of Mauritius, who are said to have described British Guiana 'as a great ice land'. That rival emigration was in full progress, and in possession of the ground. And finally, the Calcutta emigration agent could only reach the people through the untrustworthy medium of native agents; and when he had reached them was liable to be disappointed, by capricious and unaccountable changes of intention.[8]

Once again the quota of 5000 for British Guiana and 1000 for Trinidad was not met, only 541 and 178 being despatched respectively.

The West Indies were not alone in fearing the effects of competition: alarmed by the opening up of migration to the Caribbean from Calcutta in 1844, the Mauritian government had requested that emigration be restarted from Madras; but this was not authorized until 1847, and it was not until 1850 that migrants began to flow into Mauritius from Madras. In 1852 Bombay also began to send migrants to Mauritius. In that year the office of a Medical Inspector of Emigrants was created, whose duties were to exercise a sanitary supervision over the various emigration depots, to decide on the eligibility of vessels tendering for the conveyance of migrants overseas, to inspect the stores shipped for their use during the voyage, and by his presence at the embarkation, and careful inspection of the individual emigrants, to guard against the possibility of any persons being shipped whose physical condition rendered them unfit to undertake the long sea voyage.[9]

Between 1850, when the West Indian emigration was restarted, and the close of the 1853 season, 5005 persons had been embarked for British Guiana and 3574 for Trinidad. For the season 1853–4, 2500 migrants were ordered on the part of British Guiana, and 1000 for Trinidad. By 1856–7, Grenada and St Lucia had been added to the list of colonies requisitioning for emigrants, though in that season only Grenada received recruits – 375 in number – in consequence of objections to St Lucia's proposed immigration legislation. British Guiana and Trinidad continued to receive immigrants at the rate of 2987 and 1642 in that season respectively.[10]

None the less, by 1859, with the price of sugar rising and the demand for labour consequently on the increase, dissatisfaction with the organization of recruitment prompted the British authorities to recommend the separation of the emigration agencies and the nomination of a single agent for each colony:

> I am led by an examination of the correspondence to believe that it will be better that the services of the existing agents [at Calcutta and Madras] should hereafter be confined to the Mauritius, and that the West Indian colonies should have a distinct agency of their own ... I think that this measure must put an end to the idea of keeping up a division of seasons between the Mauritius and the West Indies. India will be open throughout the year to the agents of all the colonies concerned to do their best for the advancement of the service on which they are employed, with the exception only, so far as regards the West Indies, of the few months in which paramount sanitary considerations render it unfit that coolies should be [shipped].[11]

At that time, migration to the West Indies was restricted to a certain season of the year, between September and February, whilst that to Mauritius was open all year. However, the Mauritian planters also felt that they had a cause for complaint after noting that immigration slacked off during the West India season. They suspected that arrivals at the depot during that period were 'induced to go to the West Indies'.[12]

The proposal to separate the agencies was the result of intensifying competition and friction between the rival labour exporters. In 1856 the emigration agent for the West Indies at Madras, Thomson, had reported difficulty in shipping labourers for those islands, which he blamed in part on:

> the competition of a Mauritius planter, who was engaged in decrying the West Indian emigration; ... the French, who pay to their emigrants from Pondicherry a bounty of 15 rupees a head; ... and to the disinclination of the people to expatriate themselves for 10 years.[13]

The Colonial Land and Emigration Commissioners commiserated with the West Indians, who they felt were 'at a great disadvantage' compared to Mauritius, which was well known, with a short outward voyage and cheap return passage, and an industrial residence of five years, as compared to ten years for the West Indies. Mr Thomson himself declared that the Mauritian planter who had arrived with four recruiters was attempting to induce his recruits to go to that island, and:

> his people are spreading such reports about the West Indies, saying that if they go there their arms and legs will be cut off, and that they will never see their country again ... that all this deters the poor ignorant people of India from emigrating.[14]

Fortunately for Thomson, orders had been meanwhile received in Mauritius temporarily halting immigration, pending the construction of suitable quarantine facilities. As a result, the Mauritian planter, unable to despatch his recruits, offered them to Thomson, and even proposed that his men could work for the West Indian agent! In the following year, however, the new West India agent at Madras, Franklin, was reporting 'losing men who originally registered themselves to proceed to the West Indies but who are now taking Government service for Burma'.[15] He also proposed shortening the term of industrial residence to five years, to bring it into line with current Mauritian legislation.

In 1858 St Lucia came into the fold, and Act XLVI of 1860 brought the French colonies into the arena of labour exportation, thus adding Reunion, Martinique, Guadeloupe and French Guiana to the ranks of rival colonial interests. In the same year acts were also passed permitting emigration from St Vincent and Natal. In 1862 the Seychelles were given the right to recruit in India.[16] By the start of the 1860s, with a number of colonies thus competing for indentured labour, emigration agents established sub-depots upland from the port towns, in order to prevent rival exporters interfering with their recruits. The Protector of Emigrants at Calcutta explained that the old system of supplying the wants of the colonies

> through the agency of old return Emigrants and other Native Recruiters, who were duly furnished with funds in advance by the Emigration Agent in Calcutta, to enable them to defray the outlay incurred in bringing the people to the Depot

had fallen into disarray owing to the difficulties experienced *en route* to Calcutta. It was now considered necessary to employ the services of paid local agents, stationed in the mufassil, to protect each colony's interests and to receive such emigrants as they were able to procure from the arkatis who went into the recruiting district.[17]

In 1861 there were five offices located at Raniganj, one each for Mauritius, Jamaica, Demerara, Trinidad and Reunion. Arkatis were paid a premium on every migrant delivered at a rate of Rs2 per man, Rs6 for man and wife, half the above rates for children from 10 to 16 years of age, and a quarter of the same for those below 10 years. Raniganj was an important site because of its location on the main road leading from Bihar and Hazaribag, along which, it was re-ported,

> numbers of poor persons travelling down the country in search of employment are intercepted and prevailed upon to accept food and clothing on the road . . . when once they take assistance from the Agents, they are entirely in their power, and the Agents offer them to any of the Offices without much choice on the part of the Coolies themselves.

On arrival in Raniganj, the migrants were taken by rail to Calcutta. This particular observer, however, decried the labour which was being taken away from needy local employers, which may account in part for his disapproval of the overseas agency proceedings. The Government of Bengal was called upon to move the inspection and examination of recruits from Calcutta to the mufassil, but replied that:

> Government cannot interfere with the proceedings of the Recruiters in the Mofussil, provided they do nothing contrary to the Law ... To examine and inspect Coolies at Raneegunge ... would only cause the removal from Raneegunge to some place higher up the road of the other malpractices which are supposed to exist.[18]

At the end of 1861, the Agent for British Guiana complained that 'two batches of Coolies collected for his Agency had been decoyed away'. Evidently Mauritian recruiters were deemed to be at fault, because Caird, the representative of that colony's interests, defended himself to the Bengal Government by suggesting they 'call upon the Magistrate at Raneegunge for a Report of the circumstances under which he directed the Coolies in question to be forwarded to the Mauritius Depot'.[19]

In what seemed to be an endless succession of such incidents, the next clash was between the English and French emigration agents at Calcutta. On this occasion, Mr Caird considered himself the aggrieved party, informing a local magistrate that:

> a man named 'Solum', a return Emigrant from the Mauritius, had collected in his own District a band of eighty-four souls in all, and was proceeding in charge of them ... when he was met on the way by several Emissaries of the Bourbon Agency, and from what these Emissaries stated to the laborers, the latter were led to infer they would be escorted by them direct to my Depot for ultimate shipment to the Mauritius, for which place they had left their homes. ... on the party of Emigrants reaching Raneegunge, railway tickets were taken for the whole number to Howrah, but the most singular fact in the case is that, instead of being brought on to Howrah, as the Coolies believed they would be, they were taken out of the railway carriages at Chundernagore, a French settlement, detained there some little time, fed with sweetmeats, and then put on board boats and brought to a Ghat at Garden Reach (within a few hundred yards of the Bourbon Depot), and there landed in the middle of the night. The Coolies themselves say that it was so dark they were unable to discover in which direction they were being taken, or to what Depot.[20]

Learning of these proceedings, Caird went himself to the Bourbon depot, in the company of the Protector of Emigrants, and interrogated the migrants as to their preferred destination. On their stating that they wished to go to Mauritius, they were taken to his depot. In their own version of events, the French agents declared that the batch of migrants in question:

> consisting of forty for Bourbon, and 103 for Mauritius, were brought from the villages of Boondon and Comar, in the District of Lamhee, under charge of recruiters Lagoo, Ladarnauth, Cimoo, Lam, and Gopaul Missen ... Our reason for bringing the men first to Chandernagore and then by boat to your Depot, was to avoid the unpleasant conflict that arises from Mr. Caird's armed men interfering, as they always do, with all Coolies brought by us, and you know that we

have had several batches taken from us by him, and to avoid such, we have chosen this course.[21]

A month later, the French agents themselves complained of 'another case of appropriation of Coolies by Mr. Caird', whose men took charge of two bands of migrants destined for Bourbon and Mauritius, and then proposed sending them to St Kitts. The agents, Harley & Co., accused the Mauritian recruiters of coercive tactics and urged the authorities to interview nineteen men remaining at the Mauritius depot 'that would not be compelled or drugged to proceed to St Kitts'.[22]

Leaving aside the mutual recriminations, it was evident that the Mauritian agent, trading on the well-known name of that colony, tended to come off better in disputes over bands recruited. Not surprisingly then, when the Mauritian Government sent their Protector to India to investigate the system of recruitment, he advocated the establishment of a central depot to which all intending migrants could be brought, and from it be drafted to the separate colonial depots. The representatives of the other colonies roundly condemned this proposal. In a joint statement the agents of Jamaica, British Guiana, Trinidad and the French colonies claimed that the idea had been suggested by Beyts, the Mauritian Protector, 'with the evident object of diverting the Emigration, now so successfully flowing into the British West Indies and Bourbon, from those Islands to that of Mauritius only'.[23]

Despite the seemingly intense competition, or perhaps because of it, migration to the West Indies and Mauritius had slowed in the 1860s. In the 1862–3 season eleven ships were despatched from Calcutta and two from Madras for the West Indies: British Guiana received 2967 immigrants, and Trinidad 1389. Two of these ships took 545 recruits from Madras to Jamaica. By the middle of the decade, Mauritius was also importing a much lower number of immigrants, and the requisitions of that colony were not much higher than for the West Indies. During the year 1866, sixteen ships arrived in Mauritius from India with 5596 emigrants, whilst in the West India season, British Guiana received 4509, Trinidad 2993, Jamaica 1705 and St Vincent 490 immigrants.[24]

Mauritius continued, nevertheless, to be held up as the best organized of the labour exporters. In 1863, the medical inspector at Calcutta, Dr Partridge, reported that he had five depots under his medical superintendence, which he visited each week or ten days. He reserved his highest praise for the Mauritius depot: 'of all the depots, the one in which the internal arrangements are most unexceptionable and to which I should wish eventually to assimilate the others, is the Mauritius depot'.[25]

Most of the colonies which imported Indian labour were still at this stage looking elsewhere for cane workers. The West Indies imported numbers of liberated Africans, and even some Madeiran and Chinese workers were periodically recruited. In 1868, for example, the government of Trinidad sought to ascertain whether a better class of emigrants could be obtained from China, and commissioned Mr Warner, their Emigration Agent at Calcutta, to proceed there to enquire into the subject. Mauritius received several contingents of liberated Africans in the 1860s, whilst Jamaica renewed its interest in India, appointing Mr Anderson to be their Emigration Agent in 1868 and instructing him to despatch 1272 migrants.[26]

Evidently by 1864 competition between agencies was still rife, for the French agents continued to complain of interference by the Mauritius depot personnel. The Protector of Emigrants scarcely knew what course of action to take. On investigating the case of the disputed band of migrants 'it was found out that they were recruited and registered for Bourbon. They were accordingly told by me to go to the French Depot'. However, he could not bring himself to blame the Mauritius agent for attempting to take the men off to his depot:

> although not approving of Mr. Eales' conduct in diverting these people from their way to the Bourbon Depot, for to that Depot he was given clearly to understand by the Jemadar they had been registered for, . . . nevertheless the unanimous cry of Maureech is some justification in his disbelief of the Jemadar's statement.[27]

In 1864 a consolidating law was passed which was designed to remove major discrepancies in legislation governing emigration to different colonies, to regulate recruitment and depot procedures for the better protection of migrants, and to define the duties of the Protectors of Emigrants. In the same year, heavy mortality on the passage from Bombay to Mauritius led to a suspension of emigration from that Presidency.

Following the passing of this act, the indentured labour-importing colonies complained against competition from inter-Asian migrations, such as those to the tea plantations. They decried the increasingly tough laws regulating the collection and despatch of their migrants, whilst countries like Ceylon and Malaysia, which shipped even larger numbers of workers, were not subject to the same provisions. After the implementation of Act XIII of 1864, it was pointed out that the depot accommodation of the Ceylon Agency in South India was inferior, and that the Ceylon recruiters could bring 'their coolies down the coast in frail country coasting vessels called dhonies ... we are required to bring our coolies down the coast by steamers or first class sailing vessels'. The West Indian and Mauritius agents had to pay registration fees to magistrates and protectors and employ a surgeon, whilst the Ceylon Agent, relieved of all these expenses, was 'able to pay a much higher premium to contractors and recruiters ... and thus obtain coolies more readily than ourselves'.[28]

By the mid-1860s Mauritius was also feeling the effects of competition from Natal, because of the higher price paid to the latter's contractors, at Rs35 a head. Natal recruited principally in the southern districts of the Madras Presidency, and the fee offered to the contractors meant they:

were better able to apply a higher premium to their recruiters than that allowed by the Mauritius Government. It was thus that Mr Burton unwittingly created a competition between our southern contractors and Natal contractors, and the consequence has been that our men first become dissatisfied – held back for some time from furnishing us with coolies – and when they did give us any, they were occasional and few; and now they are still clamorous for similar rates as the Natal contractors get.

There were similar problems for Mauritius in competition with the French, who continued to operate from their settlements of Pondicherry, Yanam and Karikal, having closed down their Madras agency some years earlier. Once again, it was represented that the contractors preferred the French service because they were permitted 'under the pretence of supposed advances, to extort Rs 13 from each emigrant out of the Rs 15 which he receives prior to embarkation'. The Indian government was exhorted to place the French agencies also under the operation of Act XIII of 1864 in all respects.[29]

Mauritius soon had other problems to be concerned with. In his report on the 1866–7 season, the Calcutta Protector noted that emigration to that island had:

fallen off very considerably during the past year chiefly from two causes: firstly, owing to the high prices of grain imported for the consumption of laborers in the Colony; and secondly, from the depressed state of the agricultural prospects of the Island, in consequence of the recent severe drought, the effects of which are likely to be disastrous. For these reasons emigration on account of Government is temporarily suspended. There are, however, a number of old emigrants returning to Mauritius at their own expense, paying their passage, – a fact which speaks for itself, as indicative of the general condition and prospects of laborers in that Colony.[30]

In that year, Mauritius imported only 478 immigrants, compared with 4509 for Guiana, 2993 for Trinidad and 1705 for Jamaica. Even diminutive St Vincent claimed 490 labourers. Immigration to Mauritius recovered slightly in the following season but continued to be lower than that for the principal West Indian islands. The prevalence of epidemic fever in the island and the resulting mortality provoked the temporary suspension of emigration operations.[31] Mauritius had seen the peak years of its immigration strategy and now became a minor player, as other colonies, like Fiji, moved in to tap the Indian labour market.

In 1871 Act VIII was passed to consolidate the laws concerning emigration of native labourers from British India. Many previous regulations were restated, and further measures instituted, particularly relating to the operations of recruiters. Under the Act, emigration agents were subject to approval by the government of India, and their remuneration was made a fixed annual salary. The Indian government was to appoint a protector of emigrants at each port, whose duties were outlined by the Act. He was to license the depots established by emigration agents and to inspect them along with a medical inspector. The Protector was also made responsible for the licensing of recruiters, who were entitled to recruit for one destination only and were required to present themselves before the local magistrates of the districts in which they were working. Emigration was authorized from the three ports of Calcutta, Madras and Bombay, and migrants were required to register with the magistrates of their home districts before leaving their region. The magistrate was to ascertain their comprehension of the contractual terms offered them; in the port towns, the Protector himself was expected to examine emigrants. If emigrants were considered by the Medical Inspector to be unfit or if found to be irregularly recruited, emigration agents were required to pay the amount necessary to return the migrants to their homes and to maintain them until they were fit to make the journey. Ships proposing to transport migrants were also required to be licensed, and for this they had to be surveyed by the Protector of Emigrants and to have adequate space to carry their passengers, including space for a hospital and separate accommodation for women and children. The Act also regulated the provisions, cooking fuel and water that such ships should carry. Emigrants who refused to embark could not be forced to do so, but were liable for debts incurred on their behalf. The usual lists of persons embarking were prescribed. Emigrants proceeding to French colonies were required to carry an interpreter. Due penalties were prescribed for infringements of the Act. The probable length of voyages was defined as follows: for Mauritius, Seychelles and Reunion, six weeks from Madras and Bombay and eight weeks from Calcutta; for the West Indies, nineteen weeks from Madras and Bombay and twenty weeks from Calcutta, and for Natal, ten weeks from Madras and Bombay and twelve weeks from Calcutta.[32]

The passing of the Act brought howls of protest from emigration agents concerned that the licensing and registration provisions would hamper their work. In their report for 1871, the Emigration Commissioners admitted that the operations of the agents at Calcutta were affected by the new legislation passed in that year. They noted that some of the magistrates who were opposed to emigration generally refused to countersign the recruiters' licences, while others delayed their signatures to make enquiries. Under these circumstances several of the sub-agents resigned their agencies, and the recruiters returned their badges. The Commissioners deprecated these actions, convinced as they were of the benefits of indenture:

> some of the magistrates in India, from false impressions as to the advantage of emigration to the Indian labourers, dislike it, and the course adopted by the Lieutenant-Governor afforded a plausible ground, of which they were not slow to avail themselves, for discouraging it. Yet it cannot be denied that as a general rule Indian emigrants improve their condition very much by emigration to the West Indies. In their own country their wages, even at the best times are very low; their employment is uncertain; they are exposed to privations which from time to time

assume the dimensions of wide-spread famines, and they are without the prospect, or even the possibility, or improving their material or social condition. In the
West Indies, on the contrary, every one who will work can obtain employment;
their labour is light; their wages are far beyond anything they could earn in India,
and it depends only on themselves to add to them by extra industry.[33]

As the supply of labour to the West Indies and Mauritius dwindled or levelled
out, complaints about obstruction and competition gave way to considerations
of cost, and attempts to pare the expenditure of the agencies. In 1873, whilst
the government of Surinam was preparing to receive its first Indian immigrants,
the governments of Natal, the West Indies and Mauritius were informed of
proposals to amalgamate the agencies.[34] The Protector felt that:

The proposed joint agency, under a thoroughly efficient and trustworthy officer,
will doubtless prove not only economical to the several colonies interested
therein, but also beneficial to the intending emigrants themselves [who] have no
ready means, prior to registration, of fully ascertaining the truthfulness of the
statements put forward by recruiters interested in recruitment only so far as to
advance their own private ends.[35]

However, the government of Bengal stressed that the case of Mauritius was
'quite apart from the West Indian colonies, and under different conditions
which are well known to the Indian population', so that it should be kept
separate from the proposed West Indian Colonies Amalgamated Emigration
Agencies.[36] In later years, in fact, the Mauritius agency was to be amalgamated
with that of other colonies.

Mauritius was generally treated as in a class of its own in so far as emigration
was concerned. In his report on the working of the emigration depots in 1874,
the Protector noted that a special feature of the Mauritius depot was that there
was always 'a comparatively large number of old returned emigrants about to
re-emigrate with their families and friends', who cooked for themselves and did
not require the same level of care as that bestowed on new migrants travelling
alone.[37]

Despite such special considerations, by the 1870s Mauritius was no longer
the model colony of the Indian indenture diaspora, and the true state of affairs
was revealed by Sir Arthur Hamilton Gordon, who, having completed a stint in
Trinidad, was able to compare the West Indian colonies with Mauritius when
he arrived as governor there. In the transmission of requisitions – that is, in
regulating the annual introduction of labour – Gordon showed that the government in the West Indies exercised a much greater control over the level of
immigration:

In all the West Indian colonies every proprietor desiring labour sends in to the
Immigration Office before a fixed day in the year a statement of the number of
coolies he wishes to be introduced for him. The Government . . . orders either that
whole number, or any less number it thinks proper, it being entirely free to them
to do so or not. In Mauritius the requisition may be sent in at any time, and if

accompanied by an engagement to pay the necessary expenses, must be forwarded to the Agent of the Colony in India to be complied with. There is no limit
to the number of labourers which may be asked for, and no direction on the part
of the Government as to the transmission of the application to India.[38]

In Mauritius, unlike the West Indies – where the allotment of labourers was left
to the colonial government on their arrival – new immigrants were indentured
in India to a particular estate. This difference was important, because in the
West Indian colonies the allotment to estates depended on conditions on those
establishments. Thus, reported Gordon, in Antigua a proprietor in arrears
would not be allotted labour, in Grenada an estate without a hospital would not
receive any immigrants, as in Demerara, where additionally the mortality of
Indian labourers on specified estates was also a factor. In Mauritius, the
government could not use these means to ensure that estates where conditions
were bad would not be allowed to recruit new labour. Instead, the planters had
virtual control over the quantity of immigrants they would introduce, no matter
what their record of labour management.

One reason for the ultra-repressive legislation implemented in Mauritius was
the centrality of sugar production on the island and the corresponding political
influence of the planters. At the same time, the perceived vital role of Indian
labourers there pre-empted measures which were imposed in colonies where
the sugar lobby was less strong, such as the 1895 law in Natal which effectively
gave the Indians a choice of reindenture or repatriation. This contrasts with
Mauritius, 'where planter ascendancy was unquestioned, such compromises
were unnecessary and land settlement by time-expired labourers was in fact
encouraged from the 1880s onwards'.[39]

In 1878 Fiji became the last of the major Indian indentured labour-
importing colonies to begin registering emigrants. The scheme was master-
minded by Sir Arthur Hamilton Gordon, ironically the same man who had
been so scathing about the Indians' treatment in his previous posting, Mauritius. Apparently, he still considered indentured labourers to be useful kick-
starters of capitalist plantation economies, despite the social problems their
presence engendered. There is no evidence that the measures he set up to
regulate the indenture system in Fiji resulted in more humane conditions and
treatment. On the contrary, the testimonies which emerged from Fiji of a living
'narak', mediated by the likes of C.F. Andrews, became potent weapons for a
growing anti-indenture lobby. The drawing to a close of the indenture system,
which was officially abolished in 1914 but did not breathe its last until a few
more ships had off-loaded their human cargoes in the 1920s, occurred at a time
when its economic significance had, in any case, greatly declined, but was
doubtless spurred on by the political agitation against it in India.[40] By then
around 1.3 million Indians had emigrated as indentured labourers.[41] When the
Sanderson Committee produced its 1910 report, indenture was considered by
its exponents and regulators to have more or less 'done its work', but perhaps its

demise was hastened at the grass-roots level by pamphlets like the following, which circulated in eastern UP (Uttar Pradesh) at around the same time:

> *Save yourselves from depot wallahs*
> *It is not a service but pure deception*
> *They take you overseas*
> *They are not colonies but jails.*[42]

Recruiters and Recruits

Gordon had demonstrated many flaws in the Mauritian system, perhaps symptomatic of a colony which was no longer really in need of imported labour and could rely on the circular migration of returnees to maintain immigrant levels. Grierson, however, opined that:

> returned emigrants do not, as a rule, succeed as recruiters. A man who returns from the colonies with money would not care to undertake the arduous and unpopular duties, and a man who returns without money would, for obvious reasons, not be desirable.[43]

This flew in the face of the evidence offered by the Mauritius emigration agents and by their competitors, who watched the stream of arrivals at the port towns accompanied by returnees. In the recruiting districts, the vital role of return emigrants was revealed by the Magistrate of Patna, who explained:

> The coolies who emigrate to Mauritius and elsewhere generally return with comparatively handsome fortunes, and their good luck is noised abroad. Coolies working in the Colonies send information of their well-doing to their friends and relatives by the return Coolies, and the first information called for by those who feel inclined to emigrate is as to the climate of the country they have served in. Intending Emigrants being satisfied on that point have no objection to cross the 'Black water' and sell their labor in the dearest market. Irish Emigrants remit money to their friends in Ireland and send information of their well-doing. The Indian Coolie does the same, only his love of country is as great as he always returns to it, after putting by a handsome provision for his old age.[44]

The important role of returnees is paradoxically demonstrated by the problems they created for labour exporters at times of competition, when returnees from one colony were lured into the recruiting service of another. Differential rates of remuneration naturally tempted recruiters to take the highest offer. In 1861, the Mauritian agent taunted Marriott, the British Guiana representative, with the contention that 'there is not on your establishment a single recruiter who had not been employed by this agency for the last 17 years in recruiting coolies for the Mauritius'.[45] The Governor of Mauritius drafted a Minute in which he deprecated the departure of recruiters into the service of other colonies and the tactics they used for their new employers:

It would seem that many of the Recruiters who are employed at the other Colonial Depots, have been in the service of the Mauritius Depot, and have, no doubt, been generally known as having been attached to that Service, and they are the principal persons who practice these frauds on intending Emigrants. Among the devices they employ, they appear to be in the habit of representing the Depot of the West Indian Establishments as the 'New Mauritius Depot' at Calcutta, into which Indians coming down from the Country for the purpose of emigrating to Mauritius are decoyed, under pretence that they will be forwarded from thence to this Island, while in reality they are shipped for British Guiana, or some other West Indian Colony.

It seems also beyond doubt that many old Immigrants of Mauritius who have been sent back to India for the purpose of aiding the Recruiting Service of this Colony have been bought over by the Recruiters of other places.

It also appears that the newly appointed Emigration Agent of the French government, and his partner at Calcutta, are largely employed by Planters in this Colony in recruiting for them; and, for the reasons given by our Agent, he seems to have good grounds for apprehending that many Indians who had been recruited for Mauritius will have emigrated to Reunion under the impression that they were going to Mauritius.[46]

The Governor suggested that since a considerable effort had been made to separate the West Indian and Demerara Agencies from those of Mauritius, in order to guard against all possible conflict of interest, and nefarious practices on the part of recruiters, it was equally necessary that agents employed either at West Indian or Foreign depots should have no links with the Mauritius depots in any of the Presidencies.

However, if Mauritius had always relied on return migrants, did this make the island a special case, or was this feature shared by other indentured labour-importing colonies? By the 1870s the Demerara migration was certainly beginning to exhibit some of the same features as the Mauritius indenture system, with increasing numbers of returnees featuring in annual emigration. In his report for 1873–4, the Calcutta Protector speculated:

> the fact that 96 were found willing to return to Demerara during the year may in part be explained by the large remuneration which labour finds there, the average sum brought back to this country by each emigrant having been no less than Rs 293 during the past year. It is a new feature that among the returned emigrants to Demerara several should be found proceeding to the colony as private passengers and paying large sums for their passage.[47]

It seems plausible that the information networks which operated in the recruiting districts had registered the declining economic position of Mauritius and the harsh legislation recently enforced there against time-expired immigrants, and that British Guiana was usurping the favoured position of Mauritius. If further research proves this to be the case for the West Indies and other colonies, we might need to consider the redefinition of the indenture system in terms which bring it closer to the kangani model of Sri Lanka and Malaya.[48]

Returnees worked alongside the local recruiting hierarchy: agents, sub-agents, duffadars, arkatis and maistries. The operations stretched across three distinct zones: the recruiting districts, the mufassil half-way stations where sub-depots were located, and the port towns where the main depots were sited and from where migrants were embarked for the various colonies. The emigration agents were usually European officials who liaised with contractors and sub-agents, and employed returnees and local recruiters. In the mufassil the duties of the sub-agents included superintending the operations of the recruiters, providing for the lodging and feeding of emigrants and their registration before the local magistrate, and despatching them by railway to the depot.[49] The ordinary recruiters came from a range of backgrounds: visiting the Demerara depot in Shahabad in the early 1880s, Grierson met with four recruiters whose previous employments had been respectively as a peon to a zamindar, a servant to a mahajan, a watchman, and a return emigrant from Mauritius.[50] A list of recruiters employed for the West Indies in 1866–7 reveals the range of districts across which the agents were spread, and the varied ethnic background of recruiters. The vast majority were Indian born, but Table 1.2 does not reveal how many were returnees.

The work of recruiters, and the characteristics of those they collected, depended on a number of factors. Socio-economic conditions in India affected the ease with which labour could be mobilized, whilst successive legislative reforms determined both the methods employed by recruiters and the types of

Table 1.2 Sub-agents and recruiters employed in the Mofussil by the Emigration Agencies for British Guiana and Jamaica, 1866–7

Name	District	Native of	Employed as
Noorkhan	Lucknow	India	Sub-agent
M.C. Bose	Dinapore	India	Sub-agent
Vanspall	Midnapore	Surinam	Sub-agent
Hobeeboolla	Chupra	India	Licensed recruiter
Soopun Khan	Gurbeta	India	Licensed recruiter
Richard Walter	Midnapore	Jamaica	Licensed recruiter
A. Renben	Bhangulpore	India	Licensed recruiter
Budree	Dinapore	India	Licensed recruiter
W. Dickson	Bancoorah	India	Licensed recruiter
Jacob Solomon	Arrah	India	Licensed recruiter
Kollon Khan and 8 others	Oude	India	Licensed recruiter
Hosseinee	Midnapore	India	Licensed recruiter
M.J. Manasseh	Benares/Arrah	India	Licensed recruiter
Rumjaun Khan	Cawnpore	India	Licensed recruiter
B.C. Soor	Sasseram	India	Licensed recruiter
Saligram	Benares	India	Licensed recruiter
W. Goddard	Bancoorah	India	Licensed recruiter
Meer Moordikie	Goruckpore	India	Licensed recruiter

Source: BEP 432/21

individual they were likely to target. Finally, recruiters worked within the constraints of a profession which was not always appreciated.[51] According to Grierson, 'they dare not go into the bustees to recruit for fear of being maltreated, or of having false cases brought against them. It is for this reason that they can never leave the bazaars or open streets'. Recruiters also reported that the police frightened intending emigrants away. In Bihar, a sub-agent named Badri Sahu complained that:

> when he recruits men of respectable castes, the police find their way into the depot and turn them out, saying that the Government is going to make Christians out of them, and that they would be eaten up by maggots and leeches.[52]

Perhaps this was an instance of caste solidarity, but in other cases obstructive tactics by police were due less to their disapproval of emigration than to their greed for bribes. Thus Grierson's informants noted that constables habitually stationed themselves at the Howrah bridge in Calcutta, refusing to let bands of recruits pass unless a bribe of Rs2 or Rs3 was paid.[53]

Other obstacles placed in the way of recruiters included the intervention of Europeans whose servants had been kidnapped, the delaying tactics of sceptical magistrates, and the anti-emigration lobbying of Indian capitalists, anxious to prevent the flow of labour overseas. In 1856, for example, the West India Emigration Agent complained that the Assistant Collector of Salem refused to pass the emigrants collected by his maistry (Morla Meerah), and put a peon as a guard over the maistry until they were dispersed. In his reply, the Magistrate explained that he did not pass the coolies referred to, because the maistry stated that he had engaged them to go to Mauritius.[54] Magistrates did not hesitate to use agents' rivalry amongst themselves to block the migration process. Thus, in 1857, migration was interrupted at Madras:

> on the complaint of the emigration agent that a number of persons 'licensed' by his maistries were making an improper use of their office in carrying coolies to the French Settlements. Orders were issued to the several Collectors to put the law in force against such parties. The proceedings instituted under these instructions appear to have put a stop, for a time, to emigration altogether. The Agent's maistries, honest and dishonest alike, were obstructed in their proceedings, weeks passed without the arrival at Madras of a single laborer and emigration was virtually at a standstill.[55]

The large-scale emigration and rising numbers of colonies competing for labour in mid-nineteenth-century India did not go unnoticed by local capitalists. The Bengal Landholders' Association, in 1861, viewed 'with alarm the strenuous efforts which are being made by the various Agencies established in Calcutta, for the encouragement of Native Emigration to the West Indies, Mauritius, and the French Colony of Bourbon', and plans to grow cotton in Australia using cheap Indian labour. They considered that an 'erroneous impression appears to exist in these various Colonies, and in England, that

India is over-populated'; this they refuted, adding that natives of India disliked sea travel, and accusing the overseas agencies of deceiving:

> the simple agriculturist, who in many Districts is little removed from the ignorant condition of savage life. He is not made to understand he is wanted to labor in countries only to be reached after a long sea voyage, but with specious promises, or other less justifiable means, is induced to proceed to the Capital, and there shipped off in comparative ignorance of his destination and engagements.[56]

The Association therefore sustained its anti-emigration campaign by casting doubts on the real willingness of migrants to proceed overseas. Their representative asserted that the Protector of Emigrants could not in practice ascertain the actual knowledge possessed by the intending migrants, and described the process of confirming consent thus:

> The intending Emigrants, prior to embarkation, are usually asked in gangs if they are willing to proceed to Mauritius, Demerara, or other parts for which they are recruited, and mixed in those gangs or around them are Native decoys who vociferate loudly their willingness to proceed to the Port they are wanted for, the rest or some of them ignorantly join in the cry, and thus the general assent is considered as given and the people are embarked.[57]

In 1867 the British Guiana agent complained that the Collector at Kanpur would not register his recruits, 'saying that I was sending all the strong people out of India, and that I had taught the people to speak all in one tongue', meaning that the intending emigrants had been all taught to express their willingness to emigrate, and their satisfaction with the terms of the engagements.[58]

The delaying tactics of magistrates continued to be a source of irritation to labour exporters throughout the nineteenth century. In 1871 the Jamaica agent reported that some of these officials kept intending emigrants waiting for two and three days before they would register them:

> Obstructions are thrown in the way of registering the emigrant, and at times it has been with the greatest difficulty that they could be got registered at all; so bad has it become in some districts that it has been reported to me that batches of coolies have been removed from the district in which they were collected, and taken to another, where the magistrate had the reputation of being a fair dealing man, and one who attended to his duties himself without the intervention of subordinates.[59]

If the local capitalists were motivated by purely economic interests, magistrates and other British Indian officials who came into frequent contact with intending emigrants were actuated also by the desire to prevent unrealistic promises from being made to naive villagers. These complaints prompted the labour exporters to issue notices – translated into Indian languages – for intending emigrants which purportedly described average wage rates, contractual terms and working conditions. Whilst not strictly inaccurate, they continued to paint a rosy picture of the indenture system, as the following notice issued by the Trinidad Emigration Agent reveals:

The Bearer of this
(....
.... Badge No.
....)
is employed by the undersigned to recruit Agricultural Emigrants for the Government of Trinidad in the West Indies, in which Colony they will be treated with kindness and always enjoy Government protection.

Emigrants will be provided with a free passage from Calcutta to Trinidad for themselves and their families, with proper food, clothing, and Medical attendance during the voyage.

On their arrival in Trinidad they will be located on such Estates only, the proprietors of which have produced medical Certificates that proper and healthy lodgings are ready for their reception.

The Island is exceedingly fertile, and the rates of wages for work, which is principally ... by piece work, vary from ten Annas to one Rupee, and an industrious laborer can easily earn double the latter sum in a day.

In no case is the daily pay less than ten annas; during the crop (the season for manufacturing the Cane juice into Sugar) the ordinary wages for all employed are thirteen and a half annas, those laborers employed in keeping up the fire for boiling the juice of the Cane, superintendents of work, and trenchers, are paid at a higher rate, as those varieties of work require greater attention.

Whilst ill the Emigrants are provided with Medical attendance, medicine, and nourishment gratis.

They are provided at all times with houses rent free, and in most instances with as much garden ground as they can cultivate at their leisure hours for their own benefit. The climate and soil are favorable to the production of every description of grain and vegetables grown in this country.

Emigrants can always communicate with their relatives and friends in India through the medium of the Protector of Emigrants in Trinidad and the Agent here. Great care is taken by the Protector of Emigrants in Trinidad in locating the Emigrants on their arrival, not only not to separate blood relations, but to respect as well the more distant ties of kindred and of even local acquaintances.

Whole families, men, women, and children, can go together.

Any further details will be communicated to the Emigrants on their arrival here. The undersigned will be thankful for any assistance rendered by the Authorities in the Mofussil, or their subordinates to the bearer, who is particularly cautioned against misrepresenting his position or deceiving intending Emigrants in any way.

Trinidad Emigration Agency Office,
Trinidad Emigration Agent.
Calcutta, 186-

What kinds of people were tempted by such notices into registering as migrants? Individual explanations for migration reveal an intriguing blend of economic necessity, chance encounters, trickery, and traditions of labour mobility in defining causative factors (see the individual accounts in Chapter

2). However, these decisions or circumstances cannot be considered in isolation from the broader defining features of indentured migration. The characteristics of the overseas Indian populations depended on the location and networks of recruiters, the level of influence of returnees in the targeting of specific villages, externally imposed restrictions on the migration of certain caste or ethnic groups, and gender requirements, to name only some.

The legislation governing sex ratios in indentured migration is a good example of the effects of externally imposed requirements on the make-up of the migrant population. In 1843, when Mauritius began to recruit labour, on average only 13 women were despatched per 100 men. A year later, when the West Indies joined the ranks of the labour importers, women formed around 21 per cent of migrants. This fell to 16 per cent at the close of the 1840s, but following legislation which prevented ships from departing without a required proportion of women, the annual rate rose to 30 per cent and 40 per cent of male emigrants.

The determination of the imperial authorities to secure a due proportion of women and children to accompany male indentured migrants was demonstrated by Russell's threat, in the mid-1850s, to put a stop to emigration if this was not achieved. Russell pointed out that in European emigration to North America and Australia, the proportion of female migrants had been 80 to 100 or 4 females to 5 males. This remained a major difference between the two contemporaneous migration streams. The issue of sex disproportion was considered even more important in the West Indies than in Mauritius, as underscored by the Secretary of State when he informed the Governor of British Guiana that measures proposed for Mauritius:

> are to be considered as equally applicable to the West Indies, where indeed, it is still more important to redress the disproportion, inasmuch as the immigrants being brought from a greater distance, and for a longer term of service, must be regarded as constituting a more permanent population.[60]

However, the problems of legislating for a desired sex ratio in immigration were outlined by the Land and Emigration Commissioners in their report on migration in 1866:

> In the course of the year a question arose as to the minimum proportion of females to males to be required in the emigration. This question is attended by considerable difficulties, because, on the one hand, a small proportion of women gives rise to strifes and jealousies, if not to worse crimes among the men, while, on the other, to require a large proportion leads either to the acceptance of a very inferior class, or to an injurious limitation of the whole number of emigrants.[61]

In the convention which had been set up with the French government in 1860, it had been agreed that for the first three years the proportion of females in the emigration should be fixed at one fourth the number of males, for the next two years at one third, and after that time at one half. By 1866, therefore, women

Table 1.3 Proportions of female to male migrants, 1866–7

Countries	Males	Females	Proportion of females to males %
Mauritius	3,718	1,898	51.05
British Guiana	3,072	1,437	46.78
Trinidad	1,979	1,014	51.24
Jamaica	1,156	549	47.49
St Vincent	306	184	60.13
Total	*10,231*	*5,082*	*49.67*

should have been emigrating in numbers equivalent to one third, or just over 33 per cent, of the whole number. The Indian governments, however, expressed doubts as to the expediency of enforcing this rule. The Bengal government proposed that the proportion should be reduced to 25 per cent, and the Madras government that it should be fixed permanently at 35 per cent. Eventually it was decided to fix the minimum proportion at 33 per cent of the whole number, or 50 females to every 100 males. The greater the migration, the more difficult it was for the colonies to achieve this ratio. In the 1866–7 season, the proportion of female to male migrants was as shown in Table 1.3.

In 1872, when the 40:100 female/male ratio was applied, the West Indies only managed an average proportion of 37.83 to 100.[62] Eventually, the rule was relaxed to provide for a 25 per cent sex ratio of women to men. The ratio of women to men in migration was also a function of the encouragement given to family resettlement in the colonies, of the level of activity of returnees in bringing female relatives overseas, and of the type of labour required.[63]

The requirements of employers, as articulated in their requisitions or in the instructions given to emigration agents by the colonial states, also helped to define the characteristics of indentured populations by restricting recruitment to certain castes, age ranges and ethnic groups. Thus the British Guiana agent at Calcutta was instructed to reject all intending migrants who showed signs of disease, were aged more than 35 if male or 30 if female, or were of the castes of Fakirs, Kayeths, Brahmins and Baniahs. This did not stop high-caste migrants from concealing their real status or prevent contemporaries from issuing blanket generalizations about those who went overseas. When Grierson made his survey of the castes of 1226 migrants and found that only one-third could be characterized as of a low social position, he noted that this contradicted what he stated was the universal belief: 'I have been assured by every native from whom I have enquired, and by most Europeans, that only the lowest castes emigrated'.[64]

Naturally, assumptions about the caste and social status of recruits were often made to serve other ends. The tortuous logic of one member of the Police Enquiry Commission in Mauritius, who sought to explain (as a reason for harsh colonial vagrancy legislation) both that migrants were composed of 'the scum of the Presidencies', including 'a large infusion of the criminal class', and that many emigrants after 1857 were mutineer sepoys, who would not generally deign to emigrate, is a case in point:

> I have met many old soldiers who, to my personal knowledge, must have been actively concerned in 1857 in the mutiny of an army in which they and their forefathers had for a century eaten the salt of the Honorable East India Company ... it requires but little knowledge of the Bengal sepoy and his history to show he would not emigrate to work as a coolie from choice, on the contrary, he would, if he did leave his country, naturally finding the work distasteful, I may almost say impossible, run off, and pass his time vagabondising, preying on his neighbours.[65]

A number of studies have drawn upon statistical evidence gleaned from migrant certificates and registers to re-evaluate the caste background of indentured migrants.[66] This volume, using case histories documented in the following chapters, demonstrates that individuals from a very wide range of social backgrounds found themselves drawn into the recruiter's net.

As with caste, nineteenth-century officials did not tire of speculating on regional differences in migration and ascribing preferences for particular colonies in explanation. Thus in his report for 1873–4 the Calcutta Protector noted:

> the detailed returns given show that the native of Oude, as a rule preferred to emigrate to Demerara; while natives of Bengal and Behar preferred the Mauritius, which also attracted a large number of men from North West Provinces. It is noticeable that of the lower provinces of Bengal, the eastern districts with their large population supply but a very trifling quota to the emigration agencies for the colonies. The probability is that these districts find a nearer and more convenient field for their surplus labour in the tea plantations of Assam and Cachar.[67]

In 1862, the Magistrate of Patna offered a climatic explanation for the popularity of overseas emigration amongst the Biharis:

> The Native agricultural population of Behar have an extreme horror of the climate of Bengal, particularly the North-Eastern Districts and Assam, and I do not think the Assam and Sylhet Tea Companies will ever succeed in securing Coolies, Natives of these Districts, unless they pay them very handsomely, so as to enable them to return home after an absence of a few years with a competency. The climate is bad they think, and not adapted to their constitutions, therefore they prefer a certainty in a good climate to an uncertainty in a bad climate, or, in other words, they prefer emigrating to the Mauritius and elsewhere, to serving in the Assam and Sylhet jungles.[68]

The Commissioner of Chota Nagpur described the reasons which motivated the denizens of that district to migrate as a mixture of drought-induced poverty, rack renting and the lures of recruiters:

The country is capable of supporting a very much larger population than it contains, but in bad seasons the Ryots are unable to meet the heavy rent demand in some parts of it and reduced to poverty ... they are in that condition easily persuaded to accept the tempting offers of the Agents of the Emigration Companies. The Subordinate Agents of those Companies have no scruples about suiting these offers to the wishes of the Ryots, always recruiting for whatever place they are most likely to agree to go to. The Mauritius, as best known, is most popular, and ... I have myself come across Agents for the French Emigration Committee unscrupulously recruiting for the Mauritius.[69]

In fact, for the early period, Bihar ranked as the most important supplying province, followed by the NWP, Oudh and Central Bengal. Geoghegan, who compiled region-of-origin figures from information provided by the Calcutta Protector of Emigrants, observed that the earliest recruiting grounds for the colonies were in the so-called 'hill coolie' or adivasi areas of Bihar and Chota Nagpore, but that the proportion of tribals in overseas migration had declined as a result of heavy mortality and their subsequent recruitment for local tea plantation production. His findings are reproduced in Table 1.4.

The research of Ralph Shlomowitz and his collaborators confirms that susceptibility of tribals to the disease environment of Calcutta was a factor.[70] Geoghegan also observed that:

recruiting operations seem to have been pushed further westward into the North West Province below Cawnpore, and, since the suppression of the mutiny, into Oudh. The tracts which now figure most largely in the lists are Arrah, Gyah, Patna, Allahabad, Ghazipur and Oudh.[71]

As regards southern India, the largest recruiting districts were considered to be Godavery, Vizagapatam, Ganjam, Madras and Chingleput. Geoghegan had little data concerning Bombay; however, recent research suggests the pivotal role of coastal districts such as Ratnagiri.[72] A decade later, Grierson reported that few residents of Calcutta or its neighbourhood were recruited, most

Table 1.4 Regional origin of north Indian migrants, 1842– 71

Region of origin	Colonial destination					
	Mauritius	Guiana	Trinidad	Jamaica	Natal	Reunion
Bihar	108,156	24,681	11,278	4,496	356	4,027
Bengal:						
West	33,131	14,028	8,396	3,214	216	1,667
Central	8,951	2,166	1,305	341	24	171
East	1,118	238	176	106	0	29
NWP, Oudh and Central Provinces	47,286	25,551	16,027	4,654	370	4,469
Orissa	3,116	719	378	147	2	19
Other	3,619	1,164	853	377	16	262

migrants being drawn from the ranks of 'up country men who have come down here for work'.[73]

The relative importance of eastern, western and southern India as zones of recruitment depended on a number of factors: local competition for labour and attitudes of Presidency governments towards colonial emigration (generally favourable in Bengal and disapproving in Bombay), legislation which decreed the opening or suspension of various ports for emigration, and preferences expressed by labour importers all played a part in defining and circumscribing recruiting operations. Between 1844 and 1850, for example, Madras and Bombay were closed to Mauritius, which recruited only from Calcutta, and after 1862 the West Indies also took its recruits chiefly from that port; but when Natal began to recruit labour in 1860, it was almost exclusively from Madras.[74] The French colonies took a large proportion of their recruits from ports in the French Indian comptoirs (see Appendix A).

The statistical data outlined above, and findings from new historical research, have helped to redefine some of the broader parameters governing just who migrated, but such work has done little to clarify the murky waters surrounding the extent of coercion and deception in indentured migration. Lal used evidence of levels of recruitment outside natal villages to claim that migrants had already made a break with home before going overseas, and the mobility of labour in nineteenth-century India is no longer seriously questioned.[75] However, it is also evident that throughout the period of recruitment for indenture, migrants were often either unaware of their real destination or unable to reach the colony of their choice. As late as 1883 Grierson was reporting 'I have heard of coolies who were enlisted for Natal, imagining that they were going to Nattore in Rajshahye'.[76] The evidence presented in this volume also suggests that relatives had difficulty in following migrants to specific destinations, and that returnees were frequently prevented from reaching specific colonies or estates by misrepresentation arising from competition between labour exporters, or poor labour allocation practices.[77]

The Voyage

Ship mortality rates were closely monitored in the nineteenth century as an indicator of the organization of indenture and the well-being of recruits. They have been scrutinized as intently by historians for similar reasons. The purpose of much of this work has been to situate indenture in the context of other diasporas by comparing death rates with the middle passage of slaves and the shipment of Europeans to the Dominions. As Dr Bakewell, the health officer of shipping in Trinidad, stressed in 1869 when he produced a report on the causes of sickness and mortality in Indian emigrant ships: 'I wish to explain why over a period of 8 years more than eleven times as many immigrants died on board Calcutta ships going to Trinidad than on board English ships going to Victoria.[78]

Yearly figures compiled by the Immigration Departments of the various colonies were sent back to Britain for analysis by the Emigration Commissioners. There were wide fluctuations in the data: in the 1852–3 season, the voyage mortality in the West Indies was reportedly around 5 per cent of the number shipped. In the 1865–6 season, the mortality in ships to Trinidad was 10.74 per cent, and 6.65 per cent on ships to British Guiana.[79] Ship mortality deaths on the voyages to Natal after 1860 averaged only 0.5–1 per cent. The number of deaths on board ships heading for Mauritius in 1866–7 was 31, equal to a mortality of 5.5 per cent, while that on the West India voyages in the same season was 4.63 per cent for British Guiana ships and 4.42 per cent for Trinidad ships.[80] The mortality of the 1866–7 season dropped to just over 5 per cent and, although still larger than in the years before 1864, was felt to be a considerable improvement on the seasons of 1864–5 and 1865–6: given that famine conditions continued to prevail in the Bengal Presidency, the Land and Emigration Commissioners concluded that 'great care was exercised by the agents in the selection of emigrants'.[81]

High shipboard mortality was attributed to a number of causes. In 1857 a report was published which analysed the reasons for high mortality on ships proceeding to the West Indies. The report did not attribute any blame to the Protector or his assistants for poor selection of immigrants, and turned its attention to other causes cited, such as the introduction of platforms, the absence of a sick bay, the increased proportion of women and children, and recent changes in diet. The author of the report felt that platforms on the ships were unsuitable: 'they are very liable to harbour vermin, and sure to accumulate dirt; they certainly obstruct very materially and injuriously the air of the space beneath'. He supported the conclusion of the Committee appointed to investigate the mortality of emigrants to Mauritius, which had decreed that a cause of the increased mortality was the higher number of women and children migrants, 'whom it is more difficult to keep on deck, and therefore have the between decks clean'. In fact, the report, as often occurred, was careful not to discount any possible cause, recommending that the introduction of biscuits was not desirable and should be discontinued, that ships carrying grain cargoes should have air-tight hatches, and that privies should be outside the ship in the forechains, properly secured. More pertinently, the report considered that the brackishness of the water of the Hughli river was a possible cause of unhealthiness. In seeking to understand why ships departing from Madras suffered less mortality than those from Calcutta, the report dived into the realms of fantasy, suggesting that the native of Madras was not so fearful of sea travel, but resurfaced with the sensible conclusion that the position of Madras was more healthy, with no comparable river voyage. The report ended with their lamenting the inadequate statistics:

> the conduct of the present enquiry has been much embarrassed by the absence of proper records. Not only are the reports and returns kept on board in themselves

meagre and insufficient, but they are rarely forwarded to the Emigration Agent in Calcutta. The consequence is, that it is now impossible to determine what castes and classes are most liable to sickness and death.[82]

Discussions about the nature of the cargoes carried was gradually superseded by the observation that the proportion of women and children had a direct effect on mortality rates. It was also recognized that where distress – that is famine – produced an increase in emigration, this also implied 'a lowering of their habitually low diet, and a still further enfeeblement of their usually feeble constitutions'. Thus the 10 per cent mortality on West Indian ships in the 1865–6 season was blamed on the migrants rather than the emigration service:

This mortality was in part attributable to the large proportion of young children, which was much more than double the proportion of any recent year, but still more to the privations under which the labouring classes in Bengal had been suffering during that and the preceding year from the failure of the harvest. Where a people, like the Bengal coolie, are generally but ill fed, there is no room for a reduction in their dietary. Any such reduction brings with it enfeeblement and disease, if not absolute starvation. Much, therefore, as we regret the extent of the mortality in the emigration of 1865, we cannot consider that it implies neglect on the part of the emigration agents in the selection of the people or the fitting of the ships, or default on the part of the surgeons or officers of the ships on the voyage.[83]

Fortunately, present-day analysts of shipboard mortality have been able to interpret the statistical evidence with improved tools of enquiry.[84]

Ship mortality figures were regularly increased by accidents at sea when storms, fire or navigation difficulties led to the wrecking of ships and heavy loss of life. In 1866, the *Fusilier* dragged its anchors and went ashore at Port Natal, where twenty-six of the migrants perished by drowning or exposure to the weather, and the *Eagle Speed* was wrecked on the Mutlah Bank in the Hughli river, when 262 out of 497 of her emigrants were drowned. In this latter case an enquiry was held by the Indian government, the pilot was dismissed, and the surgeon was disqualified from again serving in an Indian emigrant ship.[85] These enquiries rarely considered the effect on migrants of such momentous and dangerous journeys. In fact the cramped living quarters on board ships, and the often nightmarish experiences generated by outbreaks of epidemic disease, encounters with squalls, and the brutal treatment meted out by tense and drunken crews, led to many complaints by indentured immigrants on their arrival in the colonies. Some examples of their depositions are given in Chapter 2.

Life in the Colonies

The experience of the indentured labourer depended very much on the provisions enshrined in the contract he or she had signed and the manner of its enforcement. Contractual terms were not uniform across all labour-importing colonies. In 1871, Sir Arthur Hamilton Gordon summarized important legislative differences in colonial contract regulations: in Grenada, Antigua, St Lucia and St Vincent, immigrants were paid wholly in money, no rations being allotted to them. In Demerara they were fed for the first four months after their arrival, in Trinidad for the first two years. In Jamaica labourers had the option after three months to convert their ration entitlement into money wages, but in Mauritius, 'the feeding is continued for the whole period of the first or any subsequently renewed indenture, without any option to either party'.[86] Women immigrants, who were invariably indentured in the West Indies, were not indentured in Mauritius and consequently did not receive rations. In Natal, the employment of women on sugar plantations, never important, was negligible by the beginning of the twentieth century.

In 1860 the French colonies were legally authorized to ship migrants from British ports in India. This did not mean that the first indentured labourers destined for French territories arrived only after that period, since emigration had previously been carried on from the French ports in India. The system adopted was slightly different from that employed by the British colonies. The immigrants to Reunion were reportedly:

> pre-engaged in India to serve during five years any one to whom they may be transferred by the speculator who brings them over. The terms of the contract are, it is said, four rupees a month, with allowance of rice and salt . . . The planter pays the full value of the labour he obtains, but a portion of it goes into the pockets of the middle-man.[87]

The period at which wages were paid also differed between colonies: in Jamaica and Demerara they were paid weekly, in St Lucia and Trinidad fortnightly, in Mauritius, Gordon noted:

> the contracts provide for the monthly payment of wages, but an enactment of the Colonial Legislature prohibits any immigrant from suing for the cancellation of his contract, on the ground of non-payment of wages, until after the expiration of three months beyond the time at which such wages become due.

As regards housing provision for indentured immigrants, Gordon pointed out 'in all coolie-employing colonies the obligation to provide suitable and sufficient lodging is uniform, but the modes of enforcing it, as also the estimate of what constitutes suitability and sufficiency, varies very greatly'. In Trinidad and Demerara the Governor could remove immigrants from estates where their accommodation was bad or insufficient, whilst in Mauritius the law depended on the opinions of the various local magistrates, who could order that lodgings be repaired.

Medical care was better defined and more elaborate than housing provisions in colonial legislation. By 1871 immigration law in all the West Indian colonies and Mauritius provided for a hospital on estates, and for medical attendants; in Mauritius and most of the West Indies these were appointed by the proprietor of the estate, but in Jamaica and Trinidad the attendants were government officers. In so far as the return passage was concerned, in the West Indies immigrants were entitled to a free passage home after ten years' residence, or to a small grant of land; in Mauritius this right had been withdrawn in 1853, although in cases of sickness the Protector could issue a free passage.

The contractual obligations of immigrants also varied from colony to colony. Immigrants were bound to work for five days a week and seven hours a day in Demerara; in Trinidad for 280 days of nine hours; in St Lucia, Grenada and Jamaica six days a week, excluding holidays; and in Mauritius, every day, that is for two hours on Sundays and nine hours on the other six days. Absence from work was punished in Trinidad by imprisonment for seven days, whilst five days' absence in Demerara could lead to two months' imprisonment. In Mauritius the labourer absent without justifiable cause (and unless the labourer was admitted to hospital, sickness was not admitted as a reasonable cause) in Gordon's words:

> loses not only his wages and rations (which latter are, in the West Indies, given whether he works or not), but also a halfpenny on every shilling of his monthly wages, which may be deducted by the employer himself; or he may, at the option of his employer, be imprisoned for fourteen days, or have his contract prolonged for a period corresponding to that of his absence. If he is absent for three days from the estate he becomes a deserter, and may be apprehended not only by the police but by his master or his master's servants, and imprisoned for three months.

In Trinidad the punishment for vagrancy was seven days' imprisonment. Gordon reported that in all the West Indian colonies, the:

> great agencies to prevent abuses and insure obedience to the law are the inspections and returns, and the powers of removal vested in the Governor. In all these Colonies returns more or less elaborate are required quarterly from estates, under penalties which are in some cases heavy. No returns of any description are by law or regulation exacted from the employers of labour in Mauritius.

In Mauritius only the Protector had legal powers to inspect estates, but he was not bound by law to do so, and neither he nor the Governor had any power to suspend immigration to a particular estate.

Mauritius and British Guiana came in for special scrutiny in the 1870s when concerned individuals – de Plevitz in Mauritius and des Voeux in Guiana – drew the attention of the authorities to abuses in the law and administration of those colonies concerning Indian immigrants. In both colonies, Royal Commissions were appointed to assess the truth of the allegations, and it was found that vagrancy legislation and the intervention of the judiciary had been used to pressure immigrants to re-engage and to limit their opportunities for mobility. Many of the petitions presented in this volume to highlight aspects of the living and working conditions of indentured migrants were drawn up to attract the attention of the Commissioners (see Chapter 3).

One of the recommendations of the British Guiana Commission had been that medical attendants at estate hospitals should be government servants. This was quickly effected in Jamaica and Trinidad, and recommended for Mauritius also.[88] The Guiana Commission remarked on the difficulties of conducting efficient inspections of estates when magistrates were effectively the guests of the proprietors, but the close personal relationships which existed between officials and planters were not so easy to undermine. The reindenture of migrants was also addressed by the Commissions. In the West Indies no re-engagements were allowed until the previous contract had expired. In Mauritius the labourers had been 'exposed to many acts of petty tyranny' if they refused to re-engage with some months of their indenture left to run, and the West Indian provisos were proposed for adoption in Mauritius. The British Guiana Commission also recommended that no reindentures run for longer than twelve months.

The colonies thus also differed in their attitudes to labourers once the indentures were terminated. In Natal, many time-expired Indians were repatriated; in Fiji, Indians were barred from purchasing land. In the West Indian colonies the immigrant received, on the expiration of his or her contract, a certificate of industrial residence, by which he or she became free to work on his or her own account or to re-engage. The reindenture was optional and the immigrant at this stage was in theory 'as free a man as any other inhabitant'. In Mauritius, although a certificate was given, this had to be purchased and the immigrant then had a week in which to re-engage:

> If he does not re-engage, and does succeed in proving that he has means of living, he must obtain a police pass . . . If he fails to comply with either of these conditions he becomes, in the eye of the law, a vagrant . . . If at any time he declines to re-engage, and desires to live by free daily labour, he has to pay an annual tax of 1l. for the privilege of so doing. Every Indian immigrant in the Colony, as long as he lives, is subject to these restrictions. He must not leave the district within which he lives without the permission of the police . . . He must not change his place of abode, . . . and his house may at any time be entered without warrant by the police.[89]

The hardships to which such time-expired labourers, or 'old immigrants' as they were called, were exposed are detailed through an analysis of their petitions in Chapter 3.

Once the indenture system was well established, reports were annually or twice yearly called for relative to the size of the Indian population in the colonies, the mortality rate on estates, and the numbers reindenturing or returning to India. The number of immigrants under indenture in British

Guiana on 1 January 1865 was 32,150. By the first half of 1867, the Immigration Agent of British Guiana reported that 2765 Indians and Chinese had reindentured themselves for a second period of five years' service, receiving bounties worth $137,075; that the number of immigrants employed on estates was 42,166; and that mortality had been at the rate of 2.17 per cent over the first six months of the year. In 1870 the Indian population on estates in British Guiana numbered 52,598, of whom 40,220 were under indenture and 12,378 were not. Unlike in Mauritius, where the 1871 census recorded that the vast proportion of women were not contracted to estates, in Guiana 10,429 women were indentured, and 4859 were not.[90]

In 1868 it was reported that the death rate of Indian immigrants in British Guiana in that year stood at 29.4 per 1000 per annum. The Emigration Commissioners pointed out that this return dealt only with 'the lowest class of unskilled labourers' and, comparing it with the available urban mortality returns of all classes in Britain, which apparently averaged about 24.56 per 1000, concluded that 'the mortality of the lowest class of the labouring population, if taken by itself, would scarcely be less than that of the Indian immigrant in British Guiana'. This comfortable conclusion, however, failed to take into account the more restricted age range of the Indian overseas population at this period.[91] Since most of the statistical surveys of indentured populations have used data which identify the Indian only at the onset of the indenture, much research remains to be done in this field. Shlomowitz has used statistics of annual mortality from the Pacific to compare death rates of Indians and Polynesians in Fiji.[92] My own research, using a sample of around 7000 individual register entries, has revealed that 14 per cent of adult male, 12 per cent of adult female and 13 per cent of child migrants died within the first five years on Mauritius, after which period, survival rates increasingly improved.[93]

What did the indentured labourers earn for their pains? The Royal Commissioners appointed in 1870 to enquire into the condition of Indian immigrants in British Guiana found much to criticize concerning the promised and actual or likely earnings of indentured labourers, their comments upon which subject attracted some attention in India. This prompted the Emigration Commissioners to seek to rectify what they considered misinterpretations of the evidence. They sought to clarify that 'the wages earned depend so much on the ability and industry of the individual labourer that it is difficult to frame any scale that shall be at the same time general and precise', but went on to offer realistic scales of pay which could be circulated to Indian recruiting agents.[94] There has been little research specifically on the movements of wages and prices over the nineteenth century in the field of indentured labour studies, but there is general agreement that one of the effects of intensive immigration was to depress wage rates in the labour-importing colonies, which then stagnated well into the twentieth century in most cases.[95]

The prosperity of indentured labourers, as measured by records of their remittances and declared savings on returning to India, was considered by Geoghegan to have 'been too laxly kept' to be of much use. However, he did report that over the first three decades of government emigration, returnees from British Guiana brought home ten lakhs of rupees, averaging 300 rupees per person. The comparable figure for Trinidad was 166 rupees.[96] The statistics concerning savings and remittances were certainly irregularly kept, and many remittances sent home were not received by the payee because of inadequate addresses and the like. This was a major cause of concern, as expressed in the letters between migrants and their relatives (see Chapters 4 and 5). In 1868 regulations were drawn up to regularize the sending of remittances. It was provided that amounts to be remitted to India were to be deposited in sums of not less than $10, or more than $100, with the Colonial Treasurer or other officer to be named by the colonial government for this service. Individuals making such deposit had to fill in a form which specified the full name, age, occupation and address of the remitter, the amount deposited, and the name, age, occupation and address of the intended payee in India. The remitter was then furnished with a money order for the amount payable by the government in India at the local government treasury nearest to the residence of the payee, converted into rupees. Before payment of the money the payees were required to furnish name, address and other such particulars relating to the remitter as well as to themselves. The remitters were responsible for sending the money orders at their own risk to the person intended to receive the amount in India, and payees were given twelve months in which to present them. Migrants returning to India could deposit their savings in return for money orders in the same way.[97]

In 1871, the Protector of Emigrants reported that 1588 individuals had returned from Mauritius, twenty-eight of whom remitted Rs13,738 through the Emigration Agent's office. Others brought bills of exchange for various sums, sovereigns and other sterling money, and jewellery. In the same year 416 migrants from Demerara brought savings amounting to $58,994, and 393 from Trinidad had savings valued at Rs127,368. The Protector of Emigrants' annual reports consistently show that whilst the numbers of return emigrants from Mauritius were generally higher than arrivals from the West Indies, a smaller number of them brought money. In his report for 1872–3, the Protector noted that seventy-four returned migrants from Mauritius brought Rs42,774, a small proportion of more than 2000 individuals travelling back to India. This was a striking contrast to Demerara, where of 846 returning, 551 remitted money. In 1873–4, 1522 Mauritian returnees carried savings valued at Rs23,709, whilst 473 returning from Demerara brought back Rs138,920, and 376 leaving Trinidad brought back Rs107,294. The discrepancy was no doubt in part due to the fact that at this stage free return passages were offered only to pauper

Indians in Mauritius, who therefore accounted for the greater proportion of returnees. The Protector, however, explained it in these terms:

> it appears that the Mauritius emigrants do not adopt so largely as the emigrants in the West Indies do the practice of remitting monies through official channels, but prefer bringing their savings personally in the shape of bills of exchange, gold coins, and jewellery.[98]

However, as indicated above, not all of those who returned were prosperous, time-expired migrants. There were also many who through infirmity or other causes were sent back in an indigent state. The petitions presented by the elderly and impoverished, pleading for a return passage to India, make heart-rending reading; a selection of such missives is presented in Chapter 3. By 1872, the Indian government was considering the advisability of alleviating their distress, particularly as some migrants found it difficult to be reintegrated into their own communities:

> In some cases, no doubt, they return poor and helpless, in consequence of their own imprudence in the colony; nevertheless their condition, aggravated possibly by the loss of their relatives and caste in this country, gives all of them a claim to consideration. It would be a great boon if a fund could be raised for their support.[99]

When the Indian government queried whether the colonies should not be made responsible for the relief of emigrants permanently injured in that colony, or otherwise unable to maintain themselves, they received a firm 'no' from the British Secretary of State for the Colonies. Kimberley was of the opinion that this would be quite contrary to the usual principles on which emigration was carried on from one country to another. He stated:

> If a debtor and creditor account is to be struck between the colonies and India, it would be necessary to estimate the value of the advantage which India derives from emigrants who leave India, practically paupers, and return with considerable sums of money amassed in the colonies, by means of which they become contributors to the wealth and revenue of India ... if the liability of the colony were admitted in the case of loss of limb it might on similar grounds be extended to cases of ill health from disease contracted in the colony, and a colony might become responsible for the maintenance in India of an indefinite number of paupers without having any means of knowing whether they were making reasonable efforts to procure a livelihood.[100]

By the close of the 1860s, when indentured migration to the West Indies and Mauritius had been in operation some three decades, attention was turned to the numbers of Indians who had not exercised their option of return passages, and could therefore be considered as having settled overseas. Guiana was calculated to have a population of around 15,000 Indians who had declined to exercise their right to a free return passage, whilst in Trinidad an equivalent figure of 7887 immigrants was estimated.[101] In Mauritius, the size of the old immigrant population was assessed more in terms of those still working on estates and those who had taken up other pursuits. It was this latter class which became an increasing source of concern to the colonists. Following the promulgation of a highly restrictive anti-vagrancy law in 1867, the freedom of time-expired Indians in Mauritius was greatly circumscribed, as their petitions indicate (see Chapter 3).

The concern of officials was thus redirected towards assessing the social conditions of these overseas Indian populations who could now be regarded as settled permanently. Violence on estates, particularly the crimes of wife-murder and suicide, of which there was a high rate, preoccupied colonial officials and generated a voluminous correspondence. The statistics revealed that the overseas Indian populations were committing a greater number of wife-murders and suicides than other ethnic groups in their various territories. Officials in this Victorian age of scientific racism then debated the question whether this was a statistically significant phenomenon, a peculiarity of the Indian people, or a by-product of the socially dysfunctional living conditions within the indenture system. Information was accordingly sought from Indian officials as to the frequency of those acts in the various Presidencies. In 1870, the Bengal Secretary reported that 'in Bengal, among the class which furnishes emigrants, suicide is not uncommon among females, but among males, or taking the population generally it is not very usual'. He annexed an extract from the Annals of Indian Administration for 1866–7, which revealed that in India the proportion of suicides in a population of 55 million was 1 in 25,300, against 1 in 15,200 in England. The most common causes of suicide in India were apparently:

> jealousy, family discord, destitution and physical suffering. Jealousy, with all the bitter feelings which it engenders, is the cause of a large number of female suicides. The undivided family of a Hindoo numbering many members of different degrees of relationship, is unquestionably a fruitful source of the most serious quarrels.[102]

The Madras government, for its part, submitted a statement showing the number of cases of suicide which had occurred in the Presidency in the five years prior to 1870 in a population of 26,539,136 (see Table 1.5). The Presidency Government believed that this statement:

Table 1.5 Cases of suicide in the Madras Presidency, 1865– 9

Year	Male suicides	Female suicides
1865	482	760
1866	594	794
1867	492	798
1868	516	784
1869	566	829

shows that . . . the proportion of suicides to the entire population is far less than in the case of the emigrants at the Mauritius. But in India the poorest class, from which emigrants are supplied, is the class which is most prone to suicide, and this circumstance may partially account for the contrast between the two rates; still the extreme prevalence of the crime in the Mauritius demands, in the opinion of this government, rigid investigation.[103]

The fact that the Madras government offered an implicit criticism of the indenture system in Mauritius, in comparison to the Bengal government, may in part have been a function of its greater concern for the labour needs of local capitalists, and hence noticeably less enthusiasm for overseas emigration than the Bengal government consistently demonstrated. The response of the Bombay government was terse and to the point: 'it does not appear from the reports of the different officers who have been called on for opinion that the classes from which the emigrants come are notorious in this country for their propensity to commit suicide'.[104] It was difficult to compare rates between India and even between the colonies. For example, by the beginning of the twentieth century the suicide statistics of indentured populations in Mauritius and the West Indies were considerably lower than in Natal and Fiji, but this no doubt bore some relation to the date at which indenture began in the various territories.[105]

On the second issue, that of the frequency of wife-murders, statistical information was once again called for from the Presidency governments, the results of which were as shown in Table 1.6. The conclusions which the government of India drew from the material collected were that:

the statistics bearing on the question of murders of women in the cooly importing colonies are so absolutely fragmentary, that we are not in a position to form any opinion as to the relative frequency of woman and wife murder amongst the people of India and amongst the Indian emigrants in those colonies. But the statistics now forwarded show that in this country slightly more than one fourth of the persons murdered are adult women (female children having been excluded from the statements), and that of the women murdered about one half are wives murdered by their husbands.[106]

Table 1.6 Frequency of wife-murders

Province	Population	Total murders	Murders of women	Wife-murders (by husband)
Madras	27,105,020	1,166	340	154
Bombay	14,309,131	974	314	164
Bengal	42,865,569	2,486	804	399
NWP	29,985,590	1,421	329	148
Punjab	17,596,752	1,716	476	168
Oudh	10,854,755	656	95	52
CP	8,119,081	430	122	67

Historians have latched onto this phenomenon as evidence of the darker side of plantation life, but until more sophisticated statistical comparisons of wife-murder in India and overseas are available, the interpretation remains emotive rather than analytical.[107]

Having survived the violence of the plantation, did indentured Indians lose all ties with India? Contemporaries often thought so: Grierson believed that even those individuals who returned to India had often broken 'with all their home ties'. In proof of this he cited the West Indian Emigration Agents' comment that returning Indians from those colonies were required to make a will and that they left their property to a wife or relation in the colony rather than to a person in India.[108] It could be argued instead that many migrants created two sets of ties rather than replacing the old social obligations with the new. The letters which passed between migrants reveal that in many cases, despite absences of several decades and the acquisition of new families and property overseas, migrants continued to be involved with and interested in the domestic squabbles, financial and marital arrangements of their relatives in India (Chapters 4 and 5).

Nevertheless, at least two-thirds of all migrants failed to return to India on completion of their indentures. Some went elsewhere: time-expired labourers in Reunion went to Mauritius, old immigrants in Mauritius went to Natal and Madagascar, Indians in the West Indies travelled between the islands, and some overseas Indians even journeyed from Mauritius to Brazil and China. It was obviously cheaper for employers to import Indians who were already working in neighbouring colonies rather than to recruit them from India. For their part, the governments where the ex-indentured labourers were settled would be freed from the obligation of providing a return passage to India. Thus in the 1860s the government of Reunion authorized a Major Andrews to seek recruits for Mauritius from among the Indians in Reunion who had completed their industrial service, had demanded their passages back, and were therefore regarded as lost to the colony. However, Major Andrews extended his operations to all time-expired Indians in the island, and local planters complained, leading to the abandonment of the scheme.[109] In 1873 the Mauritian Colonial Secretary reported that an attempt had been made to embark some old immigrants in Mauritius to go to Madagascar to work on a sugar estate. The wage offered was high, but in view of the slave laws still operative there, the government of Mauritius had refused permission. Some Indians nevertheless managed to make their way to Madagascar. The Mauritian government sought advice from India with respect to the legality or desirability of such migration. In reply the Indian Secretary outlined his strong objections to Indians going to a country where there was no guarantee of due protection against ill-usage, oppression and improper coercion. He recommended that the Mauritian government should prevent secondary migration to non-British territories.[110] Further examples of such new diasporas – the remigrations of Indians to more uncharted territories – are given in Chapter 5. As one diaspora spawned another, the indenture experience paved the way for new forms of labour migration in the British Empire and into the post-colonial era.

Notes

1. Hitchens, 1931: 290.
2. Parliamentary Papers 1840 XXXIII Letter from Russell appointing the Emigration Commissioners.
3. Parliamentary Papers 1837–8 (669) Thomas Blythe & Sons to Bettington & Co., Sydney, 22 Apr. and 7 Oct. 1836.
4. Parliamentary Papers 1841 (45) Appendix to the Calcutta Commission Report, Tabular Statement of Ships which have sailed from Calcutta.
5. Geoghegan Report, pp. 9–15.
6. 7th GRCLEC, 1847; 8th GRCLEC, 1848.
7. 12th GRCLEC, 1852, Appendix No. 42, Extract of a Report from Mr White to the Governor of British Guiana, 8 Nov. 1850.
8. 12th GRCLEC, 1852.
9. Range 188 vol. 67 Captain Burbank to Secretary, Government of Bengal, 21 July 1863.
10. 14th GRCLEC, 1854; 17th GRCLEC, 1857.
11. Appendix to 19th GRCLEC, 1859.
12. Parliamentary Papers 1859 31 I Stevenson to Stanley, 12 May 1858, encl. Report of Immigration Committee, 6 April 1858.
13. Parliamentary Papers 1859 xvi (2542) Murdoch & Rogers to Merivale, 25 Nov. 1856.
14. *Ibid.*, Thomson to Walcott, 15 Oct. 1856.
15. *Ibid.*, Thomson to Walcott, 29 Oct. 1856; Franklin to Walcott, 14 Jan. 1857.
16. Geoghegan Report, pp. 16–28.
17. Bengal Emigration Proceedings, Range 15 vol. 76, Eales to Rivers Thompson, 13 Mar. 1861.
18. Bengal Emigration Proceedings, Range 15 vol. 76, J.H. Young, Esq., Commissioner of Burdwan, to the Secretary to the Government of Bengal, 6 Feb. 1861; J.D. Gordon, Junior Secretary, Government of Bengal, to the Protector of Emigrants, 8 Apr. 1861.
19. Bengal Emigration Proceedings 15/77 T. Caird to C. Eales, 11 Jan. 1862.
20. Bengal Emigration Proceedings 15/77 A.M. Monteath to H. Bell, 17 Feb. 1862, encl. Caird to the Magistrate of the 24-Pergunnahs, 19 Jan. 1861.
21. Bengal Emigration Proceedings 15/77 F. Harley and Co. to F. Lamouroux, 22 Jan. 1861.
22. Harley & Co. to F. Lamouroux, 10 Feb. 1861.
23. Bengal Emigration Proceedings 15/77 Grey to Bell, 30 Jan. 1862, encl. Emigration Agents of Jamaica, British Guiana, French Government and Trinidad, 5 Apr. 1862.
24. 24th GRCLEC, 1864; 27th GRCLEC, 1867.
25. Report of Partridge, 27 June 1863.
26. Emmer, 1993: 248–9; Laurence, 1971: 163–178; 28th GRCLEC, 1868; 29th GRCLEC, 1869.

27. Bengal Emigration Proceedings 15/81 Captain C. Burbank to S.C. Bayley, 29 Aug. 1864.
28. Bengal Emigration Proceedings 432/17 correspondence with the Indian Emigration Agents, 1865.
29. *Ibid.*
30. Bengal Emigration Proceedings 432/18 Burbank to Secretary, Government of Bengal, 5 Apr. 1867.
31. Bengal Emigration Proceedings 432/20 Baker to Secretary, Government of Bengal, 8 May 1869.
32. 32nd GRCLEC, 1872, Appendix: Act No. VII of 1871.
33. 32nd GRCLEC, 1872.
34. See Hira, 1987: 190.
35. Bengal Emigration Proceedings vol. 170 Protector of Emigrants, Calcutta to Secretary, Government of Bengal, 9 June 1873.
36. Secretary, Government of Bengal, to Secretary, Government of India, 9 July 1873.
37. Bengal Emigration Proceedings vol. 171 Protector of Emigrants' report, 1 Sep. 1874.
38. CO 167/534 Gordon to Kimberley, 18 Aug. 1871.
39. North-Coombes, 1991.
40. See Kelly, 1991, Ch. 2. For a personal view of the ending of indenture see Samaroo, 1987b: 25–38.
41. Bhana, 1991a: 17.
42. Tinker, 1974: 311, 335; Gupta, 1971: 33–4.
43. Report on Colonial Emigration from the Bengal Presidency, G. Grierson, 1883, Diary, p. 19.
44. Bengal Emigration Proceedings 15/77 E.F. Lautour to G.F. Cockburn, 31 Jan. 1862.
45. CO 167/426 Caird to Marriott, 8 Nov. 1860.
46. Bengal Emigration Proceedings 15/76 Colonial Secretary, Mauritius, to Secretary, Government of Bengal, 6 Feb. 1861, encl. Governor's Minute of Jan. 1861.
47. Bengal Emigration Proceedings vol. 171 Protector of Emigrants' report, 1 September 1874.
48. For further details on the role of returnees in recruitment see Carter, 1992a: 231–41. For views on the indenture/kangani divide see Salleh, 1990: 21; Jain, 1993: 6–9.
49. Bengal Emigration Proceedings vol. 432 W.J. Jeffrey, Esq., Emigration Agent for British Guiana and Jamaica, to Captain C. Burbank, Protector of Emigrants, 11 Mar. 1867.
50. Report on Colonial Emigration from the Bengal Presidency, G. Grierson, 1883, Diary, p. 34.
51. For further details on the mechanics of recruiting in various colonies see Lal, 1983: 15–31; Mangru, 1987a: 53–108; Bhana, 1991a: 11–17. For my personal views of this issue see Carter, 1992a: 229–31; Bates and Carter, 1992: 205–47, and 1993: 159–185.
52. Lal, 1983: 25.
53. Report on Colonial Emigration from the Bengal Presidency, G. Grierson, 1883, Diary, p. 68.

54. Indian Public Proceedings Range 188 vol. 45 Magistrate of Salem to Chief Secretary to Government, 3 Dec. 1856.

55. Indian Public Proceedings Range 188 vol. 58 Chief Secretary to Government Fort St George to Secretary, Government of India, 20 Nov. 1857.

56. Bengal Emigration Proceedings 15/76 W.F. Fergusson to E.H. Lushington, 30 Dec. 1861.

57. Bengal Emigration Proceedings 15/77 W.F. Fergusson to E.H. Lushington, 7 Mar. 1862.

58. Bengal Emigration Proceedings 432/18 Emigration Agent of British Guiana to Protector of Emigrants Calcutta, 8 July 1867.

59. Bengal Emigration Proceedings vol. 168 Extract of a letter from the Agent General of Emigration for the Government of Jamaica to the Protector of Emigrants, Calcutta, 28 Apr. 1871.

60. Parliamentary Papers 1859 xvi (2542) Russell to Higginson, 25 May 1855; Russell to Wodehouse, 23 June 1855.

61. 27th GRCLEC, 1867.

62. 32nd GRCLEC, 1872.

63. The Mauritian state paid particular attention to the proportion of families recruited, see Carter, 1992b: 1–21. For British Guiana see Mangru, 1987b: 211–30. The proportion of women migrating to tea plantations was generally higher than for sugar because of the more important role for women in tea production; see Chatterjee and Das Gupta, 1981: 1861–8.

64. Report on Colonial Emigration from the Bengal Presidency, G. Grierson, 1883, p. 35, and Appendix, p. 5.

65. Report of J. Gorrie on the dissent of J. Fraser from the Police Enquiry Commission, 1872. Callikan-Proag, 1984: 223–72, has demonstrated the progressive deterioration in attitudes and representation of Indians in the colonial press of Mauritius. Bolt, 1971: 75–205, discusses the impact of the Jamaica revolt and the Indian mutiny in changing British attitudes towards Asians and Afro-Caribbeans.

66. Lal, 1983: 70–1; Bhana, 1991a: 60–83; Carter, 1995: 98–103.

67. Bengal Emigration Proceedings vol. 171 Protector of Emigrants' report, 1 Sep. 1874.

68. Bengal Emigration Proceedings 15/77 E.F. Lautour to G.F. Cockburn, 31 Jan. 1862.

69. Bengal Emigration Proceedings 15/77 Major E.T. Dalton to H. Bell, 14 Mar. 1862.

70. Shlomowitz and McDonald, 1990: 35–65; Shlomowitz and Brennan, 1990: 86–109.

71. Geoghegan Report, p. 67.

72. See Carter, 1995: 104–7; Yamin, 1989: 32–53; Chandavarkar, 1994: 128.

73. Report on Colonial Emigration from the Bengal Presidency, G. Grierson, 1883, Diary, p. 69.

74. For region of origin data concerning individual colonies see Lal, 1983: 45–67; Bhana, 1991a: 34–59.

75. Lal (1980); Jain, 1993: 1–2; Bates and Carter, 1992: 205–47; Washbrook, 1993: 68–86.

76. Report on Colonial Emigration from the Bengal Presidency, G. Grierson, 1883, p. 33.

77. Migrants could also be prevented from embarking if they were rejected on medical grounds; this could then lead to their embarkation for another destination where employers were less fussy or more needy. Two boys, rejected by the West Indian and Mauritian agents, were thus sent on to Cachar tea plantations: Bengal Emigration Proceedings 15/77 S. Wauchope to Secretary, Government of Bengal, 3 July 1862.

78. Bengal Emigration Proceedings 432/21 T.W.C. Murdoch, Esq., to Sir F. Rogers, Bart, 16 July 1869, encl. extracts from Report of Dr Bakewell, the Health Officer of Shipping in Trinidad, on the causes of the sickness and mortality in cooly ships, June 1869.

79. 14th GRCLEC, 1854; 26th GRCLEC, 1866.

80. Bhana, 1991a: 19–20; 27th GRCLEC, 1867.

81. 27th GRCLEC, 1867.

82. Indian Public Proceedings Range 188 vol. 57, Report on the Mortality of Emigrant Coolies on the voyage to the West Indies in 1855–1857, by the Inspector of Jails and Dispensaries, Lower Provinces.

83. 26th GRCLEC, 1866; 27th GRCLEC, 1867.

84. See Shlomowitz and McDonald, 1990: 35–65; McDonald and Shlomowitz, 1990: 84–113. My own data on ship mortality to Mauritius is given in Carter, 1995: 120–50.

85. 26th GRCLEC, 1866.

86. CO 167/534 Gordon to Kimberley, 18 Aug. 1871.

87. 11th GRCLEC, 1851, Report of Hugon, Protector of Immigrants.

88. CO 167/535 Gordon to Kimberley, 2 Sep. 1871.

89. CO 167/534 Gordon to Kimberley, 18 Aug. 1871.

90. 26th GRCLEC, 1866; 28th GRCLEC, 1868; 31st GRCLEC, 1871.

91. 31st GRCLEC, 1871.

92. Shlomowitz, 1990: 116–127; Shlomowitz, 1986: 289–302.

93. Carter, 1995: 280–1.

94. 32nd GRCLEC, 1872.

95. For an analysis of Guyana which could be replicated across the indenture diaspora see Rodney, 1981: 331–51.

96. Geoghegan Report, pp. 68–9.

97. 28th GRCLEC, 1868, Appendix No. 32, Regulations for the Remittance to India of the Savings of Coolies in the West Indies and other Colonies.

98. Bengal Emigration Proceedings vol. 168 Grant to Secretary, Government of Bengal, 28 Sep. 1871; vol. 170 Protector of Emigrants to Secretary, Government of Bengal, 18 June 1873; vol. 171 Protector of Emigrants' report, 1 Sep. 1874.

99. Bengal Emigration Proceedings vol. 169 Protector of Emigrants, Calcutta, to Secretary, Government of Bengal, 29 Feb. 1872.

100. Bengal Emigration Proceedings vol. 170 Herbert to Secretary of State for India, 8 July 1873.

101. 32nd GRCLEC, 1872.

102. Indian Public Proceedings vol. 506, Apr.–June 1871, Secretary, Government of Bengal, to Secretary, Government of India, 29 Dec. 1870.

103. Chief Secretary, Government F.S.G., to Secretary, Government of India, 25 Jan. 1871.

104. Chief Secretary, Government of Bombay, to Secretary, Government of India, 17 Mar. 1871.

105. Bhana and Bhana, 1991: 137, 151.
106. Indian Emigration Proceedings vol. 691, 1871–2, Secretary, Government of India, to Secretaries, Governments of the Presidencies, 30 Aug. 1872; Government of India to Secretary of State for India, 2 Sep. 1872.
107. For discussions of the phenomenon see Mangru, 1987b: 217–19; Kelly, 1992: 259–62.
108. Report on Colonial Emigration from the Bengal Presidency, G. Grierson, 1883, p. 36.
109. 29th GRCLEC, 1869.
110. Indian Emigration Proceedings vol. 692 Colonial Secretary to Secretary, Government of India, 18 June 1873, and reply, 9 Aug. 1873.

CHAPTER TWO

Experiences of recruitment and the voyage overseas

Historical studies of the mobilization of Indian indentured labour for the overseas sugar plantations have tended to adopt positions along a theoretical scale which is labelled 'coercion' at one end and 'voluntarism' at the other. Famine-induced registration at depots coupled with physical sequestration of unwilling recruits was the favoured scenario in works like *A New System of Slavery* (Tinker, 1974) and its advocates. This model was countered by studies which promoted a thesis of mobile proletarians and marginalized women seeking a better life overseas.[1] Both schools of thought accepted the received wisdom that in going overseas migrants lost contact with home and family in India and underwent a period of domestic instability abroad. On the one hand it is difficult to sustain the premise that migrants should continue to be in a state of ignorance about the nature of the indenture system over an entire century, whilst on the other it remains necessary to explain how the dynamic of recruiting to particular territories was maintained in spite of stagnant or declining wage rates. My own research on Mauritius has documented the incidence of circular migration and the utility of returnee recruiting within the indenture process.[2] The arguments presented here, using the statements of recruits and recruiters, seek to illustrate subaltern initiatives and the constraints imposed upon them by the practitioners of labour exportation.

The First Wave of Indian Indentured Migrants, 1834–41

The recruitment of indentured labourers was to a large extent controlled and determined by economic interests outside India: the numbers and characteristics of migrants corresponded more closely to planter demand and preference than to individual aspirations. Privately organized from 1834 to 1839, their immigration was timed to coincide with the freeing of the apprentices on sugar estates in Mauritius and British Guiana, and Indians were brought essentially to replace the former servile plantation workforce. Complaints about the use of coercion in these early shipments led to the abolition of further emigration until Commissions of Enquiry had reported on the whole question of indenture.[3] The investigations of the Calcutta Commission yielded valuable interviews with the first wave of returning migrants who had served out their five-year contracts. Enquiries at Madras and Bombay also produced some depositions of migrants.[4] These provide our first opportunity to encounter individuals who had experienced indenture and returned to recount the particular circumstances of their recruitment.

The ease with which migrants had been deceived as to their destination and the nature of the work expected of them is all too clear from the results of the Commissions set up in 1838 and 1839 at the three Presidencies. The Calcutta Commission had interviewed some return migrants as part of its remit to decide on the resumption of indenture. From the statements taken, it seems clear that migrants were often intending to seek work within India, and consented to go overseas without really understanding the location of the two colonies then recruiting. Boodoo Khan's account of how he came to migrate to Mauritius in 1836 provides a fascinating glimpse of the world of the itinerant soldier. He describes his ignorance of the whereabouts of the island, but seems fearless when told the truth of his situation. His dignity in the face of adversity is striking, and Boodoo Khan takes great pride in noting that he was not confined, as the other emigrants were, for fear that they might escape. However, it is indicative that not all were as resolved to take on the unknown as Boodoo Khan appeared to be:

I am a Pathan, and my home is at Gyah; I left my home in the month of July (Assar) about two years ago; I left my home to seek service. I entered into the service of the Rajah of Morbough, as a sepahie, for five rupees per month and food; I served him for a year, and received 15 rupees only in cash, but I got altogether nine cows, some worth three rupees, some four; I sent the cows to my home at Gyah. I have a brother in the Calcutta militia, named Sheer Khan. I got the cows for field work, not to eat. The Rajah is a Hindoo; I knew that he gave cows to many. I quarrelled with the Rajah's commissary about food, and took my discharge; besides, there was no fighting, or I would have remained. I met with a duffadar at Seersa, in the same district of Morbaugh; the duffadar's name is – I forget now; he had a beard; he took me to Beerbhul; the duffadar told me I was to get 14 rupees wages, of which seven would go for food, etc., and I would receive seven; and he told me the food I should get was 14 chittacks of rice, two chittacks dholl, half chittack ghee, half chittack salt, and two of salt fish. I should receive clothes every six months; that I should be five days on the voyage, should get there in a small boat (dinghee), and was to serve for six months at Meritch; I thought it was some island about five days' journey; this was at Seersa . . . I do not remember whether I was taken before Captain Birch; I was brought to this house (Captain Birch's) to have my arm punctured; I received my permit in another house; I was told by a very stout gentleman that I was to break stones and do field work; I forget now what else he said; I do not recollect whether he said any thing about pay; he told me to behave well. It is very probable that I was told about food, but I forget now what was said; I was told I was to go to Meritch; I said I was very willing; there were a great many Coolies; I came after the rest; I know that every thing was told me in the place where I got my permit; I received six months' wages, of which one month was cut for dustooree; one month went in plates and dishes; I gave six rupees to one man to buy me a box, a chattah, and a goorgoorie, (umbrella and hoqqah), but he did me out of it; I gave six rupees to the duffadar for khorakee; I bought nine rupees' worth of clothes, and took with me seven rupees. All who went with me got six months, out of which the duffadars gave some three, some four rupees. There were two brothers, Jundeh Singh and Futteh Singh, who had nothing to do with the duffadars; they kept their own money and have got money now at the Mauritius.[5]

His claim to leadership qualities, or superior caste status, was evidently recognized in Mauritius because he was appointed a sirdar or foreman, but he was not prepared to be a mere instrument of his employer, and was sent home to India for misconduct in 1838. The brief report of the Chief Commissary of Police in Mauritius on his case reads as follows:

The Indian sirdar, named Boudoucan, in the service of M Lachiche & Co. embarked by ship Lancier, Captain Brown, at his own and employer's request, for not obeying employer's orders, and instigating the Coolies under his command to desert.[6]

Karoo, who was also interviewed by the Calcutta Committee of Enquiry, stated that he was a resident of Khurkotta, in the district of Moongheer, and like Khan reported having been taken to the police office before his embarkation. There he was told:

that I was to remain at Mauritius five years; my pay was to be five rupees per month, of which one to be deducted. I received 20 rupees in hand, being four months' pay before embarking, but the duffadar took ten rupees out of that sum for the diet expenses on the road.

Asked what had induced him to leave home, Karoo responded:

A man of the name of Golam Ally, who is a duffadar, went to my country. He gathered 15 men and brought them down to Calcutta, he had three men with him with badges on. He asked us, 'What are you doing in the jungle? Come to Calcutta, and you will get employment for repairing roads, for which you will receive pay at the rate of four rupees per month, beside diet'. We came; he paid all our expenses on the road. When we arrived here, he told us that no employment on the roads could be got; 'You had better go forward and you will find plenty of employment'. He mentioned that we should go to the Mauritius, and said it was a good country, and that we should get good food and good clothes there. We agreed to go to the Mauritius, and went. There were 300 Coolies on board the ship in which we proceeded; we arrived in three months. The sea was so high, I could not eat anything for four or five days.

The means by which men such as Karoo were brought to the port was through the offer of employment at Calcutta itself. The significance of the men with badges who accompanied Gholam Ally, the duffadar, was the association, in the minds of the villagers, of badge wearing with government officials.[7]

The evidence of men like Karoo was considered, by the anti-coolie-trade lobby, sufficient proof of the involuntary nature of their recruitment, but J.P. Grant, who authored a long memorandum on the indenture system, pointed out that Karoo, 'though brought to Calcutta in expectation of employment here, when fully informed, agreed to go'. He added that Boodoo Khan, even when entreated by his brother to desist from the idea of emigrating, 'still went willingly and knowingly in all matters, except in having a notion that he was going to serve the Company'.[8] Ultimately the measured arguments of Grant, himself a Bengal civil servant, received a greater degree of support in Britain than the Calcutta Commissioners' conviction that the trade could not be reformed and should be abolished. J.P. Grant also organized the interview of some return emigrants on the ship which brought them back to Calcutta in 1840, commenting, 'the men all had a healthy, well-fed appearance, and were well clothed. They seemed to us to be intelligent persons, perfectly alive to their own interests'.[9]

In Mauritius, the self-appointed Free Labour Association, an organization of merchants and sugar planters who lobbied the local and home governments to secure the resumption of indenture, also perused the Calcutta Commission of Enquiry Report attentively and wrote a lengthy refutation of its important points. On the deposition of Boodoo Khan they noted that he was a sirdar who had been deported from the island, and argued, 'On these grounds it might be matter of serious doubt whether this man's evidence ought to have been admitted at all'. Nevertheless, like Grant, they concluded that the man's deposition proved that he migrated 'of his own free will, being perfectly cognizant of what he was about'. Concerning the depositions of Karoo, Seeboo and others, the Free Labour Association considered that every word uttered 'bears the stamp of falsehood', and sought to refute the Calcutta Commissioners' argument that the returnees were the 'best judges' of the questions at issue:

> To this we answer, certainly they are the best judges, and so is the culprit at the bar the best judge whether he committed or not the crime for which he is arraigned, a much better one than the magistrate who sums up the evidence, or the jury who pronounce the verdict, because he knows from certain science what they can only infer from the evidence produced. But the question is not whether he is the best judge, but whether he will be naturally disposed to pronounce the more correct judgement.[10]

Returnees at Madras were similarly interviewed before the Justice of the Peace at the Madras Police Office. Their statements indicate that to all intents and purposes they had consented fully to embark for Mauritius. Yet their emigration was only voluntary in the sense that they were not forcibly embarked at gun point; as Paravadee himself pointed out, they had no other option because of their difficult economic circumstances:

> *I am a Cooly, and as such I was employed by many persons on the Neilgherry hills. Having heard about six years ago, that Coolies were required at Pondicherry, for the purpose of going to the Isle of France, I went to Pondicherry, where I was maintained for 2 months by one Caroopayee, a respectable female of that town. A French Gentleman named Vinay engaged about 370 men, to go to the Mauritius, to work as Coolies in*

Sugar Cane Plantations – Mr. Vinay informed us, that we were to get five Rupees a month, besides daily Batta, consisting of rice, doll, curry stuff, & c. sufficient for our subsistence. We agreed to the terms, and signed them before the Police Magistrate at Pondicherry. Shortly afterwards we were embarked on a ship bound to the Mauritius . . . We are poor men of this place, or else we would not have gone on board ship, or to a foreign land, from fear of losing caste.

Paravadee belonged to a set of individuals who commonly resorted to overseas migration because their employment had already rendered them itinerants and hence more likely to come into contact with recruiters. His statement indicates, nevertheless, that the initial resort to foreign colonies was undertaken with some trepidation, because it entailed a sea voyage and unfamiliar contact with social groups which usually kept apart from each other.

The deposition of Moottoosawmy, an inhabitant of Nathum, described as a village in the district of Trichinopoly, reveals that he belonged to another common category of migrants: those small land cultivators who were effectively driven off their property by British revenue policies. Such commentaries reveal the link between the macro and micro levels – how individuals like Moottoosawmy, caught up in British commercialization policies on the subcontinent, found themselves cast adrift from traditional agrarian employments and induced to participate in British capitalist development in another part of the Empire. He stated:

I was cultivating the land of my maternal uncle Camatchee Nadanam in the village of Nathum for several years; but the produce after payment of the kist money to the Circar, proved insufficient for the support and maintenance of my family and children – consequently I left my village about five years ago with the intention of earning my livelihood at Madras – on my way I heard that labourers for the Mauritius were obtaining service at Pondicherry through the means of one Caroopayee – on my applying to her, she took me and 29 other men to a French Gentleman who carried us to the Police Office, where our names were registered and we then signed a Document expressing our desire to proceed to the Isle of France to serve under Mr. Cochin there for five years, on salary of 5 Rupees each per month as well as Batta and Clothes – we received each of us three months wages in advance and were embarked with 170 others in a vessel bound to the Mauritius, where we arrived after a voyage of 33 days – on landing Mr. Cochin got our names registered at the Police Office and employed us to work in a Sugar Cane Garden.

Other witnesses before these enquiries spoke of more directly coercive tactics – having been drugged or tricked into migrating and smuggled on board ships.[11] Few individuals were given the opportunity to recount their experiences for posterity, but some migrants spoke through their actions, running away from recruiters and guards or throwing themselves off the ships which were transporting them to the colonies. In 1838 three Indians deserted from the *Emerald Isle* when it docked at Mauritius on its way to South Australia. They were sent back to Calcutta.[12]

Relatives might also draw attention to the plight of migrants, as did Hauniff Durzee, who petitioned the Justices of the Peace at Calcutta:

The humble Petition of Hauniff Durzee;
Sheweth, That your petitioner's brother, Aumeer, about 18 years of age, who suddenly was concealed, and all the search your petitioner made for the last one month and half, it could not be discovered; at last now your petitioner finds that his said brother, Aumeer, is unjustly and forcibly detained in the custody of one Mr Dowson ... your petitioner went several times to see him, but was driven away by the servants.
Therefore, your petitioner begs that you will kindly adopt such measure that his brother be released, through one of the police constables; in so doing,
Your Petitioner will ever pray.[13]

On the other hand, there were already persons departing for the colonies as part of chain migration processes – wives and children called to join husbands, elderly relatives emigrating to be with younger family members – whose embarkation, still a product of economic necessity, was nevertheless not the result of deception or trickery. As early as 1838, one man stated his intention to join his two sons who were in Mauritius. Unfortunately, in this case, he had been the victim of fraud, having been embarked on a ship bound for British Guiana.[14]

Despite the conflicting nature of the material collected, it was decided to authorize the resumption of migration to Mauritius alone from 1842, but this time under government control. Thus abuses committed by over-zealous recruiters, leading to fraudulent embarkations, could be checked, and the general conditions of shipment, allocation to and work on estates could be regularized.[15]

Experiences of Recruitment, 1842–1910

Migrants asked to give evidence as to the circumstances of their recruitment after the new regulations of 1842 were in place continued to express ambivalent views about their experience. In fact all the abuses previously noticed by the Committees of Enquiry in the late 1830s were evidently still present in the 1840s. There were those who had undoubtedly been the victims of misrepresentation. There were others who, like Mohamed Sheriff, who migrated to British Guiana, were picked up by recruiters when away from home:

My name is Mohamed Sheriff. I was a gentleman's servant in Bombay (Colonel Adams, of the 13th Native infantry). I went to Lucknow where I was buying flowers for the table in the bazaar and was there met by a peon, who asked me if I wanted service. I said 'yes'. He then asked me if I could boil sugar. I said 'yes'. He told me then there was plenty of work for me if I would take it – boiling sugar and other work, if I like it; that I should have to go to Demerara, and should get ten annas to two rupees a day, and nineteen dollars present.

*So I went with him to Calcutta and was approved in the office, stayed there five days and
then embarked. Some of the people were allowed to take their lotas with them, but all the
others had everything taken away by the peons when they embarked, and were served
with government clothing . . . Nine men came from Lucknow with me. They were not all
cultivators – some barbers, coachmen, porters and other followings. I have not received
19 dollars and do not expect it.*[16]

Accustomed to seasonal inland migrations, some recruits were persuaded to
go to a colony which they still understood to be part of, or close to, India itself.
Such witnesses did not find it inconsistent to describe migration as an inevitable economic 'choice' whilst also complaining of deception and force in
recruitment.[17] Their apparent 'mobility' did not, at least from the available
testimonies of the 1840s, necessarily signify 'willingness' to migrate overseas.
The conviction of the anti-coolie-trade lobby that there was little understanding as to the whereabouts of Mauritius, or as to a sea journey being
involved, gained ground amidst evidence that, once confronted with the ship,
some migrants threw themselves overboard into the Hughli river rather than be
carried out into the ocean.

The Chief Magistrate of Calcutta himself saw a man jump overboard from
the *Faize Robany*, and on picking him up, ascertained that he was an unwilling
emigrant.[18] He sent the police onto the ship and a number of men and women
were removed from it. Purtaub Singh was one of those on board. His statement
indicates that, like many others, he was away from his home village seeking
work when the proposal to emigrate had been made to him.[19] Understanding
that Mauritius was a short journey from Calcutta he was happy to proceed, but
once realizing its distance, he described his fears as follows:

*I am a native of Orissa, [together with] my son, we left the country at the same time. At
Balasore we met with a duffadar who promised to procure me pay of 10 rupees per month
and I am old and feeble. On our arrival here I got some clothes the same as my son and
we were lodged 15 days in the duffadar's house and not allowed to go out unless the
duffadar accompanied us; we were told that we would have plenty of money and that if
any gentleman of the bank shall question us as to our willingness to proceed to Mauritius
that we were to say yes, also that I was at liberty to leave the place whenever I choose if
I did not like the place; I never knew that Mauritius was so far nor would I go to such a
distance at the risk of losing my life and my caste.*

The Magistrate argued that if the statements of men like Singh were to be
believed, 'they have been cruelly abused'. It was evident that the government
regulations of 1842, which required emigrants to declare their willingness to
proceed to a particular colony, were not working, and he concluded: 'if in the
face of all these precautions, the people suffer themselves to be deluded and
give credence to the stories trumped up by the cooly duffadars there appears no
help for them'.[20] Purtaub Singh and others who had been on the ship quickly
left the police office when told they were free to go. Their experience of
indentured migration had taken them no further than the depot and the

riverside embarkation. If the Chief Magistrate had not been observing the *Faize Robany*, they would have proceeded to Mauritius.

The eighteen emigrants who wrote to the Agent at Madras, however, were themselves taking steps to draw attention to their plight. Their letter described a recruiting operation similar to that which operated in northern India, whereby local maistries (equivalent to the duffadars of the Calcutta agency) would bring them to the coast, providing for their wants along the way and then passing them on to others. Once they had accepted food from their recruiters, a chain of debt was established which effectively prevented migrants from refusing to embark. The tactics used by recruiters to whittle away their pay advance were also denounced, and the emigrants complained of the number of 'old hands', possibly returnees, who were profiting from them:

We are poor and distressed people mostly cultivators of the interior countries, resolved to embark for the Mauritius for the purpose of bettering our circumstances, being so we are engaged by a maistry at Pondicherry or Karrical, some are taken up on our way to this by the intervention of these men and women, who wait at these stations. They seldom give us a batta on our journey, when arrived at Madras we are given up to another maistry for a certain profit or commission, who keeps us at some place for a time on the allowance of one anna batta per day to such as are only able to gain it from him, and that at irregular hours, and then we are tendered to some House or Agency that require men for shipment, those who agree to meet all fees and expenses of the maistries are taken before the Doctor and passed, while others who are candid are kept off for a certain time when from the want of means or friends to assist in a strange place even as much as a rupee to return back to our villages are compelled to submission and to be satisfied with one or two rupees as the remainder of an advance of 20 rupees . . . clothing, eating utensils, batta, small gold or silver trinkets are sold to us and in particular maistries fees are deducted; a batch for a ship is charged 30, 40 or 50 rupees as ceremony fees, performed at some pagoda or other, some of us losing passport apply to our maistries who recover it they charge to us another rupee for the same certificate as if it is a new one . . .

There are nearly 70 maistries, deputies, under maistries and collectors in men and women, the whole from Pondicherry come for the sole purpose of this traffic, they are all old hands who have robbed many thousands of poor fellows.

Had their friends and collectors in the interior who circulate the emigration news to us, informed us that our families could be taken together many of us should have done so but we are led to think that since their aim of making money as they will is thus encouraged they are perhaps commissioned to engage men only and thereby many of our men were embarked without having the previous idea of the government's wish that every man can take his wife and children with him.

If we are suffered to come and register ourselves it would be of very great advantage to us, but the evil of being passed from one hand to another cuts us short of 6 or 7 rupees as fee only instead of the established fee of 2 rupees a man which is publicly known.

Each maistry cheats us as he thinks proper, and exits from Madras no sooner his pocket is full, nobody knows how he came and how he went away, not one of us have yet had any intercourse or even seen the party shipping us, we are all kept in darkness, cheated to their heart's content and then shipped off without the means of putting one quarter of a rupee into the hands of parting friends and relatives who come from distant places to bid us farewell.

... Issue your orders and advices to the parties shipping us, that they may not take us
through the Pondicherry Maistries who are spread all over Madras ... but through
somebody who will act conscientiously receiving the usual fee and at the same time be held
responsible to your goodness whereby we poor and miserable wretches will be protected
from the present impositions which your goodness will be able to know on enquiry.
P.S. We could not avoid sending this by post as our appearing in a body could not be
effected without alarming the many maistries controlling us.[21]

Yet the eighteen signatories were not denouncing the emigration system *per se*;
rather they were attempting to reclaim some control over the process: specifically they wished to be responsible for their own registration. The allusion to
the intermediaries who surrounded them as 'Pondicherry maistries' probably
referred to the fact that prior to 1842 most recruits for Mauritius had been
shipped by French merchants from that port, and the return migrants had
therefore also originated from there, thereafter evidently dispersing throughout
the Madras Presidency. A particular issue raised by the letter writers was the
fact that they would have liked to emigrate with their families, and they
demanded better information to enable men to bring their wives and children.

The Emigration Agent at Madras, to whom the letter was addressed,
candidly informed the government, 'I have no reason to doubt the bulk of this
statement, and I regret that this Department can in no way check or control the
evil practices complained of'.[22] It was explained that migration was wholly
controlled by certain firms at Madras, which were commissioned from Mauritius to embark emigrants, and which therefore paid maistries to collect recruits
for them. The Agent could only suggest rather lamely that the Collectors and
Magistrates of the inland districts be notified that male migrants were permitted to take families with them, and that the 'Superintendent of Police might
be able ... in some degrees at least to check the oppressive proceedings of the
maistries'. It was resolved to circulate the emigrants' letter to police and
magistrates in the districts of North and South Arcot, Chingleput, Madura and
Trichinopoly, from where most of the emigrants came. The Chief Secretary
also informed the Magistrate of Tanjore that officials charged with explaining
the government's role to migrants should inform them that they were under no
obligation to refund money advanced, or to embark at Madras if they had
changed their minds. He underlined the importance of this by explaining
that:

the greater portion of emigrants it appears from the returns are agricultural
labourers, whose utter ignorance of anything beyond the limits of their own
village, renders them incapable of judging for themselves in this matter and they
are in consequence easily imposed upon by the maistries.[23]

In later years, when overseas migration was a better-understood concept,
deceptions could still be practised on recruits seeking to embark for one colony,

but being inveigled into the service of another. In 1860 the Mauritius Emigration Agent at Calcutta reported on the tactics adopted by West India recruiters:

> a large number of the Coolies who are picked up on the Grand Trunk Road for the
> West India Depots go there under the full impression that they are going to the
> Mauritius Depot, and the Recruiters, in order to deceive the people, style the
> Depot to which they are being conveyed as the 'Nya Merich-ka-kotee' [New
> Mauritius Depot], hence the absolute necessity of the fullest information being
> given to the Coolies individually at the time their certificates are being counter-
> signed by the Protector to check, as far as possible, the abuses that are practised
> upon them by paid Recruiters.[24]

In support of this statement, one Chummun Boolakee, one of the band initially
fed by the West India Agent and then diverted to the Mauritius depot, declared
that he had friends at Mauritius and knew no one at Demerara, hence his
determination to go to the former colony:

> *[I] came down at Calcutta with a party of eleven others from Shergotty for the purpose
> of emigrating to the Mauritius and on the road was met by the Duffadar 'Bugoo' at
> Muggra Pool, who asked [me] where [I] was going to. [I] replied 'I am going to
> Mauritius'; then he said 'I will take you to the Depot. I am the brother of the man you
> are looking for. He paid the boat expenses for myself and party to Calcutta and gave each
> of us one pice to get refreshment'.*
> *After landing he took us to a place he called a new Depot for the Mauritius at Cassia
> Bagaun, where the Baboo at the Depot entered our names in a book and remained there
> for three days, but found out, at the end of that, time, it was the Demerara Depot and not
> the Mauritius. I with my party wanted to get away but they tried to prevent us, but
> eventually we ran away and came to Mr. Caird's Depot, leaving the little property we
> had behind.*

The problem for the West Indian agents was that once intercepted by Mauritian recruiters, migrants – albeit collected by the former – would not disavow
the claim of the latter that they had ever intended to go to any other than the
Mauritian depot. Thus, on another occasion, the agent for Demerara described
how a group of migrants had been brought from Dinapore to Raniganj on a
three-week journey, under the care of a guard acting on his behalf, when they
were taken away and sent on by rail to the Mauritius depot. When questioned
by the Protector of Emigrants at that port, they all denied having been collected
for Demerara. Prior to the appointment of separate agencies, the Mauritius
recruiters had acted for the West Indies but, contended the Demerara agent,
had not differentiated between the two colonies, hence the name of the West
Indies had never been widely circulated in the recruiting districts, thereby
adding to his problems.[25]

In this case, as in many others, the Protector of Emigrants was in a quandary.
The paperwork indicated that the migrants had indeed been recruited at

Dinapore by a Demerara recruiter, but on being questioned by him they were adamant that they had been initially recruited for Mauritius. As he explained:

> In the midst of such conflicting evidence, resting as it does almost wholly on native testimony, it seems almost impossible to arrive at any satisfactory conclusion as to which of the two colonies the people were originally recruited for, and the only course open to me, therefore, was to base my decision on the final declaration made by the people themselves in my presence, and sanctioned their being sent to Mauritius; indeed, under the rules at present in force, I conceive that I could not have given a decision at variance with the present wish of the coolies, even had I had indisputable evidence of their having been recruited for other colonies.[26]

Given the ease with which the Mauritius recruiters could leave the hard work of collection, transport and feeding to the West India Agents and then take migrants from them when they neared Calcutta, the West Indian Agents took to placing guards over recruits. In this case the thirty-six labourers had been placed in the charge of a chaprasi in the employ of the Demerara agency, who wore a belt with a brass plate attached to it on which were engraved, in English and Persian characters, the words 'Hunter Marriot, Emigration Agent for British Guiana'. He had with him a written pass, signed by a sub-agent for Demerara at Dinapore, in the following words: 'Please pass thirty-six coolies for Hunt Marriott, Esq., Emigration Agent, Cassia Bagan, Calcutta, without molestation', together with a list of the men. This did not deter the Mauritian recruiters, however, as the chaprasi, Shaik Buccus, explained:

> *A gentleman in Dinapore engaged my services to escort thirty-five coolies to the Demerara depot in Calcutta; he furnished me with a badge and two papers, on one of which is written the names of all the coolies entrusted to my charge. I also receive from him Rupees 60 to defray the feeding expenses of the coolies on the journey. The gentleman and a baboo asked the coolies in my presence if they were willing to emigrate to Demerara, and they all answered in the affirmative, either to go to Demerara or to any other place the saheb was pleased to send them: this was all that was spoken to the coolies about Demerara in my presence. Shortly afterwards I left Dinapore with all the coolies. The first interruption I met with was at Gya, where there were two sircars who began to speak to my people about going to Mauritius, but the coolies refused to listen to them, stating that the saheb had only told them about Demerara; the name of 'Morich' was only mentioned to the Coolies by the sircars. I heard nothing about Bourbon; at another halting place about six miles further on, I met five or six duffadars, who immediately addressed my coolies about going to Mauritius, but without effect. We then continued our journey, and met with no further interruption until we got within two miles of Raneegunge, where we were stopped by an European gentleman, a baboo, and some peons, whom I afterwards learnt were employed by the Mauritius Agency. After they had conversed some little time with my coolies, they made all my people desert from me and follow them. In my efforts to prevent the coolies I was assaulted by the peons and pushed aside. I then went to the Thannah and complained, but could get no redress. The coolies had been seventeen days under my care when they were enticed away. The sum of Rupees 70 was disbursed on the road, ten of which, I should have before stated, was received from a Demerara chuprassee at Bogra, whom I did not see afterwards. No other recruiters were met at this place. I*

followed the coolies to Calcutta, and complained to the baboo of the Demerara depot that they had been taken from me. I repeatedly told the Mauritius recruiting agents at Raneegunge that the people had been collected for the Demerara depot, but did not shew them the two papers in my possession.

Migrants heading for the Mauritius depot at Bhawanipur were thus persuaded or deceived into bringing their recruits to other depots, and labourers collected for the West Indies were rerouted to the Mauritius depot if they stated that colony's name. To offset the better-known name of 'Maurich', West Indian recruiters also regularly intercepted bands and informed them that Mauritius was no longer recruiting, or that the depot had been removed to a new site.

The evidence of Inder indicates that Mauritius was a preferred destination for two overriding reasons: nobody had heard of other colonies, and many people believed their relatives who had migrated had gone to Mauritius. Inder was one of many migrants in the mid-nineteenth century who went to Mauritius as part of a chain, following pioneers. It was in much the same way that the European movements to the New World gathered pace in this period. Unfortunately for the recruits into indenture, however, the prospects of reaching the same colony and the same plantation as that for which their relatives had engaged was fraught with obstacles. Inder's statement recounts his near escape:

I was one of a batch of 17 Coolies who accompanied Juggon return Cooly from Gya for Mauritius, where I have a brother, I never heard of such a place as Demerara until Soopun, Golamun, and others wished us to go there. Mr Caird and Toyluck Baboo released us from the Demerara Recruiters. [27]

Thus if ignorance about Mauritius had frightened away men like Purtaub Singh two decades earlier, by the mid-nineteenth century it was the comparative familiarity of Mauritius over rival labour importers which ensured its popularity. This continued for a time even when wage rates began to compare less favourably with the newer recruiting territories; but ultimately the networks of information which had assisted the process of chain migration to Mauritius were also to act to dissuade workers from proceeding to a colony which had less and less to offer its new recruits.

When emigration to Mauritius was at its peak, the determination of migrants to go there rather than another colony in order to be reunited with family members led to extraordinary acts of courage. The experience of Ramasawmy, as recounted by him, provides a remarkable testimony to this. We first meet him in the office of the Protector of Immigrants in March 1861. He had been brought there to explain why he had jumped overboard from the *Jacques Coeur*, bound for Martinique, when that vessel had docked at Port Louis harbour. Ramasawmy explained that he had embarked at Karical twenty-eight days before, having been told he was to go to Mauritius. He had jumped overboard because he had found out, from the conversation of the officers on board, that the ship was destined for the West Indies, but had arrived at Mauritius for a short stop *en route*. Not wishing to go any further, he decided to attempt his escape. His ill treatment on the ship had strengthened his resolve to take the risk of jumping into the sea. Along with another man, Periacarpen, Rama-sawmy swam for one mile at night to reach a neighbouring ship, onto which they climbed.[28] Evidently Ramasawmy was allowed to remain at Mauritius while the ship sailed on, for one month later he was called to give a more detailed explanation of the events which had led up to his embarkation before the Depot Magistrate:

> *I belong to Watnara Chetaram, a village about ten miles from Tanjore. I left my village on the 5th January to come to Mauritius. I was induced to do so because my father who emigrated to Mauritius when I was an infant in arms, about 20 years ago, had written many letters to me telling me to come to rejoin him. My father's name is Mecken. He sent me money to enable me to rejoin him at Mauritius on three different occasions. The first time was about seven years ago. Then a man of the name of Poondemah brought me 30 rupees from my father. The second time about four years ago Saminaden brought me a second sum of 25 rupees. The third time was about three years ago when I again received Rs 15 from Poondamah, to whom the sum was entrusted by another person with whom I am acquainted. Nothing would have induced me to leave India for any other country than Mauritius. I left my house early on the morning of the 5th January to go to Madras with the intention of embarking for Mauritius, and in the afternoon met two persons, whose names I do not know. These two persons asked me where I was going, I said I was going to Madras to embark for Mauritius. They said to me, wait a couple of days and then we will go with you and ship you for Mauritius. They swore to me that they would accompany me to Mauritius, and that we should live together there. They took me to their house at Tanjore, and there induced me to conceal myself, telling me not to speak to anyone as there were crimps [commercial recruiters] about who would lead me astray. I had one rupee and twelve annas in my possession, which they took from me, promising to pay me at Mauritius. From Tanjore I accompanied these men to Coomboconum, where we stopped one night, and next day we proceeded to Karical. At Karical there was a sort of emigration depot where I was kept for ten days under lock and key. I was embarked on board the Jacques Coeur, and it was only on board that I learnt that I was going to America (the West Indies). I asked where this was and was told that it was close to Mauritius. On board ship I learnt afterwards that the West Indies were at 3 and half month's sail from Mauritius, and I then refused to go thither. When the Jacques Coeur anchored here I learnt from one of the men on board, who had already been at Mauritius that this was Mauritius, and I also heard the officers of the ship say the same thing. I was beaten and very badly treated on board and that joined to my wish to see my father and to the bad food we all got on board induced me to attempt to make my escape.*[29]

From this deposition we learn that Ramasawmy had determined to leave his village in the hope of being reunited with a father he had not seen for twenty years. Mecken had maintained contact with his son through the medium of returnees, who had three times brought money to Ramasawmy and conveyed his father's wish that the latter should join him in Mauritius. However, once *en route* for the island, Ramasawmy was deceived by 'crimps' who subjected him to ill-treatment. Meanwhile, the Immigration Office had traced Ramasawmy's father. It was discovered that Mecken was now an old immigrant, having arrived at Mauritius in November 1843 on the ship *Brahmin* at the age of 20.[30] The day following the recording of Ramasawmy's statement, his father was brought to the depot. Mecken corroborated his son's account, explaining that the small boy had been left behind because he could not look after him. Like many migrants, he received letters from his family urging him to return, but he had instead sent money, asking his son to join him. His statement was as follows:

> *I am a native of Wutnara Chetaram, which is a village a few miles from Tanjore. I left my village about 18 and half years ago, and came to Mauritius on board the ship 'Brahmin'. I left behind me in my village my infant son Ramasawmy who was then about three years old. I left my son with my brother Ramsamy, because he was too young to travel, and because I had no one to take care of him on the voyage, having lost my wife. After I arrived here I three times sent money to India to have my son sent to me. I received two letters from India, during this time, pressing me to return there. The first time I sent money to India I sent 30 rupees, the second time 25, and the third time 15 rupees. I only heard of my son's arrival here when he was at the Immigration Depot.*[31]

When Ramasawmy was brought in, the boy Mecken visualized in his memory stood before him transformed into a man, one whom he nevertheless instinctively recognized. As they stood face to face Mecken said 'This is my son. I recognize him perfectly'. Ramasawmy, for his part, stated that he knew his father at once by his likeness to his uncle.

Thus was a potential tragedy averted, and a reconciliation effected by the courage and daring of the younger man. The remarkable experience of Ramasawmy and his father speaks volumes about bonds of kinship and affection between migrants and their families, which are all too often lost in the conventional historiographies of indenture. It also demonstrates both the importance of micro-level chain-migration initiatives to the overall pattern of indentured recruitment, and the constraints placed on such migrant-sponsored strategies by the competing claims of labour exporters. Deception and the will to migrate were not mutually exclusive categories. Coercion continued to be a factor recognized by agents and migrants alike: particularly in the form of economic necessity, which pushed individuals and families to allow themselves to be indentured in return for a square meal. At the same time, the voices of those who took part in this voyage reveal to us that indenture was in some respects seen as an option for those who fell on hard times, just as struggling Irish tenant farmers knew that the emigrant ship was one avenue to a fresh start. The indenture contract came to represent for some a necessary sojourn in a faraway country where the means of subsistence could be procured for oneself and a sum of money to be sent home for one's family, and where, despite the hardships to be endured, one had countrymen also labouring.

Agriculturists and craftsmen, whose trades were declining, were among those who migrated. The statement of Madho, a Kahar of Naseni, is indicative of the prospects and working lives of the labouring caste groups of Bihar and UP, who were common recruits:

> *Ours is the only family of Kahars in the village. I have father, mother, two brothers, two sisters, grandmother, maternal uncle and his son. I cultivate 25 bighas with two ploughs, paying rent at Rs 2 per bighas. Have sown 12 bighas with wheat. I eat bread twice daily of barley, gram or juar. The family expenditure is five or six seers daily. I never eat wheat. I sell my wheat to pay my rent. I got Rs 1 a month for supplying water to certain villages. I sometimes work as palki-bearer, getting half anna a kos. I also make something at weddings. I borrow seeds at sawai rates: have not yet paid anything. I have just enough to get on with. My clothing consists of a pagri, a dhoti, and a body-cloth. My father . . . carries the zamindar's palki as a begari: he gets no pay for this, but something in kind. . . . I have two bullocks and one cow. I have not yet paid my rent, but have set off to claim for work done in carrying the zamindar's palki.*[32]

The existence of agrestic servitude in Bihar in the form of kamia bonds, might make of overseas migration an acceptable exchange of one form of debt bondage – indefinite in length – for the more finite term of an overseas indenture. Prakash has described the attempts kamiatis made to escape from ill treatment – to Calcutta, to work on the coalfields in Chota Nagpur, or simply to another village. It is quite plausible that some of these runaways from a life of serfdom found their way into the emigration depots.[33] Alternatively, the bond-holder could conceivably have been exchanged for a cash payment and handed on to a recruiter, with little say in the matter. A typical kamia bond was that of Bhinak Bhuiya:

> *The bond of Bhinak Bhuiya, son of Chamari Bhuiya, residing in village Palaon, pargana Champa, Hazareebagh district (executed in 1870's). Whereas in time past I borrowed from Sital Ram, mahajan (trader) and ilakakar (landlord) of village Chai, pargana Champa, the sum of Rs.20, bearing interest, on the security of my personal labour as a kamia (bondsman) according to the usage and custom of the neighbourhood. I now execute this deed and agree that, until the sum of Rs. 20 be repaid in full, I will in lieu of the interest thereon, continue to work as a Kamia for the mahajan aforesaid. I will raise no objection to so working, and will receive my bikma and bhunja (a double handful of cooked food distributed to kamias in the morning), and wages according to custom from the said mahajan. If I am ill for five days or ten days, my son will labour in my stead. When I grow old and can work no longer, and if I dispute the debt, the mahajan aforesaid is free to sue me in court for the amount of the loan. But if my son shall then taken upon himself my debt and obligations to work, the said mahajan shall have no further claim against me. If at any time, I repay the principal, I shall be free to go where I please. Wherefore, I have executed this kamiati bond to be evidence of the agreement, if need be.*[34]

Thus even when the misrepresentations exercised by duffadars and maistries had been reformed by the stricter regulations implemented in the 1860s and 1870s, the decision to migrate cannot be said to have been taken freely. Indentured recruitment often took place in circumstances of humiliation and poverty.

The combination of indebtedness and rural marginalization which preceded the initial departure from home and subsequent meeting with the overseas recruiter is underscored by the evidence of Saivaroodian, who went to the French colony of Bourbon (present-day Reunion):

I hold one and a half valy of land in the above-mentioned village. I was involved in debt to the extent of about 100 rupees and had no means of discharging it also I was unable to maintain myself and family. I therefore determined to proceed to Mauritius, make some money there and return home ... I set out alone from my village, without taking leave of my wife and my only child, a boy of seven years of age and proceeded taking the high road with a view of going to Madras. At the village of Audodotoray in the Coottallum Taluka, I was joined by four persons who had come from the North ... They said that they also were going to Mauritius; took me with them, and together we reached Karrical in the French settlement. As soon as we arrived at Karrical I learned that one of my comrades was a resident of that place, and that he had brought thither the other three persons. For five days I subsisted on what I had brought with me and lived in the house of the above whom I found to be a maistry. He then assured me that the coolies were to be conveyed not to Bourbon but to Mauritius ... He led me into a godown which was enclosed on all sides by walls, and shut the door after me. There were already about 100 or 150 persons in this godown ... somehow or other my wife accompanied by my little boy, came to the godown in which I had been lodged, and called to me from the outside. They refused to permit me to go out or even to open the door. The same day, some gentlemen came and visited the godown, informed me that 15 rupees would be first advanced to me for proceeding to Mauritius, and told me to accept the amount from the hand of the maistry. The maistry paid me 11 rupees ... Out of it I retained one rupee, and through a chink in the door, gave the remaining ten to my wife; she refused to take them, and threw them down on the ground. Some persons who were outside picked them up, and gave them into the hands of my boy. My wife then returned home with the boy.[35]

What must this man, weighed down by the burden of debt, have been feeling, that he was persuaded to leave his village without even informing his family? One can imagine also the emotions of his wife who tracked him to the godown in Karaikal, from which he could not even emerge to bid her farewell. Saivaroodian did not return to India until 1857 (having probably left between 1839 and 1841), when he recounted his experience. His story graphically demonstrates that the recognition by individuals of the need to migrate, and even the stated intention to proceed to a particular colony, in no way negate the claim that coercion, deception and human suffering were a recurrent feature of the indenture experience.

The experiences of the individuals whose depositions were recorded help to demonstrate the complexity of the migration process. The statements of Saivaroodian, Purtaub Singh and others represent just a few of the many individual cases of hardship which together produced the unnamed waves of migrants who proceeded to the colonies, to serve the interests of sugar producers and consumers in the British Empire. For them the experience of indentured migration was only just starting. Their words reveal that from such

unhappy beginnings migrants attempted, and increasingly succeeded, in wrest-
ing a process of settlement from what, at its inception, was intended by those
who engineered it to be little more than a new servile institution.

However, if the evidence of contacts maintained between migrants and their
families, and the experiences recounted in the depositions and petitions of
indentured labourers, reveal a phenomenon of group or chain migration which
is often absent from official sources, those migrants who testified to having
gone abroad, particularly to Mauritius, to join relatives or fellow villagers did
not always like what they found on arrival. Hesaddat had paid his own passage
to Mauritius to visit his son, who had settled there, and in the hope of gaining
material support from him. To his consternation, his son's position was not
much better than his own, and Hesaddat found himself unable to afford to pay
his passage back to India. He accordingly petitioned the Chief Clerk of the
Immigration Department to provide him with a free return voyage:

> *The undersigned Hesaddat of Port Louis without profession has the honor to submit to*
> *you respectfully,*
> *That he arrived in this colony as passenger on the 20th September 1879 on board the ship*
> *Allum Ghier from Calcutta to see his son and in the hope of having some assistance from*
> *him.*
> *That on his arrival in this colony, he has been much surprised to see his son, who is*
> *married and father of family in a very bad situation.*
> *That having had no assistance from his son and having no means to support himself he*
> *wishes to return to Calcutta, where he has family, but has not the means of doing so.*
> *Therefore he humbly prays that you may be pleased to take his poor situation into your*
> *serious consideration and allow him a free passage as coolie in order that he may return*
> *to Calcutta and join his family or otherwise, he will be in a very sad position here.*[36]

Unfortunately, because the man had arrived not as an indentured worker but as
a passenger, the Protector could not help him. The Immigration Office could
do no more than suggest that he might apply to the Governor, who 'would
perhaps allow his passage being paid out of charitable allowances'.[37]

Further, if many migrants who went overseas in the latter part of the
nineteenth century did so, like Hesaddat, following relatives and co-villagers,
this did not preclude the continuing use of coercion and fraud in recruiting. In
1862 the Mauritius depot gained unwanted publicity as a result of the kidnap-
ping of a young boy, Bahadoor. The boy was lured by the promise of higher
wages to engage for Mauritius, according to his deposition:

> *I am twelve years of age. I have for some time been acquainted with Lungut, who is*
> *employed collecting people for Mauritius. I have often heard of Mauritius as a place*
> *where Coolies can earn better wages than in Calcutta. I was engaged at a Cook Shop for*
> *twelve annas a month. Lungut told me to go with him and he would get me twelve*
> *Rupees, 'what was the use of remaining here for twelve annas?'; he took me to a shop and*
> *gave me some sweetmeats, which made me stupid, and then took me to Bhowanee-*
> *pore.*[38]

The Demerara agency was charged with a similar offence a few years later when their recruiter, Joynarain, was sentenced to seven years' imprisonment at Benares. He petitioned the Indian government for clemency in his case.[39]

In 1871 the attempts of Buldeo, a recruiter for Jamaica, to compel some women to migrate from Allahabad gained notoriety. It was a Baptist missionary, the Revd Evans, who brought the story to the attention of the authorities when his servant's aunt was one of those sequestered. He reported that she had gone out to seek work when she had met a chaprasi who offered her a job grinding corn, took her to a place with other women, gave them food and then said that their names would be written 'by the orders of the sirdar' to go to 'Miritch desh' (Mauritius) as coolies. Next day her husband went and searched for her, but Buldeo Jemadar, who was in charge of them, would not let her go unless her husband paid Rs 5, which he could not. The servant, a mochi, informed Evans of his relative's plight, and took him to the place. There he confronted Buldeo Jemadar, who told Evans they were free to go if they wished. At this all the women bolted, whereupon Buldeo reportedly flew into a rage and said he would report the matter to 'Burrah Sahib', that is, Bird & Company. Evans asked the government to consider:

> what unutterable anguish such acts as these must cause in poor families. Only think of a poor mother, maybe a widow, going out in the morning in search of work to get a few pice to provide food for their children, and those poor children never again to see their mother, she being kidnapped in the station of Allahabad and in the name of government.

Evans reported that Buldeo had eight men on the look-out to pick up individuals; they were paid one rupee per person. The Reverend also went to see Bird & Company, who 'expressed their sorrow for the way in which Buldeo decoyed the women, but said they were not accountable, and they feared they could not put a stop to it, though they would warn him'. He pointed out that such individuals did not dare state the true facts when they were registered before the magistrate because they were threatened with debt. He also recounted that Buldeo had shouted in his presence 'Ham sirkar ke hookum karte hain' and 'Ham sirkar ke nowkar hain', or 'I am a servant of government'. Buldeo was condemned to one year's imprisonment.[40]

Recruiters, as these cases show, ran serious risks when they attempted to coerce even the ordinary and lowly. Relatives were not slow to defend the interests of family members detained by colonial agents. In 1871 one Ungnoo presented a petition to the Allahabad court to the effect that his sister-in-law was detained against her will at an emigration depot in Moteegunge under the charge of Manasseh (a West India recruiter). The woman in question, Mussamut Amirtee, stated that she was on her way to her home in the Mirzapore district when she was offered work at two annas per day, grinding flour in Moteegunge. When she got there she found herself virtually a prisoner, but sent her 8-year-old child to get help. When before the deputy magistrate, she consented to emigrate because her captors had promised to set her free. The recruiters involved in the case were sentenced to one month, one year, and eighteen months' imprisonment respectively.[41]

The hostility of villagers to the work of labour exporters is shown in the folksongs of women from UP and Bihar:

> *Oh recruiter, your heart is deceitful,*
> *Your speech is full of lies!*
>
> *Tender may be your voice, articulate*
> *and seemingly logical,*
>
> *But it is all used to defame and destroy*
> *The good names of people.*[42]

This song has also been recorded as in use in British Guiana in the indenture period.[43]

On the other hand, the crushing poverty which many of the songs describe is recognized to be a major factor in the decision to migrate, and is portrayed as a better option than a life of agricultural drudgery in India:

> *Born in India, we are prepared to go to Fiji*
> *Or, if you please, to Natal to dig the mines.*
> *We are prepared to suffer there,*
> *But Brothers! Don't make us agriculturalists here.*[44]

Once in the colonies, the folksongs of indentured labourers turn the depiction of migration into a heroic act of resistance. In the following example, from Surinam, the journey overseas is turned into an escape from caste oppression:

> *I call India blessed, and the Brahmans and Kshatriyas too,*
> *Who attach untouchability to their subjects.*
> *They rule by the power of these very subjects.*
> *While keeping the company of prostitutes.*
> *The subjects escaped and came to the islands*
> *And, yes, India turned on her side.*[45]

The following song from Mauritius, by contrast, acknowledges the exaggerated hopes of emigrants, convinced by recruiters that they would find gold on the streets of that island, and stresses the reality of disappointment:

> *Having heard the name of the island of Mauritius,*
> *We arrived here to find gold, to find gold.*
> *Instead we got beatings of bamboos,*
> *Which peeled the skin off the back of the labourers.*
> *We became Kolhu's bullocks to extract cane sugar,*
> *Alas! We left our country to become coolies.*[46]

The case of Debi Ram, No. 428,378, who went to Mauritius in 1904, demonstrates that recruiters were still able to take advantage of the ignorant and the desperate, and to place them in situations which they would later find profoundly distasteful. Debi was only 19 years old when he was shipped as an indentured labourer. In Calcutta he had given his caste as Thakur and was said to be from the zillah of Dholpur, Kewlari thana. He arrived on the steamship *Surada* and was allotted to Bel Etang Sans Souci estate for five years on 20 October 1905. It did not, though, take long for Debi Ram to come to the attention of the authorities. Soon after his arrival he was sentenced to three years penal servitude for arson. The reasons for this act might have remained undiscovered had not the Protector of Immigrants interviewed him during one of his routine prison inspections. The testimony given by Debi Ram is an extraordinary account of a young man who ran away from his village home because of a Rs5 gambling debt:

I lived principally by begging in the village of Sampor Khiro in the country of Dholpore in India where I was born. I never worked for my living – my parents used to feed me, they are both alive. I stole Rs five from my mother's home and gambled with it. I had been told by my parents not to gamble, so I was frightened when I lost the five rupees and ran away from home. I thus begged my way to Agra. When I was at Agra a man asked me if I would like to go to Calcutta to work saying that I would be paid Rs 6 a month and get clothes and food besides. I said I would. I was then taken by him before the Magistrate at Agra who asked me if I was willing to go to Calcutta where I would be paid Rs 6 a month and given my food daily and where I would be given clothes. I said I was quite willing to go. The Magistrate told me that I would have to work daily and advised me not to go saying it was a cold country and I would die there. I replied I wish to go as I want to earn my living.

I used to do light work in the fields in the village where I lived. I used to drive two oxen yoked to a plough, and work the fields with a khoorpee. I never did hard work in the fields, such as I was required to do here, in India. I did not use a hoe there at all. All the work I did in India was very light. I need to look after cows and buffaloes when they were feeding. My parents had 5 cows, two buffaloes and 2 bullocks. I used to drive two oxen while they drew water out of a well -- in fact all the agricultural work I did in India was light work.

When I arrived at Calcutta a gentleman there told me that I would have to work hard here in the field and asked me if I was willing to go to Mauritius as an agricultural labourer, I said I was quite willing to go. I am a brahmin by caste – the man who induced me to emigrate at Agra told me to say that I was a Thakur. I was not taught by my father what a brahmin should do – he taught me to read but I have forgotten all about it. I can neither read nor write. Since my childhood I used to watch cattle feeding and do light work at home.[47]

It is difficult to be sure of the veracity of all parts of this statement. Was he really a Brahmin as he claimed? His immigration register gives his caste as Thakur, but Brahmins were often advised to claim to be Thakurs to avoid rejection.[48] Perhaps Debi Ram was of weak intellect – he seemed to have been given few responsibilities and a very rudimentary education; still, his testimony reveals that, even into the twentieth century, overseas recruiters continued to divert unwitting travellers in India into the exporters' hands.

Twentieth-century oral depositions have been collected from indentured labourers in the Caribbean and Fiji and published in a number of historical and anthropological studies. The accounts of such individuals naturally lay stress on dramatic personal incidents as causative factors of migration, and must be read as interpretative rather than as purely factual evidence. Thus Calcutta-born Maharani describes her experience as an abused daughter-in-law in India and her subsequent escape to Trinidad, where she eventually married again, in an interview with Noorkumar Mahabir.[49] Ram Bahadur gave the following account, to anthropologist Jim Wilson, of the events surrounding his departure for Fiji in 1906:

> His family had to leave their village after his father died, because other villagers, in revenge for his father's tyrannical ways, refused to work their land, stole their jewellery, and framed his elder brother for theft. Warned by a Muslim woman that police were coming the family fled by night, leaving a lamp burning to prevent pursuit, and leaving also all their crops and possessions. As none of them had ever left the village they went round in circles all night, but at dawn found the road to Ferozpur.[50]

At Ferozpur they were guided to the recruiting office for Fiji, were taken by train to Calcutta and embarked for their Pacific destination.

The few indentured Indians who wrote down their life stories, like Totaram Sanadhaya of Fiji, could be counted on to recount the sufferings of others:

> *I . . . saw a woman washing her tattered clothes on the banks of the river. . . . she told me her story. After seven years of marriage, her husband had died [in India], leaving behind his aged mother and a three year old son. One day she left them at home to go on a pilgrimage to Dwarika. On her way back she got separated from her companions at Mathura and ended up in Fiji. She felt very sad remembering her aged mother-in-law and son, wishing she were dead.*[51]

In 1979, to mark the centenary of Indian migration to Fiji, the *Fiji Sun* published several interviews with ex-indentured labourers. Meheboob reported:

> *I left home just looking around like young people do these days, and I met a man who said in Allahabad, there is sugar to be strained and I am looking for servants. He said every six months I come home and you may come back with me.*

Sarju's testimony is interesting for what it reveals about the difference between the nature of agricultural work in India and that expected from an indentured labourer in Fiji:

> *Lots of people came to Fiji for many different reasons, some after getting into trouble and fights, others to earn and so on. I was told by the recruiter that for 'Kaskari Kam' (agricultural work or working on the land), I would get one shilling and six pence for*

eight hours a day. In India for the same work one received only one ana for the whole day's work. But kaskari work in India, means working on the land at your time and pace. Nobody can push you around or off your land. I thought I could work in Fiji and daily save a shilling and spend six pence. It was with these thoughts that I came to Fiji. Instead over here there was task work and only nine pence after a back breaking day and I was in a 'girmit' for five years. This was 'dagabaji' (trickery).

A female informant, Ratna, described how her attempts to find her husband led to her embarkation for Fiji:

My man left the house after he had been rebuked by my father-in-law. I took my child and went looking for him in Ajodaji. I spent five or six days there, I did not know where to go and where to look for him. I was told that my husband had gone to Calcutta. I went to Calcutta by train to search for him. I was told that he had already left two or three days earlier. I went to the wharf and there I saw a steamer, some people took my son off me, and threatened me. I was put into the depot with my child and stayed there for two or three days before embarking on the ship.[52]

Ratna was one of many Indians who, searching for missing partners, and sometimes convinced their absent relatives had emigrated overseas, departed themselves for one colony or another, usually without much chance of being reunited with their loved ones.

The Punjabi recruits who addressed a letter to the Commissioner of Jullunder in 1915 were more articulate and focused in their reproaches. They were not, strictly speaking, indentured labourers, as they had paid their own passages, but as the following letter shows, they considered themselves to have been equally the objects of fraud:

We all the Punjabis now residing in Fiji Islands left our country on the inducement and representations of Wali Mohamed and Atta Mohamed, castes Sayed, residents of Karnana, tahsil Nawanshar, District, Jullundur, Punjab. They have been sending our people during the last 5 years and on each steamer 45 or 46 men are being emigrated while they take Rs. 35 as their commission for each individual and Rs. 5 from the shipping Co; – we were made to understand that in Fiji we can get work on daily wages at 5/- but regret to say that even 2/- can be hardly earned – thus we have been suffering much. We had no previous experience of such tricks and they are deceiving to the people and are also against the law. We all paid Rs. 325 as commission to them. We therefore request that enquiries be made and action be taken to stop further emigration. If possible the money be refunded to us.[53]

The forty-six signatories to this letter, all new arrivals in Fiji, were less concerned with their own fate than with preventing further misrepresentations being exercised against their compatriots. Like the new wave of South Asian migrants to the Gulf States, the last trickle of immigrants to the plantation colonies were seemingly inured to the necessity of migration, but continued to be disappointed by the inequalities between contracting parties to which they were exposed.

Settlers, Returnees and Recruiters

The migration process would always ensnare the vulnerable in the nets of the unscrupulous. Nevertheless, the misfortunes of Debi Ram and his ilk provide only one aspect of the indenture experience. The need to look beyond the official narrative of recruitment, with its emphasis on either such fraudulent cases or economic push and pull factors and the social impediments to emigration, is demonstrated *par excellence* in the issues raised by a group of Telegu migrants. The Telegus provide an important case study of a community which became closely associated with migration to Mauritius, were valued on the island, and undertook indenture as a seemingly self-aware form of group settlement. There had been a Telegu presence in Mauritius from the eighteenth century, and once indentured recruitment began in the 1830s, Telegus were amongst the earliest migrants. By 1849 large numbers had emigrated to Mauritius, and in that year the Calcutta Emigration Agent reported that Telegus from Ganjam had walked the coastal road all the way to Calcutta in order to migrate to Mauritius, because Madras was temporarily closed as a port of embarkation.[54]

The letter drafted by a group of Telegu returnees some years later reveals a vision of indenture very different from the motives and experiences ascribed to migrants in many historical accounts. The concerns they express represent a clear appraisal of the migration as a means of family settlement overseas. Their

Figure 2.1(a) Captain N.G. Hatch. Dr Welsh and leading hands of the emigrants aboard '*Avoca*.' Source: B. Lubbock, *Coolie Ships and Oil Sailers*, Glasgow, 1955.

central demands are for recognition of and respect for their group identity, regulations to protect their family status (principally to secure control over their wives), and the means to migrate as independently as possible of the local recruiters and contractors who sought to make of indenture a commercial venture. The letter they wrote to the Mauritian authorities from India emphasized:

That ourselves with ten or fifteen thousand of our countrymen are most anxious to come and settle ourselves at Mauritius with our wives and children. The Calcutta men and the Tamulians are favoured and protected at Mauritius and not those of our country. When we go and make known to the police of our welfare or our grievances our words are not transmitted to the Magistrate and wherever we go to complain, we find that all the

Figure 2.1 (b) Emigrants awaiting embarkation in the bazaar.
Source: L. Lacroix; *Les Derniers Negriers*, Paris, 1939.

persons employed there are Tamulians and Calcutta, they say 'poda Coringhy' or 'Diave Coringhys' (go away men of Coringhy) and if we come to settle ourselves there with our wives and children, we shall meet with the difficulties of receiving tidings from our relatives in India ...

In our country we are all very poor where shall we get money to defray the expenses consequent on a journey to such distant places as Madras and Calcutta to embark for Mauritius but if your Excellency would establish anywhere near our country a police presided by a good man of our nation, similar to that in Madras, then the people in our country and those of the neighbourhood shall all come to settle at Mauritius with their families. The Tamulians and the Calcutta men are great thieves, they receive and live by bribery. The people of Ganjam, Sattrapooram, Itchapooram and Coringha are not thieves, they are all hardworking men. Your Excellency can enquire from all the people in your country and you will know the truth.

God knows what miseries and sufferance we have endured from the Frenchmen and the Tamulians, they wanted to exact a good deal of bribery from us, but notwithstanding that we would have paid them, had it not been that we were much afraid that they would not have faithfully transmitted our words, we have therefore left the island and returned to our country. In conclusion we beg to request that if your Excellency will be pleased to comply with our demand in putting a stop to the evils above described and to promise to alleviate our position and will also be pleased to establish a native police in the port of Ganjam which is near our country, in the course of two years a great many of our people with our families and relatives will come and settle ourselves at Mauritius and we shall afterwards follow your orders.[55]

The Telegus were a minority group in Mauritius and their complaints against Tamils and North Indians reflect the predominance of these latter in the colonial public service, and in the principal emigration depots at Madras and Calcutta. Significantly, the Telegu returnees were expressing a firm resolve to settle in Mauritius with their families. Their main requirements before doing so were that people of their own ethnic background should be appointed to oversee and finance the migration from India, maintain a channel of communication between Telegus overseas and their relatives at home, judge their disputes, and protect their interests in Mauritius. The Telegu returnees made a special reference to women who were not punished for deserting their husbands, and this was a criticism of the current state of the law in Mauritius, which, because it failed to recognize marriages not legalized by a civil ceremony, would not prosecute wives and their abductors:

We are now returning to our respective villages and on our arrival there, we will say to our friends who are also anxious to settle at Mauritius and fifteen or twenty thousand of them will come with their wives but whenever the wife of a person is ravished or carried away by another we are afraid that no punishment will be inflicted on the perpetrator. We are not thieves, we shall not commit any crime and shall live upon our labour and all the people at Mauritius know it well and your Excellency may enquire about it.

In our country if we go and complain to the Police that our wife has been ravished or carried away, the fugitive and her ravisher are both condemned to prison and by that means they are afraid of doing so again but while at Mauritius when a woman becomes guilty of such a crime she is taken before the police and asked if she likes to return again to her husband and if she says no, she is immediately dismissed and told 'aller fou moi le camp' [go away] and what fear will the women have there? We therefore request that a police of our nation be established there to judge our own disputes, the same as in our country here and also that arrangements be made to enable us to receive tidings from our relatives and friends in our country and that we may be judged by the police which shall be established as above requested, then we shall come and settle there with our wives and children.

Perhaps as a measure of the esteem in which the Telegu immigrants were held by employers, although doubtless also because the interests of capital and patriarchy conveniently converged in this matter, the sum of these complaints was quickly addressed by the authorities. A few weeks after the reading of the petition before a Committee of Government in Mauritius, a Telegu, Bardy-sardy Rungapah, was appointed a sub-agent at Rajahmundry. Further, Ordinance 3 of 1856 was passed to establish the legitimacy of marriages contracted in India.[56] The Mauritian state was anxious to accommodate the Telegus because they were considered 'first rate labourers' who from their 'habit of keeping together would be valuable additions to the population if they emigrated with their families as they would be more likely to form villages'.[57] The episode is significant because it demonstrates that participants in the indentured labour system could actively intervene in and transform the meaning and conditions of the migration process.

Whilst the Telegus in this case acted as a self-conscious community, many others combined forces on a smaller scale, at village level, or as individual family groups, to remigrate together or to send out relatives. In this way the overseas colonies ultimately saw the arrival of literally thousands of remigrants, persons who completed contractual terms, went home to India, and came back to settle in the West Indies or Mauritius bringing their families with them, or persuading kin and co-villagers to migrate. Their activities created the nucleus of permanent Indian communities overseas. Those who returned with families were often persons who had acquired some capital or property overseas and wished to continue their economic activities on those islands with their kin.

Such settlers differed from those returnees who were forced back to the colonies they had just left as a result of being robbed of their savings or, in some cases, rejected by their families. There were not an inconsequential number of such persons, casualties of a system which had separated them from their kin and made them easy targets as they returned to their homes.[58] The following petition of a Surinam returnee illustrates the utter destitution of many of these individuals:

To the Protector of Emigrants, Calcutta,
The Humble petition of Gajadhar, Emigrant.
I am one of the returned emigrants just landed from the Port of Surinam, working fifteen years there . . . void of money . . . refused and driven, without help [for rations and train fare] . . . do me such favour as I get to my native place, Banda, by railway, as I have none here to help me with a copper.[59]

In 1920, the Secretary of the Calcutta YMCA described the conditions of returned migrants from the various colonies:

> These repatriates were scattered throughout the district crowded in bustees, malaria ridden, without work, nourishment or medical relief, a prey to the sharks of the neighbourhood who were exploiting their distress. Most of them were up-country people. Many of them, on their return from their colony, had been driven from their villages because they could not fit in with the social structure of the village community; some unable to find work, had drifted down to Calcutta in the hope of securing employment. All of them, disillusioned on their return to India, had come to the riverside with the vague hope that a ship might somehow and sometime take them back to the colony they had left.[60]

Of course there were also individuals who fitted into neither of these extreme categories but who became habitual migrants, visiting several of the labour-importing colonies and returning to India when their indenture contracts expired. By the 1860s it was common for ships arriving in Mauritius to be carrying persons who had already completed stints as workers in Burma, Ceylon (present-day Sri Lanka) or the West Indies (see Appendix B).

Some returnees were sent back by planters specifically to recruit new labour, and took over the commercial role of the local maistries and duffadars. That this was a practice set on foot from the very beginning of indenture is evident from the testimony of Ramdeen, given before the Calcutta Commission of Enquiry in 1838. He had left for Mauritius in 1834 or 1835 and had spent three years there, first working as a field labourer:

> *I was merely a Coolie; I was promoted by my master to a sirdarship . . . I can read and write and therefore I was interested in everything – was a sort of factotum . . . I had formerly five rupees per month, but on my promotion got 10 rupees per month . . . My master sent me here with Captain Real to get more Coolies . . . Mr Hughes is to supply them according to an agreement with the captain; the Coolies I came for have gone, but I falling sick, was obliged to remain behind . . . There are three relatives of mine now with me; if I go, I will take them . . . There are nine of my relatives there now, and therefore I wish to go back.*[61]

Ramdeen's deposition reveals not only the influence of ex-indentured workers in subsequent labour mobilization but the family networks already present in this early phase of the diaspora.

The role of the Mauritian returnees became particularly important once the West Indies had started recruiting, because of their ability to influence would-be migrants. The deposition given by Juggon was one of many taken by the Mauritian Agent in an attempt to persuade the local authorities of the deceptions being practised against his recruits, but which also reveal the widespread use of returnees in the collection of new immigrants:

> *I am a return Mauritius Cooly. About a month since I left Gyah with 17 Coolies whom I had collected for the Mauritius Depot in Calcutta. About six days afterwards we fell in*

with a Recruiter named Golamun who offered to pay our road expenses to the Mauritius Depot as I had informed him I was short of funds. We then continued on to a Village or Chokee called Handul where we met a second Recruiter (Soopun) who had in his charge about 40 Coolies, also reported to be bound for the Mauritius Depot. I prefer Mauritius to Demerara or Trinidad, because I am acquainted with the place and have a brother there. After we all got into the Railway carriage at Raneegunge, Soopun then commenced speaking to my Coolies about Demerara, and told them they must go to the Demerara Depot together with his own chalan of 40 Coolies who were then in the same carriage with us. Myself and all the Coolies at once refused to go to any other Depot but Mr Caird's at Bhowanipore.

Soopun had much influence over the Coolies, and whilst we were following him across the Maidan about the afternoon of the 20th we met Mr Caird, who stopped and asked which Depot we were going to. I replied I was an old Mauritius return Coolie and wished to go to Mauritius with my chalan. Mr Caird told us to go to his Depot at Bhowanipore, but we were prevented by some other Recruiters who came after Mr Caird left and compelled us all to go to the Demerara Depot. It was late when we reached it, and a Baboo at the Depot told Golamun and Soopun to take us away to his house for the night. Just then Toyluck Baboo of the Mauritius Depot, saw us and compelled Golamun and Soopun to release us, and we were taken by Toyluck to the Mauritius Depot.[62]

As the mobilization of new indentured workers successively passed into the hands of fellow labourers, some of the more blatantly commercial features of the collection and despatch of labour were modified, but the potential for deception did not disappear; in some respects, recruiting strategies simply became more sophisticated.

The experience of the eighteen Madras migrants showed that returnee recruiters, like the Pondicherry maistries, quickly saw the potential for personal enrichment, exaggerating the merits of the colony they had visited and the money they had earned. The entrepreneurial aptitudes they personified are demonstrated by the letter sent from Rama in India to his brother Latchmun in Mauritius, and translated from the 'Nagri' script:

Great inconvenience has been experienced by not having a depot to lodge the men – the people recruited in the interior by old hands are obliged to go to Battay Walla who maintains them until embarkation and receives an allowance for himself; the old hands who recruited them have nothing. If you and Hitto bring money we shall be able to recruit 1,000 people in one month.[63]

Rama had been sent back to India to recruit labourers for his employer, and in this extract from his letter to his brother, he reports the potential business they could expect. The significance of this snatch of their correspondence, however, is the reference to the existing commercial structures in which merchants with capital were crucial to the whole migration process, because they alone could advance the money required to maintain recruits until embarkation. Rama, in seeking to acquire his own capital, was attempting to wrest control from merchants and, judging from the scale of his ambitions, to set himself up in a similar entrepreneurial position. A significant number of returnee recruiters, however, took on the role in order to acquire the status of foreman or sirdar over the bands they brought with them. Their relationship with the men they recruited was more complex than that of local maistries; they stood in an ambivalent position between the employer and employees, but they did much more than simply transmit the orders of plantation owners. Sirdars and the men in their bands were in a relationship of mutual dependence, and one which effectively distanced them from the estate owner.[64] This was, in fact, to be the predominant issue of recruiting for Mauritius over the middle decades of the nineteenth century. Having set in train a custom whereby migrants were encouraged to seek out the Mauritius depots on the basis of the recommendations of their countrymen, and often accompanied by them, planters and their representatives subsequently wrestled with the conflict between a system which was undeniably cost effective, but which increasingly placed the control of new immigrants in the hands of time-expired labourers who knew how to work the system of distribution and allocation to plantations. For these 'old hands' who went back to India to pick up bands, and to collect their families and the kin of their fellow workers, also expected to extend their authority over the new recruits, through their status as sirdars over the men they had brought to the plantation. Thus the authority of the recruiter was reinforced on the estate, and a man with a knowledge of local living and working conditions was placed at the head of a band of new immigrants, whose prime use to the planter should precisely have been their dependence upon him in the new setting.

Within two decades of the commencement of organized migration to Mauritius, a momentum had therefore been created, fuelled by the activities of returnees, which prompted individuals and groups of migrants to set out specifically with the aim of indenturing themselves on a plantation in an island where they knew that co-villagers also could be found. Indeed, in their efforts to migrate to such specific destinations some undertook heroic journeys. The story of Cassiram Juggernauth is noteworthy. He was one of ten men sent from Mauritius in 1855 to recruit labourers from Bombay. On arrival at Bombay, Cassiram and others had returned home to collect relatives and then reported to the local agent, Mr St Amour. However, migration had been closed from that port since 1853, and in his statement Cassiram explained how he was obliged to wait months at the port for a ship to take them back to Mauritius:

I arrived in Bombay about two years ago by the 'City of Palaces'. Davy Churram, Jugool Moosa, Bhagoo Janoo, Ragoo Mahdoo, Cundoo and another accompanied me, also five women and seven children. We presented ourselves to Mr St Amour, who desired us to wait eight days and return to his office. I called as ordered, and was told that he would write to the Mauritius regarding us and let us know the result. After two months I again called on Mr St Amour, who informed me that he had not received the expected orders. We then petitioned Government and were informed that the Mauritius Government had not given any instruction about them, but that the Bombay Government would send them to the Mauritius if they wished. We received this reply seven months after our arrival but we remained in Bombay three months more expecting a passage and received batta from Mr St Amour for 119 days through Davy Churram who received the money from Mr. St Amour or the Parsee Gomasta.[65]

In the intervening period one of the ten returnees died, and another abandoned the plan to remigrate. The remaining eight resolved to travel to Calcutta and embark from there with their families. They set out for Calcutta in November 1855, but at Nasik a quarrel broke out and Cassiram returned to Bombay with another man. Back in Bombay they were given batta by the Parsee Pestonji Mancherji, but nevertheless 'subjected themselves to very considerable sacrifice and hardship' before eventually being embarked for Mauritius aboard the *Futtay Mobarak* in 1856.[66] The only recognition of such momentous journeys was a reprimand from the Colonial Office when, as a result of such unscheduled arrivals, Mauritius exceeded its immigrant quota.[67] For the historian, however, the individual dramas described by migrants such as Cassiram add a new dimension to the study of this labour movement.

Rajoo Narayen was another man whose attempts to reinstitute recruitment from Bombay ensure that he has left a written record of his activities. In 1873 he wrote to the Protector asking for emigration to be reopened from that port, stating that he and other returnees had arrived there eight years before with the intention of recruiting new hands for their employers, and were 'reduced to a condition of extreme want and starvation' as a result of the agency's closure. The following year he wrote again from Bombay, offering to bring labourers to Mauritius. He reported that the Bombay government would allow the workers to leave if they paid their own passage, and asked the Protector to make known to employers his offer. He requested advance payments at the rate of 1000 rupees per 100 recruits, and asked for further details as to the wage rates on offer at Mauritius and the size of his commission.[68] Evidently, recruitment offered significant pecuniary advantages, which would-be entrepreneurs such as Rajoo and Rama were not slow to grasp. Rajoo's wife, Ennabie, was also in contact with the Mauritian government, concerning her husband (see Chapter 4).

In practice, however, the role and influence of the returnee recruiter were limited by the competition between colonies at the point of departure. By the mid-1860s, rivalries between labour exporters were to prove a major obstacle to the effective operation of the returnee recruiting strategy, whose success depended upon reuniting kin and co-villagers in India and abroad. Because Mauritius was the most frequented and best known of the overseas colonies, active recruiting for the island by local trading houses had greatly diminished, and the Mauritian Agent at Calcutta relied considerably on what he termed the 'unassisted' activities of returnees, who brought their bands of new migrants straight to his depot at Bhawanipur. The commercial recruiters acting for British Guiana and Trinidad were placed at a distinct disadvantage. One remedy was to pay their men well, and by so doing they attracted some Mauritian returnees into their service. The kangani-like activities of time-expired labourers in India were thus impeded by competition between labour exporters, but their presence, in itself, is evidence of a recruiting dynamic in indenture outside the formal structures of government-sponsored emigration.

Experiences of the Voyage

An Indian doctor who travelled with a shipment of 200 Indian labourers from Calcutta in 1837, Abdoolah Khan, described the voyage to the Commission of Enquiry:

> *Did you converse often with the Coolies while on board?*
> – *Yes I did*
> *Did they seem to understand where they were going, and for what purpose they had been engaged?*
> – *Yes; they did understand that they were going to the Isle of France, and as Coolies.*
> *Did they know that they were to be separated for five years from their families?*
> – *No; they thought they were going only for two months.*
> *Who told them it was only for two months?*
> – *The duffadars*
> *Did the coolies appear to be happy and comfortable?*
> – *What happiness! they were all crying.*
> *What were they crying about?*
> – *For their discomforts, such as want of room for sleeping and for dressing victuals, and also for want of utensils for eating from.*
> *Had they a sufficient quantity of water?*
> – *It was stinking and thick, something like beer foaming up.*
> *Did the coolies say they were very sorry for having come?*
> – *They did.*
> *How did the captain and officers treat them?*
> – *They used to beat them and drive them from one place to another.*[69]

The deposition of Boodoo Khan is interesting for its casual confirmation that migrants in the early years had very little idea of the distance of the colonies and the length of the voyage, and yet they were not necessarily dissuaded once these circumstances were made clear to them. Boodoo Khan and those who travelled with him were actually relanded and then shipped out again. He seems to be proud of his courageous spirit, and to see his migration almost as some kind of 'rite of passage' fulfilled:

> *When I arrived in Calcutta I learnt that I should have to go on board a big ship, and that I was to engage for five years. I did not know how far the island was, or what time would be expended in the passage until at sea, when the mate of the ship asked me if I knew how long I should be; I said no; he then told me I should be four months. I did not mind; I am*

*a man, not a woman, and I am a Pathan's son; I had given my word, and I did not care
if it were eight months. I did come back; the ship put back from Kedgeree, and I remained
25 days in Calcutta, and then went on board another ship; I do not remember the name
of the first ship nor of the second, nor do I remember the name of the captains. I first went
on board the first time in the beginning of Assar (June) and we were 15 days in the big
water, and we remained 25 days here, and went on board the second ship at Bhadur, the
end of Bhadur (beginning of September) last year. . . . there were 64 of us in the first ship;
there were 10 Bengalees, 16 Khootthas (up countrymen) and the rest all Dhangas. We
had sufficient room on board; the Captain was a good man; we got good food and water,
and were well treated. We were two months on the voyage; all were contented on board;
we were not in sloops at all; we landed from the first ship and went on board the second
ship; in the interval we were taken to a house to the east of a baboo's house, I think the
baboo was called Hurry Chutter. I was not confined; the rest were, that is, they were not
allowed to go about as I was, for fear they should run away.*[70]

Boodoo Khan's experience contrasts sharply with that of Rajcomar, who
jumped off the ship that was transporting him to Mauritius and told his tale of
being tricked into embarking. He was himself an up-country man from Arrah,
who had been living in Calcutta for two years and was employed as a ticca
burkendauz. One of his duties was to guard coolies who were being transported
from the depot to the ship. On one occasion, in the company of two Europeans
and four policemen, he marched the coolies aboard ship. After the departure of
the other guards, he also sought leave to disembark, when he found that he had
been included in the list of intending emigrants. He protested in vain, then, in
his words:

*alighted on board one of the dhingies which were alongside of the ship; upon which the
gentleman on board ordered to seize me, and about 20 persons from the ship came on the
dhingy and seized and dragged me on board the ship; and the gentleman on board the
ship struck me five or seven blows with a rattan, and forcibly detained me on board; I
again remonstrated, and told him I would never go with him, as I was not a Coolie; and
having said this, I jumped overboard, leaving all my clothes on board; but three dhingies
being sent after me, I was taken up by one of them, and was taken on board ship with my
hands tied; I then called out 'Dohoye' [help] and said that I would kill 20 men before I
would submit to be forced away. This was explained to the gentleman on board by the
serang of the ship; upon which he agreed to send me to the European who came with us
on board . . . the European . . . ordered his servants to confine me; but having been
detained for about an hour, I was, after some consultation with his sircar, released.*[71]

One of the striking features of voyage accounts as related by migrants is their
fearlessness in the face of physical abuse meted out by the ships' crews. The
archives are replete with reports of incidents involving drunken officers, brutal
captains and uncaring or incompetent doctors. There are numerous examples
of such officials being dismissed from the immigration service, and the quality
of those employed was frequently deprecated by administrators in the colonies
and in India. It was difficult to recruit doctors and ships' officers for voyages
which were dangerous and disagreeable, with the constant fear of epidemic

disease. Mauritius was particularly disadvantaged in this respect because the short passage length meant that it was not sufficiently remunerative, and the colony was unable to employ staff recruited from the Europe–Australia service, as did the West Indies.

When the *Nimrod* sailed to Mauritius at the end of 1872, it was to be Dr Browne's last voyage in charge of Indian migrants. On their arrival in January 1873, the Protector of Immigrants heard a litany of complaints from those on board. Runnoo deposed that he had been struck by Browne. Jhoonea alleged that Browne had one day stripped her naked on the upper deck, in the presence of a large number of Indians, and that, on the same day, immediately after-wards, three other women were also stripped naked. The Chief Officer of the vessel confirmed that he saw Browne catch hold of Jhoonea's saree and push her, and that her saree did almost fall off. William Lary, the master of the vessel, stated that Browne on one occasion, at 11 p.m., took a woman into his private cabin to examine her, alleging that she had gonorrhoea. This account was confirmed by the chief officer, by the assistant doctor, who conducted the woman to the Browne's cabin, and by the woman herself.[72] Muhabully, No. 361,385, stated that his wife Peearun had been caught hold of by Browne, who attempted to take her forcibly into his cabin; he had himself been beaten. Peearun agreed that she had been unwillingly taken to the ship's hospital by Browne. The husband then went on to explain how one woman after another was abused by the doctor:

> He then turned upon Coolmonteeah; he caught hold of her; she escaped from him; he then got hold of Butcheea, took her up, stripped her of her clothes and tied her up to the rigging by her wrists. Besides my wife, Junnea is the only woman whom I saw the Doctor endeavour to take into his cabin. I was told that many others were taken into his cabin by him during that evening . . . My wife and I were so much alarmed, that we went to the serang's quarters and spent the night there. Every two or three days this scene was repeated.

Champah, a young girl who had emigrated with her parents, demonstrated that Browne's abuse of Indian women continued after the ship had disembarked its passengers at the quarantine station. She testified:

> 4 or 5 days after we were landed at Cannoniers Point, at about 10 am, Dr Browne said 'come, I shall give you some quinine'. I answered 'I am not sick'. He then ordered one Heerah to take me to his house. The Doctor returned to the house and gave me a glass of liquor to drink. I drank it; he then put me on his bed, and had intercourse with me. I began crying out; he then put his hands upon my mouth . . . I went to my father and complained of it immediately.

Browne's own very weak evidence in regard to Jhooneah's complaint was that 'I invariably promote amusements, especially dancing, amongst the emigrants, and I have frequently caught hold of those who appeared depressed or down-hearted, in order to make them dance and rouse them up'. Concerning

Champah – 13 years old at the time – he stated simply 'she is a woman of bad character'. Finally, to defend his general behaviour he argued that:

> no one who has not actually been in charge of them can form a proper idea of the difficulty that a surgeon has to contend with in preserving cleanliness and order amongst them; the Indian will do nothing of his own accord ... whatever he does he must be forced to do and the surgeon who stands in ceremony with them is not a man who can discharge efficiently his duties. They are exceedingly dirty in their habits, and unless cleanliness is rigidly enforced, there is every likelihood of disease breaking out amongst them.

Dr Browne's explanations were not considered acceptable and he was dismissed from the service.

Totaram Sanadyha has vividly depicted the trauma of departure, the humiliation of the cramped living quarters and unpalatable food, the rough treatment experienced and the scant regard paid to the needs of migrants on the voyage. As in much of his writing, Sanadyha emphasizes the shame which the Indian was subjected to by the indenture experience. Despite the polemical nature of his work, his account of the voyage to Fiji is a powerful and in many ways accurate portrayal of the conditions many of the shipmates or jehaji bhai underwent:

> *When there were two or three days left for us to board the ship then we underwent medical examinations. Both males and females were examined by male doctors. We were given tunics, caps, and pants to wear, like prisoners. We were given a tin 'lota' for water, a tin plate for food and a small bag for our few things.*
> *Then all our names were called and we boarded the ship. At that time about 500 Indians left their mother country like prisoners and slaves for Fiji. Who had an inkling of the difficulties we would face there! How many people were crying oceans for their fathers, mothers, siblings and so on. There was no one to listen to their sorrows or sympathise ...*
> *We were given a space of one and half feet wide and six feet long each to stay in. It is difficult to see how we were able to live in that little space. When some people complained then the white doctor said, 'Sala, you have to live'.*
> *When we were all sitting down we were each given four biscuits and half 'chhataank' (1/16th of a seer) sugar. These biscuits were called dog biscuits by the whites and are fed to dogs. Oh God! Are we Indians like dogs? And what shall I say about those biscuits! They were so hard that they could only be broken by our clenched fists and then dipped in water and eaten.*
> *At about 4 the ship left. This was a last 'namaskaar' to our homeland. At six the sun–god set. We slept for eight hours that night. At dawn the watchman woke us up ... As soon as morning broke one of the officers chose some of us to work, some to keep watch and some to do 'topas' job. then the officer said to the topas workers, 'You do your work now.' The volunteers asked, 'What work?' Then they were told to clean the faeces of those on board. So many pleaded. But they were beaten and then forced to clear the faeces. Throughout the ship you could hear voices yelling. 'Tahi, trahi – save me, protect me!'*
> . . .
> *Twice a day we were given a bottle of water each to drink. Then no more, even if we died of thirst. It was the same about food. Fish and rice were both cooked there. Many people*

suffered from sea-sickness. Those who died were thrown overboard. Thus, after 3 months and twelve days, calling at Singapore, Borneo, etc ... we reached Fiji.[73]

The voyage was thus for many, an unpleasant and traumatic induction into the indenture experience. This short but succinct verse from a Surinami Hindi folksong sums up the feelings of migrants about the passage into indenture:

Several months on the ship passed with great difficulty,
On the seven dark seas, we suffered unaccustomed problems.[74]

I have shown elsewhere that, despite being demand-driven at its onset, migration came to acquire a dynamic of its own as labourers returned to collect families and to recruit.[75] Emphasis on the subaltern experience of recruitment demonstrates that the whys and wherefores of emigration are more complex than demand-driven theories or accounts of variabilities in push factors allow for. The original intention of planters may have been to substitute one form of cheap labour with another, through coercive means if necessary, but for the new wave of migrants the indenture experience fulfilled a different set of needs. In this way, a labour transfer which in its early phase was characterized by commercial recruiting and the use of overt or covert force transformed itself into a more complex hybrid, which combined permanent family settlement for some with short-term work for others. Further comparative research would help to elucidate the question of whether other indentured labour-importing colonies experienced this phenomenon, which is generally seen as applicable only to the inter-Asian migrations of the same period.[76]

Notes

1. See Lal, 1983, for the notion that migrants had already severed the links with home villages before registering; and for the idea of migration as an escape from social oppression see Emmer, 1986a, and Reddock, 1985.
2. See Carter, 1992a, 1995.
3. Hansard, XLIV, 20 July 1838, 382.
4. Parliamentary Papers 1841 XVI (45) Calcutta Commission of Enquiry Report; Bombay General Proceedings, Bombay Committee Report, 20 Sep. 1838.
5. Calcutta Commission of Enquiry, Captain Finniss's Memorandum, dated 1 Aug. 1838. Boodoo Khan's desire to acquire an umbrella before leaving for Mauritius suggests that he went with ambitions to raise his status, despite being told that he was only being hired for field work.
6. *Ibid.*
7. Calcutta Commission of Enquiry, Minutes of Evidence, paras 873–82, Examination of the return emigrant Karoo, Town Hall, Calcutta, 16 Nov. 1838.
8. Parliamentary Papers 1841 (427) Report of J.P. Grant, 1 Mar. 1841.
9. *Ibid.*; see pp. 46–55.
10. Parliamentary Papers 1842 (26) Smith to Russell, 14 Aug. 1841, encl. Reply of Free Labour Association to the Calcutta Commission Report.
11. See Carter, 1995, esp. Ch. 2, for more details.

12. Parliamentary Papers 1841 (45) Appendix to the Calcutta Commission Report, Finniss to Colonial Secretary, 30 July 1838.
13. Parliamentary Papers 1841 (45) Appendix to Calcutta Commission Report, Exhibit no. 21.
14. Parliamentary Papers 1841 (45) Appendix to Calcutta Commission Report, Gurr to Birch, 17 July 1838.
15. Parliamentary Papers 1844 (530) Tennent to Hope, 21 Mar. 1843.
16. Saha, P. 1970: 93. To carry one's own lota for one's own drinking water was necessary to maintain the commensal rules that preserved caste status. To be deprived of these as well as their own clothes must have been an considered an affront by many.
17. Thus the Calcutta Commission of Enquiry Report contained harrowing accounts of fraudulent recruiting alongside evidence such as that of the magistrate of Cochin, who reported that three emigrants relanded by him remonstrated against the injustice of being sent back here where they could find no employment, and would be left to starve: Appendix to the Calcutta Commission of Enquiry Report, White to the Magistrate of Malabar, 5 Sep. 1838.
18. Bengal Public Consultations 13/44 Chief Magistrate of Calcutta to Secretary to the Government of Bengal, 21 Oct. 1843.
19. Bengal Public Consultations 13/44 Chief Magistrate of Calcutta to Secretary to the Government of Bengal, 21 Oct. 1843.
20. *Ibid.*
21. Madras Public Consultations 248/4, Mar.–Apr. 1843.
22. Madras Public Consultations 248/4 Emigration Agent to Chief Secretary to the Government, 7 Apr. 1843.
23. Acting Chief Secretary to the Magistrate, Tanjore, 22 Apr. 1843.
24. Bengal Emigration Proceedings 15/75 T. Caird to Rivers Thompson, Esq., Junior Secretary, Bengal Government, 17 Nov. 1860.
25. Bengal Emigration Proceedings 15/76 T. Warner, British Guiana Agent to J.D. Gordon, 16 Aug. 1861.
26. C. Eales, Protector of Emigrants at Calcutta, to J. Monro, Officiating Undersecretary to the Government of Bengal, 26 Oct. 1861.
27. Bengal Emigration Proceedings 15/75, Dec. 1860.
28. PB 10 Protector to Colonial Secretary, 19 Mar. 1861.
29. PB 10 Deposition of Ramasawmy before John Ormsby, Depot Magistrate, Port Louis, 16 Apr. 1861.
30. PE 9 'Brahmin', 3 Nov. 1843. His name was entered as Meeken Amdee, of the Velarin caste, a native of Vurtanadoo (Wutanara).
31. PB 10 Deposition of Mecken before Protector, Mauritius Immigration Office, 17 Apr. 1861.
32. Lal, 1983: 96.
33. Prakash, 1990: 189–90.
34. From the Statistical Account of Hazareebag District, pp. 114–15, reproduced in Saha, 1970: 169.
35. Indian Public Proceedings 188/46 deposition of Saivarodian to Phillips, Magistrate of Tanjore, 13 June 1857.
36. PL 44 Hesaddat to Chief Clerk, Jan. 1881.
37. PL 44 Immigration Office Note 11, Jan. 1881.

38. Bengal Emigration Proceedings 15/77 Caird to Secretary, Government of Bengal, 10 Mar. 1862, statement of Bahadoor. The sweets given to the boy were probably spiked with bhang (opium).

39. Bengal Emigration Proceedings 432/18 Captain C. Burbank to R. Simson, 6 Sep. 1866.

40. Indian Public Proceedings vol. 506 Secretary, Government NWP, to Secretary, Government Bengal, 24 Mar. 1871, encl. Statement of Revd. Evans, Allahabad, 18 Feb. 1871.

41. Vol. 1868 J. Robertson, Magistrate to Commissioner, Allahabad, 19 July 1871.

42. Lal, 1983: 110–14.

43. Vatuk, 1964: 224, quoted in Lal, 1980: 68.

44. This song was recorded by B.V. Lal during a field trip in eastern UP in May 1979, Lal, 1980: 67.

45. Arya, 1968: 163, translated by Lal, 1980: 68.

46. Anat, 1977: 226, translated by Lal, 1980: 69. Kolhu is a machine used in the villages in India to crush cane.

47. PL 19 Statement of Debi Ram before Protector of Immigrants, Beau Bassin Central Prison, 8 Mar. 1906. Driving the plough was acceptable for a high-caste peasant, even a Brahmin from Central India. Harder physical labour in the field, however, would involve a loss of caste status.

48. PE 155 Debi Ram was listed as a 19-year-old Thakur from Kewlari, Dholpore, when he arrived in 1905. He returned to India in 1909.

49. Mahabir, 1985: 77–88.

50. Wilson, 1987: 1.

51. Extract from Sanadhaya's 'The Haunted Line', in Lal and Shineberg, 1991: 110.

52. *Fiji Sun*, Monday 19 Mar. 1979, pp. 8–9.

53. Gillion, 1962: 131–2.

54. RA 1361 Emigration Agent, Calcutta, to Protector of Emigrants, Calcutta, 23 July 1849.

55. CO 167/377 Petition of the Telegu returnees, 1 Mar. 1856, encl. in Higginson to Labouchere, 16 Aug. 1856.

56. CO 167/377 Higginson to Labouchere, 16 Aug. 1856.

57. Protector of Immigrants' Report, 28 April 1856, in *ibid.*

58. The presence of such returnees is noted by Emmer, 1986c: 197–9.

59. Tinker, 1974: 176. The register of the *Hereford IV* revealed that Gajadhar, a Thakur aged 34, possessed as savings Rs1.

60. F.E. James, quoted in Sannyasi and Chaturvedi, 1931: 2.

61. PP 1841 (45) Calcutta Commission of Enquiry, Examination of Ramdeen, 27 Nov. 1838, p. 74.

62. Bengal Emigration Proceedings 15/75, Dec. 1860, Deposition of Juggon taken at the Mauritius Depot, Bhowanipore, 6 Dec. 1860.

63. PB 5 Protector of Emigrants, Calcutta, to Colonial Secretary, 18 Mar. 1852.

64. See Carter, 1995, esp. Chs 6–8.

65. RA 1361 Henry St Amour, Emigration Agent, Bombay, to Colonial Secretary, Mauritius, 20 Aug. 1856. Statement made to the Committee on board the *Futtay Mubarak*, 15 Apr. 1856, by Cassiram Juggernauth.

66. RA 1361 Superintendent of Police to the Bombay Committee of Enquiry, 13 Apr. 1856.

67. CO 167/369 Higginson to Molesworth, 20 Oct. 1855.

68. PA 14 Rajoo Narayen to Protector, 20 Oct. 1873, and PA 22 *ibid.*, 29 Mar. 1874.

69. PP 1841 (45) Examination of Abdoolah Khan before the Calcutta Commission of Enquiry, p. 35.

70. Calcutta Commission of Enquiry, Captain Finniss's Memorandum, dated 1 Aug. 1838. Adrian Graves's work on labour recruiting of Pacific islanders (1984), reveals the importance of migration as a 'rite of passage'.

71. Parliamentary Papers 1841 (45) Calcutta Commission of Enquiry, Examination of Rajcomar, 13 Dec. 1838, p. 83.

72. Bengal Emigration Proceedings vol. 170 Report on complaints made by the immigrants per *Nimrod*.

73. Totaram Sanadyha, quoted in *Fiji Sun*, Tuesday 20 March 1979, p. 6.

74. Lal, 1980: 68.

75. See Carter, 1992a.

76. The so-called differences between indentured and kangani labour-importing colonies have been articulated by Jain, 1993: 11.

CHAPTER THREE

The working lives of indentured Indians

Studies of the imposition of the plantation regime on indentured labourers and of their responses to it have tended to portray Indians as lambs lining up patiently for slaughter. The epithets 'docile' and 'meek' are frequently used, and the 'pre-industrial ideology' of imported Indian workers is stressed.[1] The resistance of workers has been identified as 'individualistic rather than collective'.[2] Haraksingh has emphasized that the status of 'immigrant' itself impeded organized resistance because 'physical uprooting' was a 'weapon in the arsenal of control'.[3] Saunders, van Onselen, Crisp and a host of others have amply demonstrated the several layers of resistance manifested by workers in bonded labour regimes, all of which are applicable to indentured labour.[4] In applying them, however, Indian labour historians have come close to assessing every response of the worker under indenture as a form of resistance, from 'cultural resilience and adaptation' to suicide. Haraksingh, for example, has gone so far as to attempt a differentiation between 'positive' and 'negative' forms of resistance, in which the positive aspects include saving money and the negative forms include drinking or gambling. As for what provoked Indian militancy, Ramnarine emphasizes 'illicit sexual relations', whilst others point vaguely in the direction of 'harsh working conditions'.[5] Indeed, it is in accounts of the working lives of Indians that the uniformity of description and the accumulation of stereotypes crowd most heavily on the bookshelf. The issue of leadership and the confusing and conflicting roles of the sirdar or driver as exploiter and labour organizer are symptomatic of the impasse. Perhaps the manner in which these issues have been reworked in the Indian context can offer a path forward for future studies of indenture. Dipesh Chakrabarty's illuminating account of the role of the sirdar in the Calcutta jute mills is a case in point. The subaltern historians of the subcontinent have been drawing on a wide range of sources to explore the world of the rural labourer.[6] A start has been made in this direction with the analysis of the folksongs of indentured labourers, but the discovery and dissection of other oral sources may help uncover new dimensions of the indenture experience.[7]

A fundamental condition of plantation life was the indenture contract, which not only regulated the terms of employment of labourers but also defined the workers' general standard of living, since it encompassed wages, hours and type of work, as well as providing for rations, housing and medical attendance.[8] Most significantly for employers, it enshrined the notion of a fixed wage, so that over the several years of its duration workers could not take advantage of increases in the market value of labour. Further, in cases of inability to work, the indentured worker in some colonies was liable to the 'double cut', whereby he not only lost that day's pay but was required to work a further day without pay. In some cases the double cut amounted to even more than that; as a result labourers who had been repeatedly sick could find themselves, at the end of their five-year contract, bound to work for a further period.[9] Planters some-times used this measure to induce workers to re-engage for a second five-year term. Even the medical attendance clause was used by employers to discipline the workforce: individuals reporting sick were obliged to remain incarcerated in estate 'hospitals' to avoid being classified as absent without leave. In addition, penal clauses were subjoined to the contract, so that in case of refusal to work or desertion – a term very loosely interpreted by local magistrates – indentured Indians could be condemned to lengthy prison sentences. On their return to the estate they were expected to make up the time lost through their incarceration. The indenture contract was a very powerful weapon for the planters, and they depended heavily on partial colonial judiciaries to enforce its provisions.

As the century progressed, and Indian immigrants began to develop their own sub-elite on the plantations from amongst labourers who had risen through the ranks to become overseers and job-contractors, employers became locked into a power struggle with their own labour managers in an effort to retain control over the workforce. In most indentured labour-employing colo-nies, the contract was signed after arrival, allowing immigrants a fictitious 'choice' of employer. After 1858, in Mauritius, this choice was removed by requiring labourers to sign contracts in India, binding workers to an employer they had never seen, for a term of at least five years. This measure was adopted to combat the influence of sirdars in the labourers' choice of employer and effectively to destroy their role as intermediaries between new immigrants and planters.[10] In those colonies which did not routinely 'repatriate' time-expired labour, growing numbers of ex-indentured Indians settled off plantations and were organized by labour contractors to undertake short-term cane-cutting contracts for sugar-estate owners, so that direct management of the workforce by the old planter class successively declined. This suited plantocracies because by the last quarter of the nineteenth century, with world sugar prices falling, the old-style management of large estates with a resident, dependent workforce seemed increasingly anachronistic, and a process of fragmentation of planta-tions gathered pace.

The documents presented here reflect the reactions of Indians to the plantation regime as it operated in the mid-nineteenth century. Their petitions, statements and letters to those in authority are in effect a litany of complaints, and express genuine feelings of betrayal at the failure of their living and working conditions to meet the standards initially offered them, and of anger towards the judicial and administrative officers who effectively connived at their ill-treatment. The documents also demonstrate the discernibly harsher code of conduct adopted by planters towards the new immigrants indentured to them, as compared with their subtler methods of dealing with sirdars and others who increasingly competed with them to use the legal system to their own ends. Finally, the material demonstrates how indentured labourers subverted plantation codes to develop individual and collective patterns of resistance.

Work Experiences during the Transition from Slavery to Indenture

The Indian migrants who arrived in the plantation colonies of the Caribbean and the Indian Ocean were experimental 'free labourers' in societies emerging from slavery. Most had little experience of cash-crop agriculture and confronted colonial capitalism head on. How did migrants engage with indenture? One of the hardest tasks of the historian is to appraise the experiences of subalterns subjected to exploitative working practices without using a value system wholly inappropriate to customs and expectations then current. Through publication of their statements and petitions, we can enable the participants of the system to speak for themselves. However, they rarely attempted to assess or provide a commentary on their experiences except at the behest of European enquirers. The evidence of indentured workers sometimes betrays the direction and concerns of their interviewers. They were often brusque and unwilling to elaborate, but their remarks were telling. Even the shortest response was revealing: 'Calcutta better', was the comment of one man in 1830s' British Guiana.[11]

In 1842, returning migrants from Mauritius were asked to comment on their experiences before the Justice of the Peace at the Madras Police Office, and to investigators at Calcutta.[12] Their detailed statements provide a unique glimpse of the indenture system, and their reactions to it, in the very earliest years of its operation, from the perspective of free labourers in societies which were reluctantly disentangling themselves from slavery. During the 1830s, when these labourers were indentured, emigration was unregulated and apprentices still worked on the sugar plantations of Mauritius and the West Indies. The ex-slaves were not fully freed until 1839. Consequently, the Indians who testified at the Police Office belonged to the small group of pioneers who had left their country in the mid-1830s as part of an experiment in the replacement with Asians of a predominantly African workforce emerging from servility. Indentured to employers who were accustomed to dealing with slaves, the new arrivals found themselves subjected to an unexpected regime of hard labour and physical punishment. Deponents stressed the restrictions on their liberty which life on the plantation entailed, and their treatment as mere working machines, in ways which suggest that they were struggling to come to terms with the capitalist notions of time and work discipline.[13] Migrants reported that they 'were expected to work without stopping a moment' and 'were not allowed to go out of the Plantation'. Teeroovengadom deposed:

> On the day we landed, Monsieur Riviere took me and 29 other labourers engaged for himself, to the Police Office, where we were registered – he then took us to his Sugar Cane Garden; there were 20 malabar men, 8 Pariahs and 2 Moormen. I and the other malabar men lived together near the house of Monsieur Riviere, in the said Garden, the Pariahs and Moormen lived in different buildings in the same Garden. Our pay and batta were issued regularly – our work was very hard, we were made to work from 6 to 8 o'clock in the morning, when one hour was allowed for breakfast, after which we worked till 12 o'clock, and again from 2 to 6 in the evening, and then we were made to cut grass for the horse of Monsieur Riviere. Monsieur Riviere was kind to those who worked well, and severe to the others. He or his Deputy, a French gentleman who superintended the work, found fault with me but once, when I was unable to work as usual, from stomach ache. The Superintendent threatened that he would take me to the Police Office, and get me punished if he had occasion to find fault again – I was never punished during my stay there, but some of my fellow workmen were flogged, and put into stocks by the Superintendent of the work in consequence of their having failed to cut grass in the evening, and sometimes when the Superintendent of the work found fault, he stopped the batta which used to be issued every evening, until the following morning. These acts of punishment continued for about a year, from the date of our arrival, after which we were treated with more kindness. The climate did not agree with my constitution – I was attacked with cold and fever several times, and I had stomach ache frequently.

Paravadee found the work so hard that after some months he was allowed to change employments:

> We went on with the work from early in the morning until 8, when one hour was allowed to us for our breakfast. We resumed the work at 9, from noon we had two hours leave. From 2, we were engaged till 6 o'clock, and then we returned home with one bundle of grass each man for the use of our Mistress's Mules. The work was too much for me, and in two months I was unable to continue it. Planting Sugar Canes is not an easy business as in our country. The Canes there are larger than ours and require constant weeding. On my becoming sick, my mistress allowed me to graze the cattle, which I did for five years. I used to receive rations regularly, besides one dram of liquor in the evening. All the Coolies who were my fellow workmen were made to work hard daily, and in case of the least negligence, or trifling fault, we were prosecuted before the Justices, and sentenced to break stones into small pieces, for a certain number of days. Stone-breaking is the ordinary punishment in the Island, but it is most severe. These broken stones are used to construct roads, just as gravel in India.

As Paravadee's statement reveals, the Indian workers were familiar with the severity of discipline meted out to sugar-cane labour in the ex-slave colonies.

They found the restrictions on mobility and liberty difficult to bear. The Indians' depositions also reveal their sense of grievance following their realization of the contempt in which labour was held by the managers of estates, men who 'showed no mercy'. Lakshmi, a female migrant, was hit on the face with a shoe. Her testimony indicates that in this period women were subjected to punishments of equal severity to those meted out to men: she also spent time in Mauritius breaking stones.[14] Mootoosawmy, like many others, remarked on the daily physical abuse to which indentured labourers were exposed:

> When workmen were less attentive or rather slow in the work, Mr. Cochin himself or his Superintendents or our Maistry Vydelingum flogged and struck us with rattans or with their fists. Mr. Cochin at two different times caused me to be confined in the Police Jail on a charge of having refused to attend to certain new or additional work, and after being released, employed me in breaking large blue stones.

The deponents however, were at pains to distinguish between physical punishment and material conditions. In Lakshmi's words: 'although I and others were so ill-treated, yet we had no cause whatever to complain about our pay and Batta'. Karoo stated:

> My master is a good man but the blacks he employs as overseers oppress us much; they used to beat us with rattans. We received good and sufficient food; we received rice and salt every day, dholl every tenth or twentieth day, but neither ghee nor oil. I got fish occasionally.[15]

Discontent expressed with the quality or variety of food seemed to have produced improvements; but migrants soon found that wages which seemed generous in India could buy them very little in Mauritius, where the cost of living was so much higher. As Paravadee stated:

> Such eatables as we get here for a few doodies, are hard to be had there for Rupees – for instance, one small Egg is sold for one anna, and three small Fish of the size of a finger, for four annas. I do not like the country.

Gooroodyal, a sirdar who returned to India in 1840 after a six-year indenture in Mauritius, commented:

> the place is a very nice place, very little sickness, and very fine water. They exact hard labour and food is dear ... We were offered higher wages, even double, when our five years were out, but we wanted to see our children, and so came back.[16]

For him, the advantages and disadvantages were clear: Mauritius was evidently recognized to be at this stage relatively free of the epidemic diseases which regularly decimated India's urban populations, but the work regime was strict, and the purchasing power of the rupee was much less than in India. The decisive factor, for Gooroodyal, seems to have been the distance from home, and the fact that he had left his family behind.

For some labourers under indenture, whose employers enforced the double cut with assiduity, a major cause of criticisms was the fact that the wages for which they had undertaken such a long journey were whittled away by excessive deductions for absence and sickness, and fines for minor misdemeanours. As Mootoosawmy reported:

> *when unable to attend to work from sickness, we were allowed Half Batta only, and the wages stopped for the number of days we were absent. A Doctor always attended the patients and medicines given. The sum of 15 Rupees being the advance made to us in Pondicherry was stopped from our wages at the rate of one Rupee per month. From the time we commenced our work under Mr. Cochin, for the first 15 months, he paid us at 3 Rupees per month and afterwards at 4 Rupees per month – the other one Rupee stopped from each of our wages, he said, was to be retained at the Police Office for the purpose of being given to us on our return to Madras after the expiration of the five years we were bound to serve under him.*

What did these Indians ultimately take home with them for their pains? Mootoosawmy fell victim to a common mistake when savings collectively made by bands of men on the plantation could not be retrieved. He had apparently saved about Rs200 from his wages and entrusted the same to Chedumbarum, one of the labourers of his set. The money was never returned despite his repeated demands before leaving the place. Paravadee claimed to have saved Rs400 (equivalent to six years' wages), because as he said, 'we were not allowed to go out of the Plantation and consequently we had no time to buy what we required. We lived upon the rations only without spending much from our pay'. Teeroovengadom reported that fellow migrants brought home sums of Rs100–200 each. Was this first unregulated immigration of the 1830s considered to have been a success? Certainly, the European plantation owners, accustomed to dealing with slaves, could have learnt something from the cautionary words of one of the few Indian estate proprietors in Mauritius. Mr Bickagee, himself an employer of Indians, had this to say in 1836:

> It is to be regretted that the better part of the planters are unaccustomed to manage the Indian labourers. In the first place, they should be mildly treated, and every encouragement given for good behaviour; a small trifle may please them; for instance, an extra allowance of ghee, dholl, fish, or fresh meat on a Sunday, ... and to the Hindoo class a little sugar and flour, ghee or vegetables. Kindness and civility are essential, but severity and harsh language are to be avoided.[17]

The treatment of Indians as above described, and the responses they engendered, belong to a specific time and place. As the migration process matured, many of the conditions of life and labour changed. Most significantly, migrants began to assume greater control over their working and domestic lives by moving off plantations and establishing themselves in small settlements nearby with their families. Increasingly, Indian women who went overseas did so as part of a family or marriage migration and did not enter field labour.

Complaints of New Immigrants

Workers' perceptions of their conditions and treatment under indenture are difficult to ascertain, because of the cursory nature of inspections carried out on estates or by magistrates. However, when indentured labourers wished to draw attention to their grievances, they had a number of options: they could withdraw their labour from the estate and submit a plaint to the local magistrate or to the Protector of Immigrants; or they could, if they had the means, have a petition drawn up on their behalf addressed to the relevant local authorities. The majority of complaints articulated by indentured Indians dealt with the humiliating and painful physical chastisement they had suffered, and with the failure of employers to meet specific contractual obligations. Narran described one form of physical abuse in British Guiana: 'when licked, they put the breast to the post with hands stretched; some tie the hands before, some behind'.[18] Labourers often expressed dissatisfaction with their lodgings, rations and medical treatment. Over-tasking and insufficient pay – usually the result of excessive deductions – were also common causes of complaint.

Indentured workers quickly learnt that collective complaints were more likely to be attended to than individual grievances. When Ramjee Koneji, a Brahmin of Poona, recounted his experiences in Mauritius to the magistrate of 24 Parganas on 2 April 1853, describing how workers' hands were tied behind them and they were whipped with mule whips and their feet put in the stocks, he added that unless ten men combining complained to the Mauritius police 'no notice was taken of our complaint'.[19] Joint complaints could be stimulated by the presence in a colony of a known sympathizer. Kerr, Bolton and de Plevitz in Mauritius all received such deputations. In British Guiana, des Voeux was approached by a group of three hundred indentured labourers, who reportedly told him:

> *O massa, plees, massa, help Coolie. Manahee too bad, massa, starve um, beat up, chuck um, so. Massa stop um wagee, take um wife. Coolie live too bad, massa: too hard work, too little money, too little food . . . no good Coolie go court – mahitee friend manahee: always for manahee, no for Coolie.*[20]

In less formal settings, facing the conflictual situations which developed on the plantation, shipmates or jehaji bhai could be the first persons a new immigrant would turn to. When an indentured labourer in Fiji was picked on by the estate sirdar and his wages reduced: 'my shipmates and I got hold of the sirdar responsible and beat him up. Only my shipmates and I were involved, the other inhabitants of the line kept aloof'. He was then assisted by the 'women of the lines, whom I called mother or sister and who treated me well', who 'took up their hoes' on his behalf.[21]

Where a group of labourers had migrated together, or where return migrants and reindenturing workers had established a working band from the same background, ethnic solidarities became an important feature of resistance on estates. The petition of V. Pydayaya and his group is typical of many collective complaints. Their joint petition declaimed against the barrack-style accommodation they had been given and the inadequate food, but also pointed out that the estate had been transferred and that their consent should be required to any new partnership:

> *We the here undernamed most humbly expose our grievances to you and hope you will do your best not to allow the new proprietors of Mon Choisy Estate to infringe the law to our prejudice.*
>
> *We engaged on the 2nd March 1882 our services to Messrs Perdreau & Co. for the purpose of working their fibre estate; that since the day of our engagement up to this day we had no proper lodging; we have been living all under the same roof, in the same house, living together mixed-up except four people whose names are the following: Boddopully Appadu, Jogiah, Ramegadoo and Lutchia.*
>
> *And still the floors of our houses are muddy and unwholesome and the place is unhealthy and unfit to be inhabited by any person. That the rice given to us had not the quantity required and we received three times eleven pounds instead of twelve pounds. That Perdreau & Co. have transferred to our belief their lease of Mon Choisy to a new partnership just created and we have heard and verily believe that this company has lodged a complaint against us before the Stipendiary Magistrate of Pamplemousses for having refused to obey a lawful order.*
>
> *That we were not officially warned that the Estate has changed hands and could not receive any order from any new comer except if beforehand we should have been warned by the Magistrate, by you or an Inspector of Immigrants sent by you. That in order to make the transfer of our services to the new partnership our consent is necessary and must be given and signed before the Magistrate. You have the right to object to such transfer and therefore we must know from you which are our rights and privileges.*
>
> *We hope in consequence that you will be good enough to take our claim into consideration and take care that justice be done to us.*

Vazilada Pydayaya, no. 377,570

Lutchiah No. 237,789	Shangahi Appadoo No. 355,899
B. Appadu No. 354,903	Jogiah No. 296,074
Pundavaloo No. 276,488	Arun Mooliah No. 377,574
Chengebroyen No. 768,429	Ramegadoo No. 338,342
Kankee Surmegadoo No. 355,806	Ravadu Satiah No. 355,036

All signed with a 'Cross' except Patayah (Creole)[22]

The petitioners were principally Telegus from Vishakhapatnam and surrounding areas who had migrated to Mauritius between 1856 and 1875; four of the group were shipmates, having arrived on the *Evelyn* in February 1872, whilst Vazilada and Mooliah had also emigrated on the same ship, the *Latona*, arriving in 1875. Arun Mooliah and Pundavaloo are pictured in Figures 3.1a and 3.1b. Their decision to engage themselves as a band and to take collective action was commonly adopted by immigrants in order to articulate grievances more effectively as a group. The shared ethnic identity of band members also acted as a means of reinforcing a region-based subculture in the overseas context.[23]

In reply to their petition, however, an Immigration Officer penned the following note:

> I have explained to these people that an Inspector of Immigrants has just visited the estate and that the Manager has promised to make arrangements at once for providing them with proper lodging. That if in a week's time they are not provided with proper lodging they may return to this office to complain – that they are bound to work with the new proprietors as they are engaged to the estate and not to the proprietor.

The Protector followed this up with his own marginal note: 'I have seen these people also and have advised them to return quietly to their work'.[24]

The potency of group solidarity was not lost on planters, who consciously recruited Indians from diverse regions in order to foster ethnic and communal

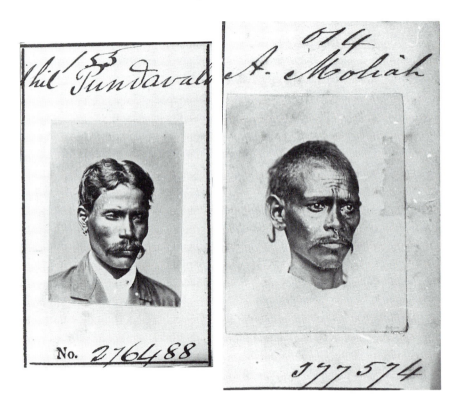

Figure 3.1(a) Pundavaloo, described as a Gentoo from Chittoor, arrived as a 10 year old in 1861 with his 43-year-old mother, two brothers and two sisters. He died in Mauritius in 1892. Source: PE 92B and PG 32.
Figure 3.1(b) Arun Moliah was a 34-year-old man of the Kapu caste from Vizagapatnam. He came to Mauritius in 1875 and returned to India in 1887. Source: PE 125 and PG 18.

divisions. If a band of Telegus or Tamils complained against an estate owner, witnesses could usually be found from north or west Indian bands to contradict their case, and vice versa. Estate managers were not averse to inflaming ethnic or communal tensions in their bid to subordinate estate workers. The petition of Ramachetty and others, who claimed that they were abused by overseers on the Beauchamp estate in Flacq, Mauritius, and complained to the Immigration Office, is a good example. One of their witnesses in the case, another south Indian called Arnachellum, had been killed. The purpose of their petition to the Protector was to denounce the murderers of this man, who were alleged to be 'Calcutta' Indians working on the estate:

> *I am very humble to inform you that is we came from Industan to work in this Mauritius for get some monies and also bring some monies to our parents that which is in India, But now we got some cases about us, that is we are in the establishment of Beauchamp in the district of Flacq, in that estate there is one gentleman to oversee, is called Mr Lulvet and another is called Mr Desir and another is called Mr Marthan these two gentlemen gather one against us, in beating, in abusing . . . and so one Calcutta man killed one man called Arnachellum that who is witness to us for our plaintings unto you in Port Louis, in the day of January 1873 . . .*
>
> *If you please send us one humble answer to us in to Flacq Court. If not we cannot work and we cannot stay in there if you willing to condemn us we are wishing to work in Police Prison . . . if you please send one letter to call us and demand on this killing case. And therefore we send this humble petition to you because you are my father and mother for us.*

Murdemootoo	*Ramachetty*
Paleanyandee	*Mooneesamy*
Nagamootoo	*Veeramen*
(3 others illegible)	

> *These men are working in Beauchamp and we knows on this killing. That man was killed between Riviere Seche and Grand River in railway.*[25]

The signatories stated that they wished to be called before the Flacq Court to discuss the matter, otherwise they could not remain on the estate, and would prefer to be condemned to hard labour rather than stay there. The simple style of the petition barely conceals the highly charged emotion which prompted its composition, and is a dramatic expression of the trauma of migrants who had come from India merely to work 'for get some monies and also bring some monies to our parents'.

Simple attempts by estate Indians to resist the petty tyrannies of their overseers and managers could escalate into suit and counter-suit once the legal process was invoked. Indians were fairly quick to take advantage of the legal mechanisms available to secure redress, once indentured migration had become established in a particular colony. But in the rare cases when they took their employers to court and won, it was usually a Pyrrhic victory, because the owners would then take steps to punish those concerned by other means, and the dispute could develop into a veritable power struggle. The petition of Bhurtun, a Muslim who had been in Mauritius since 1843, demonstrates how his son's arrest for stealing grass on Clemencia estate in 1879 led to a spiral of revenge acts.[26] Planters were well aware that Indians needed fodder for their animals and firewood for their cooking places. It became a general policy to demand money for the collection of such materials from the estates, and when Bhurtun's son was detected gathering grass, and imprisoned, his brother Dortally was asked to pay for his release. Evidently, Dortally considered this tantamount to extortion and refused to yield; the blows he received were then used by the family to demonstrate ill-treatment on the part of estate employees. When the estate guardian was fined, steps were taken to exact revenge on Bhurtun's household. A counter-plaint was made against him alleging he had stolen two doors. The subject of Bhurtun's petition was that his new complaint against the estate for invading his property had been dismissed:

> in the beginning of the month of August last, one of my sons, Ameerally, was arrested by a guardian of Clemencia Estate, for having, said he, stolen some grass in the said Estate. He was arrested and conducted before the owner of the estate Mr. J. de Villecourt. The brother of the son arrested is under contract of engagement with the said Mr de Villecourt. He was called by him and asked to pay him a fine of 20 rupees if not that he will send his brother at the Police Station, Dortally, such is the name of my second son, refused to agree, then Mr de Villecourt ordered him to be beaten, and received from the guardian called Callechurn blows with a sagaie which blows has been constated by the Stipendiary Magistrate of Flacq in absence of the Government Doctor. I then brought an action at the Stipendiary Court against the guardian who had beaten my son and was sentenced to pay a fine. Fifteen days about after the judgement rendered by the Magistrate, at about nine o'clock in the morning two guardians of Clemencia Estate went to my place and wish to enter my house under the pretext that I had stolen doors belonging to the said; they found in my premises two doors belonging to me, I was absent; on the protestation of my daughter they throw down the two doors and placed a guardian to look at them. At night about ten o'clock the accountant of the Estate along with police and three guardians of the said, went to my place to make a new perquisition. I request from them to produce the warrant which authorise them make perquisition in my place but they did not produce it and proceeded with the perquisitions. I brought a new action against Police and the other persons who without any right and contrary to the law had made a perquisition at my place. The affair has been dismissed by the Magistrate I do not know why? and I should wish you would inquire what for?
> signature of Bhurtun no. 51798.[27]

His appeal to the Immigration Office was in vain: the Department noted 'Mr Courtois informs me that this man saw the officer in charge who on learning that the case had already been enquired into by the Magistrate did not think it necessary to interfere further in the matter'.[28] It was less the outcome than the moves and counter-moves in the litigation process which are revealing of the climate of tension prevailing on estates where the petty tyrannies of the plantation regime were resisted.

Towards the end of their indentures, new immigrants faced pressures to re-engage which could make the last months of their contracts even more unpleasant. Colundaveloo's statement, made at the Immigration Depot in 1872, describes an ordeal which was not an isolated example of the type of chastisement meted out on estates in Mauritius to workers who were unwilling to renew their contracts. Plantation owners who were not able to induce labourers to re-engage by promising cancellation of debts or a small bonus sometimes resorted to physical chastisement. At La Rosa estate in Mauritius, one inspector found a group of Indians chained in a makeshift prison, to 'help' them make up their minds. Others were wary of inflicting visible signs of corporal punishment – the owner of La Rosa estate was briefly imprisoned by the colonial state for that offence – and so devised other methods of dealing with insubordinates. An effective way of humiliating and cowing a worker was by targeting the religious and cultural taboos of estate Indians, such as forcing Hindus to clean up excrement or to eat food cooked by a man from a lower caste. That undergone by Colundaveloo, however, combined the psychological punishment of solitary confinement with a polluting concept: proximity to dead bodies. He was locked in the 'dead house' for almost three weeks. In his statement made before the Protector of Immigrants, Colundaveloo describes his ordeal and his reactions:

> *I ran away from my Master's Estate 2 months ago. I had been beaten by Mr. Boulle the Manager, with a rope, because I had refused to renew my contract. I was beaten 20 days before I ran away. After beating me Mr. Boulle locked me up in a room in the hospital: the room in which corpses are generally placed (the Dead-house). The door was locked up night and day during the 20 days. I received only one meal a day during the time I was locked up. I was not even allowed to go out to the privy: a chamber-pot was placed in the room and the hospital servant used to remove it every morning . . .*
>
> *When let out I went to the Stipendiary Court to complain. I spoke to the Creole Guard. He told me to go back to my work, and that if I did not, the Magistrates would make me break stones. I did not speak to the Magistrate, nor to the Clerk, I was afraid of doing so. I did not go back to my Master. I went and saw my friends who allowed me to live with them, till I went to Moka to complain.*
>
> *I did not come to the Immigration Depot. I did not know that I could find redress by applying to the Protector. My friends advised me to go to the Governor.*[29]

His statement clearly reveals the plight of the new immigrant; he did not know to whom he could apply for redress, having arrived from Trichinopoly in south India a few years previously.[30] When finally he applied to the Protector the latter asked for the case to go to the Stipendiary Magistrate of Riviere du Rempart for investigation. His complaints were not addressed, however, once it was revealed that Colundaveloo had previously worked for three years at

Labourdonnais estate, from which he was declared a deserter in December 1868.[31]

Aside from the pressures to re-engage, many new immigrants felt cheated, on completing their contracts, by the derisory or non-existent remuneration offered them. Moorjaralli had apparently been offered a piece of land in Bengal as a payment for five years' work in Mauritius, only to discover that the claim was illusory. On his return, he found that the local Collector and Zamindar had not considered the document to be a satisfactory proof of his title to the land, and Moojaralli requested either that such proof be furnished from Mauritius or that his pay be restored to him. In a letter addressed to the Governor of Bengal he made the following plea:

Honored Sir,

With most humble submission I beg to bring to your honor's kind notice that having been emigrated to the island of Mauritius, I was employed under the Protector of Immigrants for 5 years at Lacoodohur. That after having been freed from employment, a certificate to retire to Bombay in a ship named Allamgeer, and a piece of paper written in the Nagree language, mentioning it to be the certificate of a piece of land granted to me instead of my pay in Pergunah Futtehpore in Zillah Purneah, were granted to me by the chief clerk of Mauritius – But on my showing the said papers to the Collector of Purneah and also to the Zemindar of the said Pergunah they asked me a proper certificate for the land if any. Under these circumstances I humbly solicit your honor will spare a mercy upon your honor's this poor petitioner and kindly pass such an order as I may succeed either to recover my pay or to obtain the land mentioned above.

I further humbly beg to state that I had applied verbally to the Emigration Agent of Alipore whence I was emigrated but his worship refused my prayer.

s. of Moorjaralli, son of
Mahomed Adum.
Immigrant no 352001
Inhabitant of Ponach
Pergunah Sreepore
Zillah Purneah.[32]

Enquiries were made of the Emigration Agent for Mauritius at Calcutta, who reported that:

The petitioner was brought to me by the Police about 2 months ago charged with having travelled on the East India Railway line some distance without a ticket. The petitioner thereupon asked me to refund him his savings without specifying the amount he supposed had been remitted from Mauritius, out of which he said he intended to pay his railway fare. He also mentioned the story of a piece of land which he stated that he had been promised by somebody before leaving Mauritius, and although the petitioner failed to produce the usual deposit receipt invariably given to all remitters when depositing their savings for transmission to India, or to furnish any other evidence in support of his extraordinary claim for money or land, I nevertheless had the records of this Agency examined and could find no trace of his name among the lists of remitters or otherwise, and was consequently led to infer that the petitioner must have been laboring under some hallucination.

On pressing him to state the exact amount of his savings and the means by which he had accumulated the money, he admitted that he did not know the amount but that it must be considerable because he had earned it by breaking stones for five years in Mauritius, or to use his own words 'Pathur tora paunch harus'.[33]

The Protector of Emigrants advised that the Mauritian authorities be asked to investigate Moojaralli's claims. Eales, the Agent, sent on the original enclosure written in the Nagri language which Moojaralli claimed was his title to the land, together with a covering letter to the protector in Mauritius. The land claim stated:

> *Certificate granting a piece of Lakheraj land, in Arrareah, in the Futehpore district, to Shake Mozor resident of Ponas, Baha Durgunge in the Purneah district.*
>
> *Dated 19 Bhado 1244.*
> *s. of (Illegible)*

Perhaps the returnee's plaint was compromised before even enquired into, however, because the Agent added 'the petitioner, who appeared from personal observation to be laboring under some mental delusion, furnishes no reliable evidence or proof whatever in support of his extraordinary claim'.[34] If employed in breaking stones, it may have been the case that the latter had been condemned as a vagrant. If so one can sympathize with his feeling that some money ought to have been forthcoming after five years' such labour. His passport, however, noted that he had completed his industrial residence. The immigration register also confirmed his story that he had spent five years on the island: it listed him as a Muslim from Bakerganj who had arrived, aged 32, in 1870, and had returned at the end of 1875 to India.[35] If the claim was fraudulent, the deception probably did not therefore originate with Moojaralli, but rather with the person who gave him the Nagri document granting the land.

That conditions for new immigrants did not change significantly, despite new labour laws implemented after the Royal Commissions in British Guiana and Mauritius, is evident from the complaints of men such as Venkata Subbiah, who arrived in Mauritius in September 1902, aged 25. Venkata claimed that he and a fellow worker were beaten when they were sick:

> *I am living with Subbeah in the same hut – we arrived on the same vessel and are working at 'La Barraque' Estate – on Friday night last, we suffered violently from diarrhoea – when the night guardian came, at day break, to awake us, as usual, I told him that we were sick and should go to Hospital – a moment after the Colombe (the chief employe probably) who goes to the fields – a white young man whose name I do not know – entered the hut – I was lighting the fire, and Subbeah was lying down – he struck him with his stick: I asked for pardon and explained we were sick – he struck me on the right leg and dragged us violently outside, then he kicked Subbeah who fell on the ground and bruised his head. On seeing the wound bleeding; he went away. We called on the employer who gives the rations and related what had taken place – he took a big stick &*

threatened us – whereupon, we ran away and left the Estate. We were stopped at the Police Station, and released when we explained that we were going to complain to the Protector – We beseech him to have pity on us, and inquire from our master why we were so ill-treated, whereas, since our arrival to the Estate, we always worked very well – Rameeah & Nangayah who arrived in the same vessel, on hearing our cries when we were beaten in our hut, came and witnessed the employer striking us.[36]

What is remarkable about his testimony is that it demonstrates that the lot of a labourer in the twentieth century, towards the close of the indenture era, was little different from conditions experienced by the first Indian immigrants in the mid-nineteenth century. The reaction of officials supposed to represent the welfare of Indians was equally predictable. The Mauritian Protector, J.F. Trotter, simply minuted: 'Men given usual papers and sent back to estate'.[37]

The prison statement of Debi Ram, taken in 1906, reveals that recruits at the tail end of the indenture system continued to include individuals who could not be considered to have taken a reasoned decision to migrate, but who were there because they had few options open to them. Ram's statement indicates that a common response to physical coercion and ill-treatment on the estate continued to be the individual escape route of self-destruction:

When I arrived at Sans Souci Estate I worked for 2 days only. No one ill treated or abused me on the estate. I reached the estate on Friday and spent the night with my comrades in the hospital. The following day I looked after my house and in the evening the Manager gave me a rupee – in the morning I had been given dholl, rice, oil, salt etc. On Sunday I did nothing and I worked on Monday and Tuesday. On Sunday I asked two men who were seated together what work I should have to do, one of them, said if you work well you will be well paid – the other said if you don't work you will be ill treated and you can either put fire to your house or hang yourself. When I went to work on Monday and Tuesday the sirdar beat me and several others of the coolies. I felt mad on Wednesday morning and made up my mind to kill myself and did not cook my food. When my comrades were going away I said to Mutloo, one of them, I am going to answer a call of nature; he thought I had gone but I slipped back into the house as I had resolved to set fire to the house and hang myself. Mutloo locked me in and at 7 O'clock I tied my neck with a cord and set fire to my house. I felt quite mad and did not know what I was doing at the time.

Since I was a child 10 or 12 years I have been of weak intellect. Once in a month or once in 2 or 3 months I cannot sleep and my head goes round and round. When in this state I can do nothing for a day or two and then I get well again. The deep scar on my left eyebrow was caused through my falling down when my head was going round and round, this happened in my parents' house in India, when I get these mad fits I can do nothing, but I wander about here and there. I used to run away from home in India times out of number when my mad fits came on. When I recovered I used to return home. When I am about to go mad I feel a great pain in my ears and head. . . . When I am well I am quite sensible and can work. I break 12 and 14 baskets of stone every day in prison and will even be able to break 22 as I am getting used to the work.[38]

Were the symptoms – akin to epilepsy – that he described in his statement real, or imagined for the benefit of his interlocutor? In any event, the Protector evidently believed that he was not suited to plantation life and suggested that he be allowed to return to India. The Governor of Mauritius informed him in reply that:

> the man must be left to serve his time; but that in view of your report as to his mental state the attention of the Prison Surgeon will be specially directed to the case and the Prison Authorities will be requested to keep him under constant and close supervision. If Debi Ram does not develop symptoms of insanity he may at the expiration of his sentence be treated as an undesirable immigrant and sent back to his village in India as suggested by you.[39]

The responses of Indian immigrants to their treatment on the nineteenth-century sugar estates mirror those of other workers in bonded labour regimes that have been so eloquently described by van Onselen and others. The indentured workers also had recourse to the psychological arsenal developed by slaves to subvert their position of inferiority: the cultural weapons of religion and song. There have been few studies of the folksongs and religious rituals of Indian workers under indenture, but those that have been recorded are revealing tools for the analysis of Indian perspectives of indenture. Mesthrie recounts the following song from Natal:

> *They've given you the name 'coolie', they've given you the name 'coolie'*
> *You've come to Natal, give thanks in song, brother*
> *with a cambu in your hand, and a hoe on your shoulder*
> *Let the foreigners go home.*

Much of the interpretation of these songs hinges upon a sympathetic as well as accurate translation. Thus Mesthrie speculates on the possible irony of this statement and the significance of the use of loanwords and appellations such as 'kuli'.[40] Lal has similarly collected folksongs from India which describe the work of indentured labourers, and the monotonous poverty of life in the coolie lines:

> *I hoe all day and cannot sleep at night,*
> *Today my whole body aches,*
> *Damnation to you, arkatis.*

> *I have toiled day and night*
> *from the moment I entered your house.*
> *The skin of my body has dried*
> *and happiness has become but a dream.*
> *Your elder brother is so keen on fashions*
> *and his wife is the malkin (boss) of the house.*
> *Your body aches from ploughing the fields*
> *and yet we remain so poor.*
> *I shall go away to my father's house*
> *and look after my brother's children.*
> *I shall build myself a little hut*
> *but will not see your door again.*[41]

Totaram Sanadhaya's description of a Fiji sugar estate on a Sunday is valuable because the small details he conveys of activities build into a larger picture of the nature of domestic and work relationships. The prose is of interest also because it creates an idealized portrait and then juxtaposes it with glimpses of the coarser and more violent aspects of estate life. Finally, there is a sense that Sanadhaya is fashioning a stylized image of a quietly productive overseas Indian population suffering in exile, designed to appeal to an abolitionist-minded audience:

> *On Sunday I went to the other lines for a walk. Someone was singing from the Alha and another reading the Ramayana. One was beating a hand-drum and another playing the tambura, while others were singing bhajans. Some were using obscene language. Some were entertaining their friends while others were practising the different holds of wrestling. One was standing before the sirdar with his head down while abuse was showered upon him . . . I sat under a mango tree on a piece of ground surrounded by the four lines. I saw women busy everywhere. Some were washing up their cooking vessels and utensils, some were busy in the preparation of food, while among themselves they were asking for news of their husbands, parents, etc., and weeping.*[42]

Strategies of Control and Resistance Involving Ex-Indentured Immigrants

Misrepresentation of contractual obligations remained a common cause of complaint of migrants, even amongst those who had completed their in-dentures but had chosen to continue to work on estates. The case of Coupen and Vythee concerned not the owner but the estate where the labour was to be performed. Although written in the singular, two men signed the petition addressed to the Protector of Immigrants in Mauritius, which described their obligation to work as gardeners on an estate which was not the one they had contracted for:

> *Respected Sir,*
>
> *The humble Petition of Coupen and Vythee respectfully sheweth:*
>
> *That your Petitioner has been employed in the service of Mr. Desjardin; after he discharged from his service he entered into contract of service in condition to work as a gardener in his own service; yet, your Petitioner's master owes him four months wages and further your Petitioner begs to bring to your notice, although your Petitioner engaged to work as a gardener on his own property he makes your Petitioner to work as labourer in a foreign Estate, Thereby he applied several time to the Stipendiary Magistrate at Pamplemousses about his circumstances, which he replied your Petitioner three or four times to fetch money to lodge his plaint which he could not able to pay the same of the court fees on account of not having been paid by his master four months wages which he unable to pay the fees of the court. Through this, after your honor has been appointed and perform the duties as a Protector of Immigrant, hoping that your honor will take of your*

Petitioner's case into your serious consideration and to refer the same as your honor think proper.

I am Sir your most obedient servant

Crosses of X Coupen
X Vythee.[43]

Paradoxically the petitioners, having applied for legal redress, found themselves unable to pay the court fees to lodge the plaint on account of failure to
pay wages on the part of the employer.

The means by which planters circumvented the judicial process were many
and various. Magistrates could often be relied upon to go along with charges
trumped up to coerce labourers, and subsequently dropped if the worker
agreed to re-engage. But where this was considered inappropriate, planters
devised numerous other ways of subduing workers and of forcing re-
engagements on those who had completed their first indenture contracts.
Goordyal emphasizes that he was promised, at the time of re-engaging, that he
would not be ill-treated, but goes on to describe a beating with a cane following
the overturning of a cart:

*I was under engagement with Mr Poulin for three years, at the expiry of this term of
service I re-engaged for another year, on the promise from my master that I should not
again be beaten or ill treated. He had been in the habit of ill using me, tying my hands
and beating me, sometimes with his fists at other times kicking me with his foot. A short
time after the second engagement of service, my master had me tied up in the sugar boiling
room and there I was beaten with a rattan on my bare back on which sirop had been
previously smeared by my master. This was because a cart drawn by oxen had been upset
in a canal. I had charge of the cart with another man named Soodoo who also was beaten
and has run away. Besides this ill treatment the master deducted from my wages two
months' pay. I ran away and have been a vagrant ever since. I have no papers and
during the last four years have been constantly taken up by the police and condemned to
break stones. My life is miserable and I want my papers to protect me from being always
sentenced to break stones. I am very unhappy. When I made any complaints I was
refused a hearing by the Magistrate of the District.*[44]

Old immigrants who refused to re-engage could thus be reduced to an impecu-
nious position. The situation of those who were too infirm to undertake field
labour was equally precarious, and many requested free licences to enable them
to sell produce at bazaars and the like. Thus, one old man, named Suruppeet,
petitioned the Protector in 1899, explaining:

*I have the honor most respectfully beg to submit before you my poor position. I'm an old
Immigrant in this colony, and aged 75 years and I have arrived in Mauritius at the time
of Mr Hugon was Magistrate, and I was engaged to Mr de Robillard, my first master to
my arrival in Mauritius. But at present I am without employment and had become old
and in a poor position. I solicit you to be good and charitable enough to grant me a free
license for selling vegetables and charcoal, in order to get my livelihood, as you are the*

good protector for the Immigrants in this colony, for this purpose I thus address to you, in order to recommend me to His Excellency the Governor to have a license. Hopeing sir that my will be entertained into your favourable consideration. An answer if you please.[45]

The Protector upheld Suruppeet's description of his physical condition, minuting that the petitioner was 'old, eyesight bad and unable to maintain himself in any way'.

However, for those able-bodied individuals like Goordyal who refused to succumb to physical chastisement and left the estate, condemnation as a vagrant was the inevitable result. Many statements and letters of migrants speak of having been 'sentenced to break stones'. This was in effect a punishment of hard labour, involving the breaking up of rocks into smaller chippings suitable for road building. Individuals condemned as vagrants would be entered in the Deserters' Book, an instrument by which planters kept local officials up to date with missing estate workers so that the individuals concerned would not be able to contract engagements elsewhere. Details of physical appearance, work history and the all-important immigrant number were given. The police were also given the task of ascertaining that any Indians seen travelling outside plantation boundaries were *bona fide* old immigrants or, if still under indenture, on an errand for their employer. Thus any individuals caught without papers, or not provided with an estate pass to explain their business, would be taken into custody pending enquiries with the employer concerned. It was the particular problems this caused to ex-indentured Indians who were self-employed as hawkers or market gardeners which provoked a number of high-ranking individuals in Mauritius to take up the cause of the old immigrants, ultimately leading to the institution of a Commission of Enquiry in Mauritius, shortly after that held in Guiana.

Planters had long insisted that high rates of return were an indication both that wage levels were too high and that the supply of labour in the colonies was inadequate.[46] They also declaimed against those Indians who failed to remain in sugar cultivation on the expiry of their contracts, but took employment in a variety of other trades, or even set up in small businesses on their own account. In 1847 in Mauritius a law was passed taxing immigrants who chose to engage in anything other than plantation labour.[47] Unfortunately the tax was also claimed from Indians temporarily out of work, as a means of combating what was seen as an increasing problem of vagrancy. Nevertheless, when it was found that the monthly tax of four shillings was not decreasing the outflow of plantation labour, the planters despaired of such indirect means of retaining their estate workforce, increasing instead, in 1863, the contractual term from three to five years. For those Indians still under such contracts the penalties for desertion were stiffened. In 1864, an absence of one or two days without leave could be punished by a prison sentence of six to nine months.[48]

By 1867, the planting interests, aided by a succession of sympathetic governors, had been able to gain such influence with the Mauritian Council of

Government – with the notable exception of W.W. Kerr – that the most far-reaching moves against the large ex-indentured population were ready for implementation. The pass system, introduced in its fullest form by Ordinance 31 of that year, required all old immigrants to possess a ticket with a photograph which denoted a place of residence and an occupation. Anyone found outside the allotted area was liable to arrest; the police were given powers to demand papers from any Indians whether in their homes or in public.[49] It was the sheer intrusiveness of the law and the potential criminalization of any Indian who could not produce papers which finally prompted W.W. Kerr to make a public stand against what he felt had become 'a general feeling of hostility against the Indian in this Colony'.[50] Explaining his lonely position in the government to Sir Henry Barkly, the Governor of Mauritius, he pointed out that nearly all the Committee members involved in the drafting of Ordinance 31 were 'more or less interested in the cultivation of sugar'. Recognizing that his activist stand – and particularly his involvement in the drafting of petitions on behalf of Indians – had incurred the displeasure of Barkly, he defended his position thus: 'while almost every one admits that abuses exist, scarcely any one, except myself, ventures to denounce them, the planting interests being paramount in the Island'.[51]

The petition of Pandoo, a sirdar, written for him by W.W. Kerr, delivers a telling condemnation of the actions of the local Magistrate, Gautier, and his clerk, and lays bare the unscrupulous tactics used by the Estate Manager, Raynal, acting in cohort with Gautier to break the resolve of Pandoo and his band:

The humble Petition of 'Pandoo' late Sirdar in the service of Mr. Preaudet, Planter, in the District of Moka, on behalf of himself and his band, respectfully sheweth:

That your Petitioner has been 28 years in the Island of Mauritius, and 27 years a Sirdar.

That your Petitioner and his band of thirty men engaged themselves on the 18th March last to Mr. Preaudet 'Bonne Veine' Estate in the District of Moka of which Mr. Raynal is the Manager.

That for three weeks after their engagement Petitioner and his band were well treated by Mr. Raynal; but that after that period they were illused by him. That he was in the habit of beating and kicking them, and that he obliged them after weeding with the hoe to gather up the weeds stooping instead of squatting. That such work continued throughout the whole day is very severe and that your Petitioner's band were beaten and kicked whenever they attempted to do this work squatting; that during your Petitioner's experience of 28 years on other Sugar Estates, malabars so employed were always allowed to squat.

That two of Petitioner's band, named Ramjee and Ramjee Malanee, went about six weeks since to the magistrate of the District, Mr. Gautier, to complain of having been beaten by the Indian Tataya; that when they arrived at the Court House, at about 2 o'clock p.m. the Magistrate had gone home, but they found there the Magistrate's Clerk, Mr. Pauqui, who told them to return to the Estate to work, which they did.

That five days afterwards they were again beaten by the Indian Tataya; that they again went to the Court House to complain; that the Magistrate, Mr. Gautier refused to hear their complaints, but ordered them to return to the Estate.

That about three weeks after this, Gunnack, one of your Petitioner's band, was beaten by the Indian Tataya because he squatted while gathering weeds, and that, on the following day, Sunday, when rice was given out to the band, Gunnack received a portion less than he was entitled to, and that, when he asked why that deduction was made, Mr. Raynal gave him a most severe beating with a stick which he always carries with him.

That this punishment which was administered in presence of the whole band, was so severe that Gunnack was bruised and marked from his hips to his heels.

That your Petitioner despairing of obtaining justice for Gunnack and his band from the magistrate Mr. Gautier, went immediately with his men to the Protector of Immigrants at Plaines Wilhems. That Mr. Beyts the Protector seeing how very severely Gunnack had been beaten, gave Petitioner a letter to Mr. Gautier the Magistrate, which was delivered to him the following day by two men of his band named Soonack and Tookah, that this letter was delivered to Mr. Gautier at his private residence.[52]

The initial cause of complaint had been Raynal's imposition of an uncustomarily severe work routine and punishment by beatings. When, after a particularly severe assault on one of their number, the intervention of the Protector was secured, a rival band of Telegu labourers was summoned to give evidence against Pandoo and his band. Once more, planters effectively used communal differences to their advantage. Pandoo's engagement was then cancelled:

your Petitioner went again with his whole band to the Court House in the hopes of obtaining justice, but the Magistrate was absent, and Mr. Pauqui the Clerk told them to go back to the Estate to work, and added that if they returned again to the Court House they would be condemned to two months imprisonment.

That on the following day your Petitioner and his band feeling certain that they had nothing to expect from the Magistrate and his Clerk but a denial of justice, went again to the Protector of Immigrants, who asked them whether they wished to have their engagement broken and that on their replying in the affirmative, he desired them to go to the Depot.

That at about three o'clock p.m. Mr. Beyts gave to one of the band named Mahadoo-Couly a letter to Mr. Gautier the Magistrate which he delivered; that Mr. Gautier on receiving it said 'toujours aller l'autre cote, encore aller, donner deux mois condamne,' and that lastly he desired the whole band to come to the Court House the following morning.

That your Petitioner and his band went to the Court House the following morning as desired, but that on arrival there they were informed that the Magistrate had gone to town. That your Petitioner and his band were ordered by Mr. Pauqui to return the following Monday.

That on the Sunday following at about 7 and half o'clock a.m.. Mr. Gautier came to the Estate in Mr. Raynal's carriage, who also came with him.

That Mr. Gautier called some men together, about ten or twelve Coringhy men, who work on the Estate, but not under engagement. That he told these men, if called upon to give good evidence for Mr. Raynal, to say they were well treated and neither beaten nor ill used on the Estate, to which the men replied 'Bon, Monsieur.' That on the day following the band appeared before Mr. Gautier and were, after evidence was taken, *condemned either to pay a fine of $10 each or to go to prison to break stones for a month. That no time was given to them to determine which punishment they would elect, and that they were immediately thrown into prison.*

That your Petitioner remained behind, that Mr. Gautier called him up and asked him why he had 'gate' [spoilt] the band and sent them to Mr Beyts ... That Petitioner was then ordered to go to the Estate to bring away his effects, and to return to the Court House on the Wednesday following when his engagement would be cancelled. That the Magistrate then said to him, I will break your engagement, because you are always going to Papa la case (meaning Mr Beyts).

That your Petitioner went as desired to the Court House on the Wednesday following, when the Magistrate gave him his ticket saying that his engagement was cancelled.

The petition explains how evidence was constructed to imply that witnesses were not available, and absences fabricated, whilst the planters' book was always considered 'conclusive evidence against the malabar':

That your Petitioner was forced against his will to take his ticket. That inside his ticket there was a paper stating that all wages due had been paid; that the Magistrate then offered him $12.50, that he refused to accept this sum because his band, which he had collected at great expense, consisted of thirty men, and he was promised a rupee a head per month for each, and because when the engagement was thus cancelled against his will, wages of one month and twenty days were due to him.

That the Magistrate then ordered him to return to the Court House the following day, but that he declined to do so.

That the evidence shewn to him in which Petitioner's band are made to say that they had no witnesses to the ill-treatment they received is false evidence. That one or more of the band were generally witnesses of the ill-treatment of the others, but that the Magistrate would not admit the evidence of one of the band in favor of another, and that when the men are stated to have said that they 'had no witnesses' or 'no one was present' these words are meant to imply that they had no witnesses from other bands. That thus Gunnack, according to the evidence, is made to say that there was no one present when he was kicked by Mr. Raynal is contrary to the fact, for he was beaten in the presence of the whole band.

That the Statement of Absences from the Estate is also a false statement.

Some of the band were absent from sickness, others had been beaten and were afraid to return, others again were reported absent because they were unable to complete the task given them before it was dark.

That this punishment is most unjust.

That the bell which calls them to their work is rung before 4 o'clock a.m.. That they arrive on the ground before it is light. That so soon as they can see each man gets his task, that they are allowed about a quarter of an hour to eat their cold rice which they bring with them, and then continue to work until it is dark.

That when the task is not finished they are marked absent, and their wages cut for that day.

That the task is often so hard that weak men cannot possibly finish it, the ground being stony, with roots in it, and full of weeds. That according to Law the Planter can, at the completion of the engagement, oblige these men to make good these absences either by a payment of money, or by giving two days' work for one day's absence, and as the

Planters-book is always admitted as conclusive evidence against the malabar he is thus liable to be doubly punished.

Wherefore in consideration of all the facts now brought forward, your Petitioner on behalf of himself and his band humbly prays Your Excellency to cause a full, searching and patient inquiry to be made into the whole case, and that if Your Excellency is satisfied of the truth of the facts now disclosed Your Excellency will cause the engagement of the men now unjustly undergoing the punishment of imprisonment with hard labour, to be broken, and so allow them to engage elsewhere out of the jurisdiction of Mr. Magistrate Gautier, and your Petitioner as in duty bound will ever pray.

PANDOO x his cross.

The Governor, to whom the petition was sent, asked for the opinion of the Protector. On this occasion the latter recommended that the charges against Gautier be investigated, and this was carried out. Kerr's postscript on the whole affair was a chastening one. He observed that during the time Pandoo and his men had been imprisoned their wives and children had been denied any food or firewood from the estate, and 'when these men obtained their discharge and came to my residence, accompanied by their families ... the women and children were in a most pitiable condition, one child died that night, and another within a week, notwithstanding every possible attention'.[53] The price of intervening in and pursuing the claims of Indians was high for all concerned. Nevertheless, Pandoo's petition reinforced the growing sense that Indians were prepared to pursue their complaints in spite of the partiality of the largely French creole magistracy, and in so doing, increasingly revealed the inadequacy of the judicial machinery in Mauritius.

Mr Kerr's convictions as regards the treatment of Indians in Mauritius centred on the fact that their contractual obligations had been successively widened so that 'the position of the Coolie [became] harder and harder and his choices more limited'. He pointed out that 'now, when an estate is sold, the Malabars are, so to say, sold with it. They are treated, in fact, like serfs'.[54] Kerr was referring to the fact that contracts bound labour to an estate rather than to an employer, so that workers effectively had no redress when a plantation changed hands. The cases of individuals like Mootoosamy, who complained of physical chastisement by his employer (see Chapter 5), and Pandoo, which were taken up by W.W. Kerr, mobilized planters and their supporters in the Mauritian administration against him. The Procureur General spoke in alarmist terms about Indians threatening local magistrates by bringing in Mr Kerr, and noted 'if he is not checked in some way, I foresee that we shall have trouble with the Indian Immigrants here'.[55] The Protector used the incident to report that 'little advantage is derivable from questioning prisoners as to their grievances ... but it might evidently be productive of a great deal of mischief'.[56] Finally the Governor himself was moved to warn Kerr that his 'unauthorised attempt ... to set yourself up as the special champion of the rights of the Indian Population' was both 'irregular and unbecoming'.[57] The Treasurer was ultimately dissuaded from his intention to lay his wider objections about the conditions of the indentured and ex-indentured labourers before the Colonial Office.

The importance of the intervention of courageous individuals like Kerr lay less in their conscientization of Indians – who already had an acute sense of the injustices meted out to them – than in their interpretation of events in a language and a logic which were more acceptable to the legal community. The tone of Govinden's petition, addressed to the Governor of Mauritius, again emphasizing the petty tactics of planters who used the justice system against those who opposed them, is a revealing demonstration of the self-conscious status of sirdars:

> *The humble Petition of Govinden now undergoing his sentence in Savanne prison, most respectfully sheweth:*
>
> *That your Petitioner was condemned on the 10th of September 1874 by E.J. Ackroyd Esquire, Acting Additional District Magistrate to three months imprisonment for being in possession of stolen property; viz: Hut doors belonging to 'Fontenelles' Estate, on which your Petitioner was employed as sirdar. Your Petitioner appealed against the said judgment, and the case was tried at the Supreme Court and Petitioner's appeal dismissed, and Petitioner was ordered on the 11th instant to undergo his sentence.*
>
> *Your Petitioner with all due respect to the Honorable judges who dismissed the appeal, begs most respectfully to lay before your Excellency the facts of the case.*
>
> *Your Petitioner having a large band of Indian immigrants (viz 95 men) at his disposal was engaged by the proprietors of 'Fontenelles' Estate on a salary of (£9) nine pounds per month and triple rations as head sirdar, but after having engaged his men, the manager Mr Charron (formerly Manager of 'Bel Ombre' Estate, and for whose conduct I beg to refer your Excellency to the Report of the Royal Commissioners) tried on several occasions to have him discharged, and keep the Band which your Petitioner had brought to the Estate. Your Petitioner begs to cite a case brought previously against him by the said Manager: viz a charge of having overlooked a mule and the case was dismissed by the district Magistrate.*
>
> *Your Petitioner begs most respectfully to request that your Excellency will be pleased to examine the records in the said case and your Excellency will perceive that the evidence was not satisfactory.*[58]

Govinden's petition was signed in Indian characters on his behalf by his wife Rungamah, because he was imprisoned in Savanne, as he explains at the outset. He had been condemned to three months, ironically again for purportedly stealing hut doors from the estate (the same accusation as had been levelled against Bhurtun). His appeal against this judgement had been dismissed. Govinden's petition attempts to clarify the background to this event, and appeals for a re-examination of the facts. His seniority is established by the large number of men under his charge and by his relatively important wage. The Manager of the estate is said to have attempted several times to obtain his discharge, as a means of ridding himself of a rival authority over the band led by Govinden. The petitioner notes that a case previously brought against him by the Manager Charron had been dismissed by the Magistrate, and effectively discredits Charron by adverting to the Royal Commissioners' discussion of his conduct. Most tellingly, Govinden asks the Governor to consider:

> *Can your Excellency think for a moment that your Petitioner would risk his good name and position, which your Petitioner had earned throughout his long career in this island, by committing such an act viz stealing common hut doors which at the highest price would not cost thirty shillings.*
>
> *Your Petitioner also begs to state to your Excellency that he is father of a family and has always tried to conduct himself in an honest manner, so as to be able to gain the esteem of those under whom your Petitioner served, which from the position your Petitioner held, your Excellency will not fail to perceive, he has succeeded in so doing –*
>
> *Your Petitioner most humbly prays that your Excellency will be pleased to take into your kind consideration his sad case (as Petitioner has no one to appeal to but your Excellency for protection) and grant the remission of his unexpired sentence.*

The petition is remarkable for the dignity it conveys and, by implication, the absurdity of the charge against a man of Govinden's calibre. Govinden and his wife were evidently both literate, and, whilst perhaps not drawn up by the sirdar himself, the petition reveals how powerful the Indian adversaries of the planter and his representatives had become. In their sirdars and job contractors, the indentured labourers had men of substance and potential community leaders, whose authority could be undermined only with difficulty and who were challenging the rules and methods of the employer in their own backyard.

The gulf which separated a sirdar from the ordinary labourers in status terms and in their own perceptions of themselves is illustrated by the deposition of Ramasamy, sirdar in the service of the de Montille brothers of La Rosa estate:

> *I have too much misery on the estate, when I work I get one mug of rice, when I do not work, I eat no rice. The mug produced is the same with which my rice is measured out to me; I have been Sirdar one month, but I have too much misery, and I am sent into the fields to clean, I have always had misery, when my band ran away Mr Montille told me to go and find them . . . I went to India and recruited ten labourers, and therefore, how can I work after that.*

The dual role of Ramasamy as a labour recruiter and then sirdar made it unthinkable for him to go back to field labour, and it was a powerful weapon of planters to threaten such men with the degradation of a return to cane work to keep them in their place. By employing men of high caste to be leaders in British Guiana, planters were also probably attempting to use what they regarded as traditional forms of Indian hierarchy in order to keep workers in their place (unwittingly perhaps in some cases creating new hierarchies of their own invention). This backfired in some cases, as when the high-caste sirdar Ooderman led the Devonshire Castle riots of British Guiana in 1873.[59] Ex-indentured workers of a range of castes, and particularly returnees, were another class of labour leader initially sponsored but then often later suppressed by planters.

Of course the position of sirdars, who profited enormously from their intermediary station, meant that their role was ambivalent, and they certainly did not always act in the interests of workers. Thus even when Indians secured a further degree of independence by working with job contractors rather than directly with European plantation managers, their problems were not over. The petition of Tuholoo and three others indicates that their Indian employer Seeborun had not paid their wages. They applied to be discharged from their engagement as a consequence, but found that their contracts specified their attachment to the proprietors of Beau Sejour estate and not to the contractor. However, the former would not consider their claims, since the responsibility for payment of allowances was with Seeborun. In their petition to the Protector, the men, who described themselves as 'Tuholoo no. 130,559, Gunjun, no. 130,257, Chungoo, creole, and Sauntobocus also creole, all four laborers of Seeborun a Job Contractor, on Beau Sejour Estate in the District of Riviere du Rempart', wrote:

> That Petitioners have agreed to work with the said Seeborun on Beau Sejour Estate under verbal contract.
>
> That on the 26th May last, their said Employer gave them a letter for the Police Pass Clerk of Riviere du Rempart, in order that they may get their Police Pass. That Petitioners have from the above date worked on Beau Sejour Estate, in the District of Riviere du Rempart, however their Employer is residing with them in the District of Pamplemousses.
>
> That they have always received their rations from the said Seeborun, with all his other labourers under written contract. That Petitioners having been informed that their Police Pass, bears that they are labourers of Messrs Raffray & Co. Proprietors of Beau Sejour Estate, applied to the Manager Mr Hodoul who told your Petitioner that he has nothing to do with them, they being the laborers of Seeborun Job Contractor.
>
> Petitioners therefore humbly beg that your Honor may be pleased as their Protector, to interfere in their case, in order that they may receive their wages and two weeks rations, and also their Discharge, as they are employed by a Job Contractor who has not furnished any guarantee for the payment of their wages, which is a condemnation to the Ordinance concerning Job Planters. Petitioners claim two months wages from 26th May to 26th July, the first at $5, the second at $4, and the two others at $2 each, and also two week rations.
>
> And Petitioners as in duty bound will ever pray.

> Tuholoo X his cross
> Gunjun X - -
> Chungoo X - -
> Sauntobacus X - -.[60]

Yet again, workers sometimes found themselves in difficulty because the laws respecting contractors were not as effective as those against established planters. Estate owners, in lean times, protected themselves from seizures of their property by shifting responsibility onto such Indian intermediaries, who were often 'men of straw' without the means to guarantee their workers' wages.

Tuholoo and Gunjun, probably brothers, as they shared the same surname, had arrived together from the same Bihari village in 1854, but still had not, twenty years later, the security of a permanent income in Mauritius.[61]During those years they had exchanged a European master for an Indian employer, but the outcome was the same.

The pass system meant that Indians who ventured outside their village or estate without their tickets were liable to arrest as vagrants. Destroyed or lost tickets, which needed to be replaced as a matter of urgency, obliged the Immigration Officers to check through voluminous registers to verify the details of individual emigrants. The traffic in stolen tickets, and the impersonation of old by new immigrants, meant that the verification process needed to be thorough and exhaustive. Whilst such enquiries were being made, Indians hardly dared venture out for fear of arrest.

Ex-indentured Indians working as gardeners and hawkers faced other problems in addition to the nuisance of the pass system. Rungen's drolly written petition is a revealing account of the struggle of one man to establish a small market garden on a plot of leased land, only to find that the owner sold his plot before he had even been able to market his produce:

Most Honored Sir,

With due respect the humble petition of Rungen sheweth
I beg to inform to . . . you five times since before your honor company O my lord about my poor Distress that is long time I was a mirchant to selling vegetable thing and for the named Madam Frances; last 26th October 1872 this grount about three quarter of arpens for lease she gave with me for five years. Shee maid a deemand papper with me and so I was worked in it about two month cutting the . . . and put some vegetable in it, for that I lost much money for cutting grount and building a house and putting some vegetable things in it and then shee neaver tell with me, Shee sold the garden with one man Ramasamy shopkeeper at Bellerose and so my Lord I got more fore years and five month from that grounts. They will push me out of the garden how can I go O my Lord and then I went with Mr Gonuss at the Polis I told with him and there he gave a letter for the madam and I carryed that letter with madam shee not accept that letter and put down. Another time I went to Mr Goness and told the sircumstance by Mr Goness at the Polis and then he told to take a plaint with before the magestrat and so my Lord, I am a poor and grate family man therfor I have no eny single cause to my wants to tke a plaint before the magestrate my Lord therfor I implore you since to accept my poor things and give me a good order to my poor Belley for my suffisint. Just now the vegetables are much grow I am very sorry for that . . . O my Lord, the man of Ramasamy he took all the vegetable and then he told to me do not go in-side the garden and so I beg by your Honor Company Magestrat to give me a garden about my time that she made a papper for me till fore years and five months O my Lord.
I remain your most Humble and obdeints sirvant and slave.[62]

Subsequently, the new owner of the land had barred him from harvesting the vegetables he had grown. Individuals such as Rungen, often still with a poor or non-existent command of English and French, were now required, as would-be proprietors, to wrestle with the legal documents and transactions which they paid for, without really knowing whether the title to their land was thereby assured. In this case the Immigration Office sent a complaint note on his behalf to the District Magistrate, but we do not learn its outcome.[63]

The petition of Dwareeka and Gooroodyal tells a similar story. Having, they believed, purchased a plot of land, when they wished to sell it they found that the notary who had drawn up the bill of sale declared that they were not at liberty to dispose of the plot as they wished:

Sir,

The humble petition of Dwareeka and Gooroodyal of Vacoua.

Most respectfully sheweth:
That your humble Petitioner having been brought a painfull necessity of trubeling your honour's precious time; is as follow that your two Petitioners having on the 16th September 1872 three acres of ground at Vacoua from one Volsy Ambrose for the sum of $150 which bill of sale was drawn by notary V. Barry. Who charged the Petitioner $25 for drawing of the said bill of sale.

Sir, nowe your two Petitioners in desire to sel the same plot of ground before the said notary to a party desire to purchas; the said notory totelly refuses to sel our part.

Your Petitioners therefore begs that your honour will look in to our poor circumstances, and know from the said notorey the reson for what Defeculty he nowe finds on our desire, if the said plot of Ground was not fit to be sold or purchast, than did he sel to us. We therefor beg for your honour justice.[64]

Once again, the Immigration Office could do little more than provide Dwareeka with a covering letter to take to an attorney at law.[65]

The absurdity of the pass laws, and the harassment suffered by those whose papers were in order but who experienced daily demands to verify their identity, brought forth champions of the Indians in the persons of Adolphe de Plevitz in Mauritius and des Voeux in British Guiana. De Plevitz lived at Nouvelle Decouverte, where many old immigrants had settled. He saw at first hand the vexations they experienced as a result of the active attempts by police to weed out vagrants. With the help of Vellyvoil Rajarethnum and others, he drew up a petition which presented a general account of the grievances of the ex-indentured Indians, signed by 9,401 persons, and enlarged upon the experiences of a number of them (Appendix C).

The 'Petition of the Old Immigrants', as it was entitled, recounted in graphic detail the hardships endured by the signatories if their papers were lost or inaccurate, the restrictions on mobility which the regulations enforced, and the interference with their work which the hawkers and market gardeners in particular experienced as a result of continual requests for their papers. The Petition was printed and circulated in Mauritius, exciting the indignation of the planters and their spokesmen. An assault on de Plevitz was planned at an organized meeting, and the assailant Jules Lavoquer, although convicted and fined, was commended by his peers. The Governor's opinion of the printed pamphlet, containing the petition and some remarks penned by de Plevitz, was that it:

> contains a good deal of exaggeration, many inaccuracies, and some statements absolutely erroneous, but, on the whole, its tone is not so immoderate as that of many similar publications, and some of the assertions it contains cannot, I think, be denied with truth.[66]

The individual cases appended to the main petition included those of Ramluckhun, who, in spite of producing papers, was locked up on the day of his marriage; Rajchunder, who was turned away four times from the depot when he went to get his photograph taken, travelling 100 miles on foot before he was eventually given it; and Jadhaya, who waited five days to obtain a police pass, until he was persuaded to bribe a white man and given it immediately. A Police Commission, set up locally to investigate the criticisms of police action which were implicit in the petition, surprisingly agreed that the arrest of Ramluckhun on his wedding day was 'exceptionally hard, as all the man's fault was, that while living on the boundary of Moka district his police pass was that for Pamplemousses'. Less sympathetic to the complaint of Rajchunder, they pointed out an inconsistency in his evidence of ill-treatment at the immigration depot, whilst the allegations of Jadhaya were dismissed for want of evidence.[67]

The impact of the petition in the short term was negligible. Conditions for the old immigrants did not improve until after the new Labour Law of 1878, which even then did not satisfactorily address many of the problems they faced. However, by indirectly prompting the appointment of the Royal Commission, the petition had the long-term effect of drawing attention to the conditions of the Indian community in Mauritius. In the meantime, as Chumbhee's letter to the Protector shows, old immigrants continued to address correspondence and petitions to the authorities in an attempt to regularize the passes without which they could not carry on their daily lives in Mauritius. Chumbhee's plea was for a new document which would allow him to work in another district:

> *Sir,*
>
> *I have the honor to apply to you in order that my Pass be changed. I left the property which I leased at Flacq on the 22nd February 1872 on account of serious illness and it is now that I am in a position to get my livelihood.*
>
> *As I intend to work in the district of Pamplemousses as a gardener I humbly pray that you will direct the Police inspector of Flacq to discharge my pass.*
>
> *I have the honor to be Sir,*
> *your obedient servant*
>
> *Signature of Chumbhee*
> *no. 10,493.*[68]

Chumbhee had been in Mauritius since 1843, when he had arrived as a 27-year-old from Belaspur, Arrah. The Immigration Office, however, finding that he could not produce his original pass, directed him to ask for a duplicate.[69]

The difficulties for indentured Indians whose papers were stolen or lost are highlighted in the petition of Newah and Bagnea to the Protector of Immigrants in Mauritius:

Sir,

> *The Humble Petition of Newah a native of India, about 60 years (aged) a labourer, and of Bagnea his daughter both of them residing in the District of Pamplemousses on Mr. Langlois' property (Fair Fund Estate).*

Most respectfully sheweth:

> *That, in a fire which took place on the said Fair Fund Estate on the sixth day of November in the present year, your Petitioners, who reside on the said place, lost their immigrant papers which were burnt down together with their huts.*

> *That, owing to that circumstance, they are left without any immigrant papers. That, their poverty prevent them from withdrawing them from your Department. That one of your Petitioners, the Indian Newah, is now daily exposed to be arrested by the Police Force for not being provided with his immigrant papers and thereby subjected to a condemnation from a Stipendiary Magistrate.*

> *That your Protectorship, may, as a test to the above mentioned facts, cause an inquiry to be made on the said Fair Fund Estate as to whether there was a fire or not, and whether your Petitioners do reside or not on the said property.*

> *Therefore, your Petitioners humbly pray that your Protectorship may be pleased to order that their Immigrant papers be given to them free.*

> *And your Petitioners as in duty bound shall ever pray*

Newah X   Bagnea X.[70]

The loss of their immigrant tickets in a fire on Fair Fund Estate meant that Newah was subject to daily harassment by the police. To combat fraud in the use of duplicate papers, the Immigration Office had imposed a hefty charge for the issue of replacements, and the petitioners were therefore pleading for free documents on the grounds that their loss of papers was not a result of negligence. Sadly, the effect of their petition was simply to draw attention to Newah's previous convictions. He had already been listed as a deserter from an estate – that of Mr D'Arifat in Flacq. As a result, the Immigration Department minuted tersely, 'the woman to have her ticket and the father to be sent to the Inspector of Police, Pamplemousses'. Within four days of drawing up the petition, Newah's name was listed in the Registry for Embarkation 'by order of the Honorable the Acting Protector'. He was shipped out as 'an incorrigible vagrant' on the *Glenroy* in December 1874. This was the last resort of a state which was increasingly intolerant of Indians who dared to change employers and move from one estate to another without official sanction, and a final means of depriving labourers of a right to decide their own destiny.

The Infirm and the Insubordinate

The colonial state saw little value in Indians rendered unproductive through accident or age, and labour-importing colonies were happy to provide free passages back for the elderly and infirm or for those whose absences or insubordination earned them the label 'incorrigible vagrants'. This policy was adopted from the very onset of the indenture system. In 1838 Suboo, of Hazaribag, deponed before the Calcutta Commission of Enquiry as to his experiences in Mauritius:

> *I fell sick, and was in the hospital for four months . . . from the hospital I was sent to the chief of police, where I was told that as I was disabled by the fall of a tree on my wrist, I had better return to my own country, and I was put on board ship.*[71]

Whilst most labour-importing colonies offered all Indians the right to a free return passage, Mauritius had been uniquely allowed to abolish this clause of indenture contracts, and consequently it was incumbent upon Indians settled there who could not afford the return journey to convince the local authorities of their eligibility for a free passage home through unfitness for labour. This generated a stream of petitions to Governors and Protectors as migrants related their hard-luck stories. The resulting documents are potent testimonies to the dangers inherent in sugar manufacturing and the hardships endured in an age when compensation and insurance did not cushion the worker's declining productivity. There are thus numerous depositions and petitions from individuals maimed by machinery, blinded by or losing limbs as a result of explosions, or even crushed by carts. Potun's case was by no means an unusual one. His petition, addressed to the Governor of Mauritius, calls for free passages for himself and his son, both unable to fend for themselves, he as a result of infirmity and his son following an accident. They looked to relatives in India to 'succour them in their misery', and asked to be sent back to rejoin them:

> *The humble Petition of Potun, no. 180,164, old Immigrant, of the place called 'Les Pailles', District of Moka.*
>
> *Respectfully sheweth:*
>   *That your Petitioner is in this colony for the last sixteen years. That your Petitioner has fulfilled his industrial residence as a laborer, and has since up to the present time, been earning through honest means his livelihood in this island.*
>   *That he has a son aged about 17 years, who in February last met with an accident whilst Employed with Mr. Marceau at 'Les Pailles' Moka (a nail penetrating deeply into the sole of his foot) by which accident he is now become lame and unable to work, after staying under treatment at the Civil Hospital of Port Louis, for considerable time;*
>   *That your Petitioner is now old, and can scarcely, by his personal labor maintain himself and his son, for whose wants he must provide as he is quite a cripple as before stated.*
>   *That under these unhappy circumstances, your Petitioner has reason to believe that he would find some alleviation to the misfortune of his son and his own by returning to India, their native country, where some compassionate relatives and friends may yet succour*

them in their misery; That animated by this hope, and still more by the knowledge of your
Excellency's generous feelings towards the needy and infirm, your Petitioner craves from
your Excellency the favor of your ordering that a free passage back to India be granted to
him and his son by the next available opportunity in virtue of article 183 of Ordinance
no. 31 of 1867.[72]

For once, the Protector's enquiry confirmed their story. He minuted: 'I have seen Petitioner and his son. The latter has been disabled by the accident he has met with, and the former is old and almost infirm. Free passages might be granted to both'.[73] The enquiry also verified the work history of Potun in Mauritius. Having arrived from Gorakhur, Bihar, in 1857, he had first worked on a four-year contract in Pamplemousses, then worked one year for an Indian named Juggurnauth in Moka, and followed this by two one-year stints with employers in Port Louis and Riviere du Rempart. Potun had then spent three years in Moka working as a gardener, a further two years in the same district on a verbal contract, and finally four years as a milk seller. However, before Potun and son's return passages could be taken, the Immigration Office received a counter-petition from one Chatten, who wanted Potun's impending departure to be annulled on the grounds that he was owed a cow and a calf by Potun. It seems that the passage was indeed cancelled pending the resolution of this matter, for Potun's immigration entry does not record his departure from the colony until 1912.[74]

Curpen's attempt to return to India was thwarted by a far more common problem: the reluctance of his employer to cancel his engagement. His terse petition, addressed to the Protector, was simply a request to the Magistrate to break the contract on his behalf:

Respected Sir,

I beg to inform you, that the following few lines the Indian Curpen no. 91,739.
I told to cancel my engagement my master he approved cancel my engagement, but the Magistrate never cancel my engagement and . . . I like to go to India therefore I beg to your honor to order the Magistrate to cancel my engagement. For which act of kindness and generosity I shall ever pray the Almighty and prosperity

I beg to remain Sir your most
obedient servant
Curpen no. 91,739.[75]

The local Stipendiary Magistrate was called in to report on the case, and he explained that Curpen was under engagement to Moonsamy, a job contractor, on Union Vale estate. His wage was guaranteed by Samouilhan & Co. It was because of an ongoing dispute between these latter and the contractor that the Magistrate had refused to cancel the engagement pending its resolution, and Curpen's return to India – he had been in Mauritius since 1851 – was thus further delayed.[76]

Even those migrants who had regularly completed their contracts and paid their passage could find their departure blocked because of the many formalities a returning Indian had to complete. The petition of Reetburrun and others to the Governor describes how, having paid their passage in the *Regina* and been on the point of embarkation, their departure was forbidden because they had not published their names in the local newspaper:

Sir,

The Petition of the undersigned, respectfully represents to Your Honour:

That they are Immigrants who have completed their time of service and other obligations to the Colony, as appears in the certificate of the Protector; that being desirous now of returning to their native country, they have taken and paid for their passage in the ship Regina.

That at the moment of embarking, they have been threatened with stoppage by the Police, owing to their names not having been published in the Government Gazette, a formality of the necessity of which they were entirely ignorant.

That they have applied in vain to the Captain and Agents of the ship to reimburse their passage money, that they may be able to fulfil the formality required and have wherewithal to secure a passage in another vessel.

Under these circumstances, Your Petitioners humbly pray your Honour's protection and assistance and that You will be pleased to order their being allowed to depart without hindrance, to which they conceive themselves freely entitled after having fulfilled all the conditions inferred on Immigrants,

And your Petitioners will every pray.

Their marks
Reetburrun no. 55,596 – 42,495 X
Rajcoomaree 5,567 – 54,391 X
Peeroo 27,852 – 20,231 X
Etwariah 27,849 – 20,257 X
Gunasah 80,346 X
Bucktoo 80,247 X
Ghoorohoo 80,345 X.[77]

This requirement was designed to prevent deserters, runaways or debtors from leaving the colony without informing creditors, employers or family. However, in the case of Reetburrun and his co-returnees, not only had they been unaware of this ritual, but they had been refused reimbursement for their passages from the Captain and Agent of the departing ship. The men were all north Indians who were amongst the first arrivals under Government-sponsored immigration: three had arrived in 1843, and the remainder in 1849. They were thus shipmates on arrival in Mauritius who had maintained contact throughout their stay, working for the same employer, and now wished to return together.[78] Peeroo and Etwariah had both arrived on the *Boadecia* in 1843 and were of the Kurmi caste. Bucktoo, Ghoorohoo and Gunasah were also Kurmis, were from the same village in Jaunpur, and had arrived together in 1849. Such men made of indentured migration not an individualized, isolated phenomenon but a group venture similar to the kangani schemes operating concurrently to Malaya and Ceylon (present-day Sri Lanka).

The Protector, having satisfied himself that Reetburrun and his companions had indeed worked out their indentures, gave them a certificate to present before the police at the port. It read:

> This is to certify that the Immigrants mentioned in the margin late in the service of Mr. Guthrie leave the colony at their own expense to proceed to Calcutta and that there is nothing in the records of this Office to prevent their leaving the Colony.[79]

The Inspector General appended a note to the effect that they were permitted to depart in the *Regina*, and the men were embarked on 2 March 1855. In this case, the satisfactory work history of the group assisted their application to leave, and their ability to pay their own passages demonstrates the financial capacity of an increasing number of migrants to terminate their indentures. The recognition that a rising number of Indians were returning home after a few years abroad marked a significant break for employers from the labour in perpetuity which they had expected from slaves, and they made concerted efforts to lengthen the labour requirement from indentured workers. Eventually a ten-year 'industrial residence' was demanded of immigrants in an attempt to stem the return migration streams, but overall one-third of all arrivals made it back to the country of their birth.[80]

Notes

1. Tinker, 1974, *passim*; Swan 1991.
2. See, for example, Ramasamy, 1992.
3. Haraksingh, 1987.
4. van Onselen, 1980; Saunders, 1982; Crisp, 1984.
5. Haraksingh, 1987; Ramnarine, 1987.
6. Chakrabarty, 1989; Prakash, 1992; Haynes and Prakash, 1991.
7. Lal, 1983: 112–14, and Mesthrie, 1991: 204–6, have led the way in the study and interpretation of folksongs sung by indentured migrants.
8. Early engagements followed a pattern set by John Shaw Sampson's contract with 151 tribals: Bengal Public Proceedings 13/11 Prinsep to Chief Magistrate Calcutta, 1 Dec. 1831, encl. Copy of Agreement. For details of later contracts see Indian Public Proceedings 186/75 Legislative Dept, 5 Apr. 1837; CO 167/253 Gomm to Stanley, 12 Apr. 1844.
9. Royal Commissioners' Report Chapter XVII, pp. 284–329.
10. Parliamentary Papers 1859 XXI (31–1) Stevenson to Lytton, 5 Aug. 1858; Evidence given before the Royal Commissioners 1873 vol. II, Q. 941, 6723–5. Contracts were initially signed for one year at a time. This was extended to three years in 1849 and to five years in 1863: Royal Commissioners' Report Chapter XVI, pp. 256–84.
11. From an article in the *British Emancipator*, quoted in Saha, 1970: 108.
12. These depositions are taken from the Madras Public Proceedings: the Deposition of Moottoosawmy, an Inhabitant of Nathum, a Village in the District of Trichinopoly,

General Police Office, Madras, 12 Aug. 1842; the Deposition of Paravadee, General Police Office, Madras, 13 Aug. 1842; the Information of Teeroovenga-dom, arrived from the Isle of France on 8 Aug. 1842, General Police Office, Madras, 12 Aug. 1842.

13. For a discussion of the confrontation of the rural labourer with the capitalist working day see Thompson, 1967; Cooper, 1992.

14. Full details of the experiences of women migrants like Lakshmi, Elizabeth and Bibee Juhooram are given in Carter, 1994. The episode in which Lakshmi was struck with a shoe would have been particularly shocking, since in India striking someone with a shoe, made of leather, is a defilement, a pollution of that person in caste terms, and not just an act of brutality. This act would have been remembered, since above all it would have been taken to symbolize the employer's contempt.

15. Parliamentary Papers 1841 (45) Examination of Karoo before the Calcutta Commission of Enquiry, p. 74.

16. Parliamentary Papers 1841 (427) Report of J.P. Grant, Examination of Gooroodyal, 7 Dec. 1840.

17. Parliamentary Papers 1836 (180) Response of Bickajee to the Government Notice concerning Indian labourers, 28 June 1836.

18. Mangru, 1987a: 42.

19. Saha, 1970: 116.

20. Quoted in Mangru, 1987a: 161. The language in this case is markedly similar to European representations of the pleading Caribbean slave. Was the material prepared by the recipient for a humanitarian public, or was this an accurate rendition of the creole English of indentured labourers in Guiana? Reformers in Mauritius had no tradition of slave narratives to work with, and the petitions of immigrants tended to be expressed either in the occasionally creolized French of the petition writer or in formal English.

21. Oral deposition of an indentured labour in Fiji, in Kelly, 1992: 258.

22. PA 50 Petition of V. Pydayaya and others, 10 Apr. 1882.

23. This information was obtained from the Immigration Registers: PE 55, PE 81, PE 92B, PE 115 and PE 125.

24. PA 50 Immigration Department Note and Note of J.F.T., Protector, n.d.

25. PA 14 Petition of Ramachetty and others, 3 Feb. 1873.

26. PE 19 Immigration Register of Bhurtun showed that he had arrived from Calcutta, in July 1843, aged 26.

27. PA 43 Petition of Bhurtun, 20 Sept. 1880.

28. PA 43 Immigration Department Note, n.d.

29. PB 15 Statement of Colundavaloo, 15 May 1872.

30. PE 109 'Theresa', 1865.

31. PB 15 Statement of Colundaveloo, 15.5.72; Note re entry in Deserters' Book.

32. PA 24 Letter of Moojaralli, 28 July 1876.

33. PA 24 Emigration Agent to Protector of Emigrants, Calcutta, 10 Aug. 1876.

34. PA 24 Protector of Emigrants to the Emigration Agent, 15 Aug. 1876; Emigration Agent, Calcutta, to Protector of Immigrants, Mauritius, 6 Sep. 1876.

35. PE 117 'Allum Gheer', 1870.

36. PL 2 Venkata Subbiah to Immigration Office, 29 Sep. 1902. Venkata was described as a Keruma by caste, from Cudappa: PE 153.

37. PL 2 J.F.T. Memorandum, 2 Oct. 1902.

38. PL 19 Statement of Debi Ram before Protector of Immigrants, Beau Bassin Central Prison, 8 Mar. 1906.

39. PL 19 Colonial Secretary to Protector of Immigrants, 4 Apr. 1906. Further details of Debi Ram are given in Ch. 2.

40. Mesthrie, 1991: 204.

41. Lal, 1983: 112–14.

42. Sanadhaya, quoted in Gillion, 1962: 122.

43. PA 14 Petition of Coupen and Vythee, 4 Sep. 1873.

44. PB 15 Deposition of Gooroopen Goordyal, 30 May 1871.

45. PA 206 Petition of Suruppeet, No. 95,050, 16 Oct. 1899.

46. Parliamentary Papers 1845 XXXI (641) First and Second Reports of the Committee of Council for Labour; CO 167/252 Bourgault du Coudray, Pitot, Hunter, Barbe, Koenig and Harel to the Governor, 16 Mar. 1844.

47. Parliamentary Papers 1847 XXXIX (325) Ordinance 22 of 1847.

48. Royal Commissioner's Report, p. 330.

49. Twenty Ninth Report of the General Land and Emigration Commissioners; Blue Book Report 1868 Part III, p. 44.

50. Mr Kerr to the Governor, 2 Dec. 1867, Annexure 1 Appendix F 22.

51. Mr Kerr to the Governor, 16 Dec. 1867. Kerr admitted his part in drawing up the petitions of both Pandoo and Mootoosamy in this letter.

52. Petition of Pandoo, Apr. 1867, Royal Commissioners' Report Appendix F22.

53. Mr Kerr to the Governor, 16 Dec. 1867.

54. Mr Kerr to the Governor, 2 Dec. 1867, Annexure 1.

55. Sholto James Douglas to H.E. the Governor, 29 Nov. 1867.

56. Memorandum, H.N.D. Beyts, 9 Dec. 1867.

57. Mr A. Barkly to Mr Kerr, 12 Dec. 1867.

58. PA 26 Petition of Govinden, 18 Dec. 1875.

59. Adamson, 1972: 156; Mangru, 1987a: 182.

60. PA 22 Petition of Tuholoo *et al.*, 29 July 1874.

61. PE 43 and PC 559B 'Shah Allum', 1 Jan. 1854. Tuholoo had arrived as a 9-year-old. He was a Chamar, as was Gunjun, who was aged 17. Both were from the village of Puchouree in Ghazipur.

62. PA 14 Petition of Rungen, 18 May 1873.

63. PA 14 Immigration Department Note, 22.5.73.

64. PA 14 Petition of Dwareeka and Goordyal.

65. PA 22 Immigration Department Note, n.d.

66. CO 167/529 Sir A. Gordon to the Earl of Kimberley, 17 Nov. 1871.

67. J.A. Robertson, Report to Major General Selby Smyth, President, Police Commission.

68. PA 26 Petition of Chumbhee, 9 Apr. 1872.

69. PA 26 Immigration Department Note n.d. For the full immigration details of Chumbhee see PE 8.

70. PA 22 Petition of Newah and Bagnea, 19 Nov. 1874.

71. Parliamentary Papers 1841 (45) Examination of Suboo, Calcutta Commission of Enquiry, 16 Nov. 1838, p. 73.

72. PA 14 Petition of Potun, 15 Aug. 1872.

73. PA 14 Immigration Department Note, 28.8.1872.

74. PE 60 'Iskendershaw', 27.9.1912.

75. PA 14 Petition of Curpen, 2 May 1872.

76. PA 14 Stipendiary Magistrate's Note, 6.5.1872. Curpen had arrived as a 10-year-old from Tanjore in January 1851: PC 419.
77. PA 4 Petition of Reetburrun *et al.*, 22 Feb. 1855.
78. PE 10 'Boadecia', 24.11.43; PE 23 'Aube', 1843; PE 32 'Punjab', 1849.
79. Immigration Office, Port Louis, 22 Feb. 1855, Hugon.
80. For details of numbers of Indians departing at their own or government expense 1856–71, see MA Annual Immigration Report 1871 Table Q.

CHAPTER FOUR

The personal lives of Indian migrants

The domestic and family relationships of indentured labourers have generated a great deal of debate, to surprisingly little effect. Since Hugh Tinker's depiction of Indian women migrants as 'single, broken creatures', historians have continued to brandish a barrage of official stereotypes designed to demonstrate that women were either 'liberated' or 'coerced' into leading sexually abandoned or non-conformist lives.[1] This occurred alongside measures taken in most of the colonial states to reassert male rights over women, through the imposition of legislation which recognized Indian marriages. Recent research has not helped to take the debate much further: Kelly's discussion of sexual violence on Fiji plantations and Mohapatra's analysis of 'wife chopping' in the Caribbean reiterate all the hackneyed clichés of the Indian women's 'wide eyed acceptance' of sexual abuse and frequent changes of sexual partners, illustrated by quotations such as 'I took a Papa', without offering a convincing deconstruction of this material.[2] Kelly asserts that in Fiji the European operators of indenture had no need to 'reproduce coolie labour, [nor] did they need an Indian marriage or family system. Coolie labour lasted for five years and was replaced by further recruiting'. However, there is ample evidence elsewhere which suggests that colonial labour exporters were concerned to encourage family immigration and Indian settlement. Statistical analysis of indentured workers' marital relationships also reveals the stability of the family unit overseas, and it would be useful if future assessments of women under indenture attempted to present a more than one-dimensional account of this issue.[3]

It is clear that, because the indenture system represented both an organized migration and a disciplined labour regime, these factors together acted to limit and constrain family settlement. The workforce solicited by planters and mobilized by colonial states essentially reflected the labour demands of plantation economies, and there was always a majority of men on the 'coolie ships'. Similarly, living and working conditions on estates, with the threat of prison for poor performers and the difficulties of earning a family wage, created a fragile environment for the development of a settled domestic life. Nevertheless, the

137

recognition that a long-term labour force called for family immigration ultimately overrode the more short-term requirements of employers and resulted in the increasing recruitment of Indian women, with the establishment of fixed ratios for batches of migrants. Thus, from a 13 per cent ratio of females to males migrating to Mauritius in 1843, up to 40 per cent and above were arriving in the several colonial destinations by the 1860s.[4] The sex-ratio requirement was an externally imposed device to increase the presence of Indian women on estates (see Chapter 1), but emigration agents also received instructions from individual colonial importers to the effect that female recruits should be below the age of 30 (35 in some cases; that is, marriageable and fertile). At another level, migrants were forging their own arrangements for the organization of their domestic lives: contracting marriage alliances – often with jehaji bhai shipmates – for their children; seeking suitable wives from amongst new immigrants; even, in an increasing number of cases, returning to India to collect relatives or deputing others to do so, thus creating out of indenture a sub-stream of chain migrants to the various colonies.

The documents collected in this section offer a perspective of Indian migration which differs from the emphasis on violence and instability articulated by Victorian officials and missionaries, and reflects instead the less sensationalist, more mundane but probably more representative tribulations and aspirations of individuals and families on the colonial plantations. The misfortunes of men and women caught up in the harsher aspects of indenture, such as the individual who lost his wife to another whilst he was in prison, or parents whose children were convicted of a trifling offence and banished to a 'reformatory' or consigned to an 'orphan asylum', as well as the efforts of migrants to establish a family life in their new setting and to maintain contacts with relatives, were all part of the social fabric of the Indian labour diaspora.

The Marital Life of Overseas Indians

Colonial states did not simply enact legislation to control migrants; they also reacted to demands for change from Indians who objected to what they saw as the loss of authority in their personal lives. Thus the petition of the Telegu migrants in 1856 (see Chapter 2) complaining about the lack of protection for their womenfolk was undoubtedly a factor in the subsequent legalization of Indian marriages in Mauritius in that year. At the same time the abduction of wives was made an imprisonable offence.[5] In Guyana, somewhat later, similar demands were made for control over insubordinate wives. The following letter was written to the Argosy by one Mahomed Baksh:

When a wife deserts a husband or a husband a wife we are helpless at law. If a man or woman go to the police or the magistrate or the Immigration Department the first question asked is: 'Were you married by English law?' and if the reply is in the negative the applicant is told, 'We can do nothing for you'. The faithless one is thus at liberty to do what she likes in the violation of the religious marriage vows, and the aggrieved one, if he is a poor, ignorant East Indian labourer, then sets thinking how he can achieve his own revenge with results which the criminal annals of the colony show. I know many of the atrocities for which East Indians are convicted, sent to prison and hanged would be prevented were the law but to recognise the validity of marriages according to the law and custom of East Indians.[6]

Ultimately, colonial officials and immigrant men came to share a common cause in the restitution of legal rights over Indian spouses. Of course this was not in the interests of those women who attempted to leave husbands they claimed had systematically ill-treated them. Once Indian marriage legislation had been passed in individual colonies, Indian women could find that they were summarily ordered to return to those men. Others were able to derive some benefit from the new laws, gaining maintenance in cases of desertion, and establishing their rights in cases where spouses had committed bigamy or were cohabiting with another partner.[7]

Along with new laws to regulate the relationship between male and female immigrants came new obligations. In order to distinguish legally married couples from men and women who arrived in a cohabiting relationship – in such cases women were inevitably referred to as the 'concubines' of the men they accompanied – marriage certificates were granted to couples claiming to be man and wife.[8] In addition, any individual wishing to contract marriage was, certainly in Mauritius, required to obtain a 'Certificate of Non-marriage' from the Protector's office, to prove his or her freedom from existing contractual obligations. A written application for such a certificate is the subject of Jhowry's petition to the Acting Protector in 1875:

The humble Petition of Jhowry no. 272,435 of Hospital street, Port Louis, servant.

Respectfully sheweth:

*   That since eight years ago I arrived in this colony and have never contracted any marriage up to this day. That I am now of thirty one years of age and have never contracted any marriage. That I am now to contract a marriage with one Deeleea no. 171,209 an old female immigrant of 1856, who has no father and mother in this colony, and has twenty four years of age.*

*   Therefore your Petitioner comes respectfully before your honor and prays that you will be pleased to deliver me a certificate in order to authorise the Registrar General of the Civil Status of this town of Port Louis to celebrate my marriage with the said Deeleea.*

*   And as in duty bound your Petitioner*
*   will ever pray*

*   X Petitioner's cross.*[9]

Interestingly, his statement in the petition conflicts with evidence from the Immigration Register that he had arrived not eight but fifteen years earlier from his native Gya, in 1860, aged 26. The recorded age of migrants was always somewhat suspect, resulting as much from guesswork on the part of the clerk as from painstaking enquiry, and perhaps Jhowry really was 31 as he said, and not the 41 years the register gave him; or perhaps the discrepancy reveals an attempt on the petitioner's part to reduce his age by a decade, possibly to render his suit more attractive to his 24-year-old intended bride! We have no record of Jhowry's eventual marriage but he did settle permanently in Mauritius, for his death at Port Louis is recorded in 1892.[10]

Jhowry's case reveals the importance of key officials, such as the Protector of Immigrants and his staff, who were called upon to research the marital status of immigrants before providing certificates. Indians who had a problem with their ticket found themselves effectively unable to function as individuals. Thus Carpanen could not marry because of a discrepancy in the age listed on his current and former tickets.[11] It was the immigrant number which defined the Indian in Mauritius and elsewhere, establishing his or her existence and regulating future actions on the basis of date and status at arrival.

In some cases, the intervention of the Immigration Department staff in marital issues amounts almost to a required tacit consent before an individual could marry. This was certainly the case for men who sought a wife from amongst the new female immigrants awaiting allocation at the depot. In contrast to the West Indies and most other labour-importing colonies, in Mauritius Indian women were not engaged as indentured labourers. As such they were theoretically free to take up work as ayahs or domestic servants, to rejoin relatives already in Mauritius, or to accompany friends made on board the ships to a particular plantation. In practice, women who were not offered employment, or had no kin in Mauritius, either were rendered dependent on the men who travelled with them – obliged to search for a 'protector' and to rely on him for subsistence on the island – or had to wait at the depot for a suitable man to present himself. In this way, the recourse to Mauritius was for many Indian women not a search for work at all but rather a marriage migration. This was not as desperate a measure as it might seem: for young widows migration offered the chance to re-enter a social role as a wife and mother.[12]

Single male immigrants in Mauritius quickly learnt of the arrival of un-accompanied women from their caste or region in India, but before going to the depot to claim them, they were obliged to submit a written application to the Protector and to obtain his prior approval as to their suitability. The number of petitions from men soliciting wives are therefore voluminous and provide in themselves a fascinating insight into contemporary perceptions of marriage and the role of the female spouse. Kumally's overriding requirements were for a woman to take care of his motherless children and to cook his breakfast in the morning, as he explained to the Protector:

Sir,

Being in want of a wife and having led to believe that there are many Indian women lately arrived without husbands, I beg that you will be good enough, as our Protector in Mauritius to facilitate me in getting one as I find in the impossibility of getting my

*breakfast cooked in the morning on account of the distance sometime I have to work, and
to take care of my orphan children.*

Hoping that my demand will be taken into your most favourable consideration.

> *I have the honor to be Sir
> your most obedient servant*
>
> *X Kumally, no. 306,519.*[13]

This latter need was not as trivial as it might sound, for the working day on a
nineteenth-century sugar plantation habitually began at 4 a.m. The estates
were large, and the means of transport limited; small bands of men would be
working in different fields, some of which could be several miles away. A break
for 'breakfast' at between 8 and 11 a.m. was the general rule, and as substantial
a meal as resources would allow (that is, of rice and dhal) was consumed at this
time.[14] In any event, we do not know whether Kumally, of the Naupit caste,
found a suitable wife, as this is not recorded on his immigration entry. He
remained in Mauritius until the end of his life, however, dying in 1883 at the
age of 43.[15]

Some migrants who had wives or fiancées in India, often those who had
served out their terms of indenture and determined to remain overseas,
endeavoured instead to bring relatives to the colony. Women, requested by
word of mouth or by letter to emigrate, had first to negotiate the obstacles of
arriving unimpeded at the correct Emigration Depot at the port of departure,
pass the requisite selection tests for embarkation, and then find the whereabouts of their husband in the colony. Inevitably some failed, and were obliged
to seek the protection of other men. Overworked depot staff could hardly be
expected to trace the current residence of relatives themselves, and immigrants
developed their own networks to find out when relatives had disembarked.[16]
Then the task of proving a pre-existing relationship before local officials began.
Boodun was refused permission to visit his alleged wife in the depot and was
consequently obliged to present a formal petition to the Protector:

> *The humble Petition of Boodun no. 258,928 an old immigrant of the district of Moka,
> proprietor –*
>
> *Respectfully sheweth:*
>
> *That your Petitioner's wife named Krissah arrived from India sometime ago and is
> now in the Immigration Depot. That as soon as your Petitioner was informed that his
> said wife was at the immigration Depot, he went there merely to see her, but he was told
> that he could not do so, without your order.*
>
> *Wherefore your Petitioner humbly prays that you may be pleased to authorise him to
> see his wife Krissah that she may come and reside with him.*
>
> *And as in duty bound your Petitioner shall ever pray.*
>
> *X Petitioner's cross.*[17]

Boodun, a Chamar from Gya who had arrived in 1859, had waited fifteen years
for his alleged wife, but the immigration department minuted on 6 February

1874 'this man acknowledged that the woman was not his wife but that she came from the same part of India, and he would like to have her'. Whether this was caused by lack of proof – many Indians at the time celebrated a religious but not a civil wedding – or whether Krissah was indeed simply a girl from his home region we do not know, or whether the couple ever married. Boodhun returned to India six years later.

As Biharis, Boodun and Kurmally – who arrived from Arrah in 1864 as a 24-year-old – had a good chance of finding women from their own region: they belonged to the largest caste grouping in Mauritius and from the region which had sent the greatest number of immigrants. The efforts made by immigrants to find a partner who conformed as closely as possible to their own regional and caste background, and the extent to which endogamous practices were diluted or filtered in the overseas context, form a fascinating sub-text to the story of indenture. Lal's statistical survey of emigration certificates in Fiji has enabled some conclusions to be drawn about the family status of migrants and the extent of caste endogamy or so-called depot marriages. However, these data deal only with migrants at their point of entry into colonial societies. Discussion of marriages of first- and second-generation Indians overseas in the nineteenth century has been conducted at a purely speculative level.[18] Marriage patterns in the overseas context can, however, be analysed more systematically from civil status data – and in the Mauritian context from Immigration Registers – to estimate the changing significance of caste and regional origin in the selection of a marriage partner among first-generation immigrants. I have in this way been able to frame some tentative conclusions regarding the marriage patterns of overseas Indians in Mauritius. In general, Indians marrying in the colony in the mid-nineteenth century contracted caste-exogamous but region-endogamous marriages; however, some single-caste groupings, such as north Indian Kurmis and Koeris, were large enough to enable endogamous marriages to be contracted right through the period of indenture; a practice which, although weakened, has led to the continuing existence of some major castes today.[19]

In many cases, however, the indenture system itself was the cause of social dislocation and the breakdown of family relationships, as the sad case of Rutnag testifies. Imprisoned for four years, he found on his return that his wife had gone to live with another man. In his petition he calls first for the restitution of his wife and, failing that, for the return of his son and goods. Knowing that legal proof of his marital status was required, he obtained a copy of his marriage certificate and of the certificate of birth of his son Moungta. His petition to the Protector declared:

Sir,

> *The undersigned Rutnag begs most respectfully to state: That he was married in Bombay to one Sacoo and had by her a male child named Moungta.*

That since their arrival in this island, they have been acknowledged by all their friends and acquaintances as husband and wife.

That he was sentenced to four years hard labour and during the time that he was in confinement, the said Sacoo carried away all his furnitures and had been living in a state of adultery with one Rama employed on the Bras D'eau Estate, Flacq.

That all amicable means used by him have been hitherto fruitless.

Under those circumstances he comes to solicit your interference with a view that you may be pleased to take the necessary steps to compel the said Sacoo, his lawful wife to return to the conjugal roof, else she should give back the said Moungta to him together with his articles of furnitures.

Insisting that you will take his request under your serious consideration.

> He has the honor to be
> *Sir,*
> *Your most obedient servant*
>
> *X Rutnag.*[20]

In cases such as that of Rutnag it was comparatively easy for the immigration staff to proceed. They generally forwarded the petitioner with the requisite documents and a covering letter to his local magistrate. From then it was a relatively simple matter to apprehend the woman and physically escort her back to her husband's home. Where, however, overseers or sirdars were involved with the wives of labourers, not only would redress not be forthcoming, but the complainant could find himself punished. When Budhu, of Blairmont estate, Guiana, complained to the Immigration Agent General (equivalent to the Protector) that an overseer was having an affair with his wife, he was sent to the estate manager. 'The manager read the paper,' said Buhdu, 'and immediately gave me fourteen days' notice'.[21] Where men were unable to gain redress from their employers or the law, they could take matters into their own hands, resulting in the murder of a spouse. To take just one example from the many cases of wife-killing across the indenture diaspora, from Natal, Mulwa's statement as to why he ended the life of Nootini is sadly typical:

Sahabdeen said if the woman would cook for him he would give her clothing – Sahabdeen gave me to the extent of 9s. I returned 8s. Sahabdeen asked me for the balance I owed and said if I did not pay I must leave . . . I said where were we I my wife and child to go where we to go to the bush – Sahabdeen then said I want you to go away but not the woman and child . . . I went to Mr Townsend reported the matter and asked for a lodging – Mr Townsend did not give us a house . . . I killed her because she went with other men.[22]

Other men took the option of suicide when they were abandoned by their wives. After the self-inflicted death of Ammakanna's husband in Fiji around 1917, she explained: 'we were married five years ago. We had quarrelled constantly. He had complained constantly of my shortcomings as a housekeeper. He placed a rope on the beam of our room a fortnight ago when I expostulated with him'.[23]

Women who wished to avoid a forced return to their husbands needed to be well out of reach of the long arm of the law. 'Lachoomoo' Chengelayen achieved that by running away with a painter, Ramalingum, to the neighbouring island of Reunion. Her marriage with Vencatachellum Appoo had been celebrated in Mauritius, when Vencatachellum, a south Indian from Thanjavur, was 30, and resident in the colony some twelve years.[24] It lasted four years before the wife departed, leaving their child behind but taking money and jewellery which Vencatachellum represented to be his own, as his petition explained:

> *The humble Petition, of Vencatachellum Appoo no. 308,547 residing in the District of Port Louis, employed in the Hindoo church, in Nicolay road.*
> *Most respectfully sheweth:*
> *That your Petitioner is married since the 17th February 1876 before the officer of the Civil Status office of Port Louis, to one Latchoomoo Chengelayen; That on the 16th day of April 1877 a child was borne from their marriage.*
> *That on the 13th day of August 1880 the said Latchoomoo Chengelayen absconded from Mauritius with one Ramsamy Ramalingum a painter per French mail steamer 'Godavery' which left on the thirteenth day of August 1880.*
> *That your Petitioner has received information that the said Latchoomoo Chengeloyen and the said Ramsamy Ramalingum have landed at 'Reunion' Island and that the said Latchoomoo Chengelayen is now living and committing adultery with this latter.*
> *That your Petitioner must also inform your Honor that the said Latchoomoo Chengelayen when she left Mauritius abandoned her said child who is only about three years of age and moreover she took away with her from a wooden box, the property of your Petitioner, a sum of one hundred dollars composed of one hundred rupees and ten sovereigns of five dollars each, four gold earrings and one gold ring.*
> *Your Petitioner hopes that your Honor will take into favorable consideration all the facts herein before set forth and will take such measures as will be consistent with the international law passed between England and France and will at the same time protect the interests of your unfortunate Petitioner by causing the said Latchoomoo Chengelayen to be arrested at Bourbon and to be sent back to Mauritius*
> *and as in duty bound your Petitioner will ever pray.*[25]

His sophisticated petition, calling upon the Protector to extradite his wife from Reunion as per international agreements between Britain and France, met with a cool reception: an official at the Immigration Department reported on 1 September 1880: 'I have laid this application before the Protector, who, after carefully considering this request, is of opinion that he cannot assist the applicant in any way whatever'.[26]

Despite this judgement, colonial laws generally appeared to give Indian men the means to compel their wives to return to them irrespective of the attendant circumstances. However, the legal spouses of wayward males could also claim their dues. When Lutchmee was deserted by her husband Marday, she petitioned the Protector to demand her right to financial support from him:

Sir,

The humble petition of Lutchmee no. 449 residing at Flacq on the Bonne Mere Estate

Most Respectfully sheweth:

That your Petitioner is legally married with one Marday, a labourer on the said Estate Bonne Mere in her native country as her act deposited in your office. That your Petitioner is ill-treated by the said Marday and he has turned your Petitioner out of his house on account of another concubine residing on the same estate and same house since this last ten months and your Petitioner has no means of subsistance, nor any family in this colony to support her than her said husband whom your Petitioner complained today.

That the said Marday earns from the said Estate Bonne Mere a monthly salary of Rs 20. Your Petitioner has already applied to the Stipendiary Magistrate of Flacq to have a complaint lodged against the said Marday – she has been informed that she cannot be granted of her demand without an order of the Protector of Immigrants.

Therefore your Petitioner hereby humbly submit that you may be pleased to grant an order to your Petitioner in order that a complaint be lodged gratis against the said Marday before the Stipendiary Magistrate of Flacq.

And in duty bound your Petitioner will
ever pray

Mark x Latchmee No. 449.[27]

Upon enquiry the Immigration Department found that Lutchmee *was* legally married to Marday: both had migrated together from Thanjavur via Madras in August 1861 as a married couple; he was 30 and she was 22 years old at the time. At nearly 50, Marday had now taken up with another woman. The Immigration Department in Mauritius decided that 'a complaint note to the District Magistrate be given to this woman. She complains that her husband has expelled her from the conjugal roof'.[28] Once again, the office was willing to intercede because the parties concerned were proven, by its own records, to be legally married, and the Protector issued such evidence to be used as the basis of legal proceedings against the defaulting or wayward spouse. It seems unlikely, however, that Lutchmee was able to obtain satisfactory redress: she returned to India only eight weeks later, on 30 December 1880, indicating perhaps that, without her husband's support, she was unable to maintain herself. Marday, for his part, would not have been able to provide for her much longer: he died in the Flacq district of Mauritius on 27 March 1881.[29]

Reshmee, also abandoned by her husband after many years overseas, found a different solution: she managed to support herself by obtaining employment. However, her estranged husband, despite living with another woman, found this intolerable and, as she deponed in her petition, came to her workplace, where he assaulted her verbally and physically. Women such as Reshmee, despite being abandoned, found that this did not prevent them from continued harassment, and it was to ask for 'protection and advice' as to how to deal with the situation that she wrote to the Immigration Office in Mauritius:

The humble petition of Reshmee married to one Babjur at Calcutta, arrived in this colony with her husband since about 12 years by the ship named Allum Gheer.

Most respectfully sheweth:
    That your petitioner, one year after arriving in this colony, her said husband has abandoned her and has been living at 'Terre Rouge' district of Pamplemousses and has taken another wife at Terre Rouge.
    That when your petitioner began to have an employment, her husband came and make a great noise where she worked and struck her where she is seen.
    Wherefore your petitioner comes on the name of God, as you are the Protector of Immigrants ask your protection and your advice.
    And your petitioner as in duty bound will ever pray.[30]

The Department found from its records that she was a *bona fide* married woman, having arrived in September 1868, aged 15, with her 22-year-old husband Buljur Roy. The matter was therefore referred to the District Magistrate of Pamplemousses, who was asked to 'see if some assistance can be afforded to her in the way of prosecuting her husband if the facts stated by her are correct'. His reply, however, was that:

> the petitioner is undoubtedly in an unfortunate position, but I do not see that anything can be done for her. She complains of *general* ill-treatment on the part of her husband without precising any particular fact. The fact is she would wish to have a divorce and this she must apply for before the Supreme Court.

The Protector advised her of this accordingly.[31] Reshmee subsequently remained another ten years in Mauritius, eventually returning to India in 1890; her husband had left one year earlier.[32] She and her husband, Buljur Roy, are pictured in Figures 4.1a and 4.1b.

In practice, then, legal understandings of the obligations of married couples were more often applied to men who sought to secure their rights over women who deserted them than vice versa. The Protector's role was limited by the sheer difficulty of tracing women who had left their husbands, but in some cases even women about to leave the colonies to which they had emigrated were stopped at the depots, and a Protector's note was used effectively to force the wife to return to her husband. Where women were the wronged party, redress was more likely to be limited to securing their rights to financial support, and as the cases above show, the likelihood of this was doubtful. The difficulties experienced by Indian men in regaining control over runaway women, and their ensuing complaints, lent fuel to the stereotypes which circulated of immoral female behaviour. Thus the comment of the Indian woman in Trinidad who told Sarah Morton, a missionary, 'when the last ship came in I took a Papa. I will keep him as long as he treats me well. If he does not treat me well I shall send him off at once' has become, through repetition, a standard depiction of women under indenture.[33] The chaste Kunti, whilst equally idealized, represents the other, less easily expressed dimension of the female experience of indenture. Kunti's story, as told by Totaram Sanadhya, was that of a young woman who resisted an attempted rape by the overseer:

On 10th April 1912, on a banana plantation called 'Tabu Kere', the overseer isolated Kunti from the rest and told her to cut grass at a remote spot where there would be no witnesses and even the screams could not be heard. Then the overseer and sardar arrived there to rape her. The sardar tried to hold Kunti's hands after the overseer threatened her. Kunti got out of his grip and jumped into a nearby river. By some miracle a boy named Jaidev was nearby with his dinghy. Kunti was saved from drowning, Jaidev got her into the dinghy and took her across.[34]

There are thus examples of women who successfully resisted sexual advances as well as of those who were forced through powerlessness to succumb. In

Figure 4.1(a) & Figure 4.1(b) Both of these immigrants were high-caste – Buljur Roy was listed as a Kshatria and Reshmee as a Rajput – and they migrated together to Mauritius in 1868. Reshmee was 15 years old at that time and Buljur was 22. They were from the same village in Gorakhpur. He left for India in 1889 and she returned in 1890. Their photographs were taken in 1882 and 1888. Source: PE 117, PG 27 and PG 18.

Mauritius, Bibee Juhooram underwent imprisonment and deportation when she repelled the advances of her employer. In Natal, Vellach complained to the Protector when she suffered a similar experience:

> *About ten days ago whilst in my master's bedroom regulating it, he came in, striking his*
> *pocket and saying he would give me 3 [rand] if I were to lie with him, as the mistress and*
> *her family had gone to town. I refused saying that my husband would beat me. He said*
> *he would not tell him.*[35]

She asked to be transferred to another employer but this, as in Bibee's case, was refused.

It is in the depositions of Indian men and the writings of European overseers and officials that we generally hear of the 'immorality' of women under indenture. Perhaps the reality of indenture for the majority of women can be found in their songs, in which women comment wryly on the stresses and strains of the marital relationship, and on the small daily struggles of their work and home lives:

> *Alas, I will have to run away with another man,*
> *For my beloved has turned his mind away from me.*
> *How eagerly, as I cook rice and dal,*
> *do I pour the ghee.*
> *But as soon as we sit for dinner, you start quarrelling*
> *And my heart is weary of you.*
> *I put hot fire in the basket,*
> *Carefully I make the bed.*
> *But as soon as we lie down to rest,*
> *you start quarrelling*
> *My heart is weary of you.*[36]

From Natal comes this telling song describing the lack of communication between an Indian couple:

> *You've painted your lips red*
> *and made your hair all curly*
> *Why, O wife?*
>
> *You go out walking down the roads*
> *I shall do the dishes myself*
> *You dab powder on your face*
> *and wear your sari back-to-front*
> *You've abandoned family traditions . . .*
>
> *My husband comes home high with dagga*
> *and raises havoc*
> *Should I say something*
> *then he makes eyes at me*
> *My heart has become disenchanted.*[37]

Women were mothers and daughters as well as wives, and a further dimension to the indenture experience can be gained from the study of family lives through the petitions, letters and oral evidence of migrants.

Family Relationships under Indenture

Given the evident limitations on suitable marriage partners in the overseas context, many Indian families contracted marriage alliances for their children at an early age, to ensure their future. The relative paucity of women of marriageable age in overseas indenture settlements until towards the end of the nineteenth century, when 'colonial born' Indians began to outnumber new immigrants in most of the territories where they settled, meant that a woman of the right age and caste was a relatively rare commodity. Many Indian families overseas replaced the traditional demand for dowry from the prospective bride with a bride-price requirement from the groom's family. Thus the possession of a marriageable daughter was a distinct asset. Parents could find themselves subject to competition for their daughters, and in such circumstances the allure of money might prove more tempting than an earlier alliance contracted on the basis of kin networks or caste suitability.

The petition of Jeeachee complains that, after having spent a considerable sum on the marriage of her two sons, the mother of the two daughters to whom they were given in a Hindu ceremony would not confirm the marriage with a civil wedding:

Honorable Protector

I have the honor to represent you most respectfully that in the lifetime of my husband Booton (deceased two years ago) an agreement was made between us Roopnaraine, Booton and me (Jeeachee) of the same caste and creed, in presence of the witnesses; whose names are written in margin, that our children of both families should when of age marry each other; that some months after, as our customary way require it; for the celebration of the marriage of our children Jaunkypersad two and twenty years old and Aunauth twenty now; according to our rite, both creoles of this island, with the two daughters of Roopnaraine also creole: Booton and I spent about three hundred rupees for the general expenses thereof and which Roopnaraine promised to return or reimburse to us if ever his two daughters should change their natural dispositions.

That now it happened notwithstanding my reiterated claims to have the same marriage legally confirmed by your local law; he (Roopnaraine) declines to accede to my request and wishes. Wherefore I deem it my earliest duty to call first upon your protectorship in order that he may be pleased to prescribe me the way to get that sum of money which will now ease or better my poor and difficult way of living with my children or to address me to the competent Magistrate to that matter.

I remain Honorable Protector
your most obedient humble servant

    Jeeachee.[38]

In this case, however, an official in the Immigration Department noted:

I do not see how the Protector is to interfere in this case. Petitioner had better place her case in the hands of an attorney, but at the same time to be warned her case is a hopeless one – and to which – as she has stated it – there is no redress.[39]

The plea of this widow, for whom the expenses of the intended marriages had proved ruinous, reveals the continuing recourse of immigrants to the jurisdiction of the Protector in these domestic issues, in the absence of a powerful sanction from within the Indian community to punish such behaviour. Unfortunately the Protector could not effectively take on the role of arbiter: he was notably unwilling to initiate any action which properly belonged to the domain of the court. However, the immigration office could, as in this case, dispense some advice to petitioners to dissuade them from embarking on costly litigation where the chance of success was small.

Given the scarcity value of women in the early phase of the Indian diaspora, male relatives in particular sought control over their daughters in the same way as they endeavoured to restrict the mobility of their wives.[40] Arnaselum's petition noted that the District Magistrate of Plaines Wilhems in Mauritius had already ordered one Khodabacuss to return his daughter to their house. However, the couple had run away together a second time:

The Humble Petition of Arnaselum of the district of Plaine Wilhems at the place called Rose Hill, without profession.

Respectfully sheweth:
That since ten months ago my daughter Sobrathun no. 361,226 has been absconded from my house, and went with one Khodabacuss, that since that aforesaid ten months I have lodged a complaint before the District Magistrate of Plaine Wilhems in order to have my said daughter back to me. The said Magistrate has ordered the said Khodabacuss to return me back my said daughter.

That since that time the said Khodabacuss has absconded again my said daughter.

Wherefore your Petitioner comes respectfully before your honor and prays that you will take in consideration the foregoing petition, and to authorise the said District Magistrate to recall the said Khodabacuss and my said daughter Sobrathun again before him, and order my said daughter to come in my house.

And as in duty bound your Petitioner will ever pray

X
Petitioner's cross.[41]

By implication, Sobrathun, the daughter, was not an unwilling participant in these events, but it is not recorded whether she was restored to her parents' domicile a second time.

As with husbands' rights over absconding wives, parental control over the daughter's choice of a partner was taken very seriously by colonial states. In cases where the state proclaimed itself legal guardian over individuals against the claims of parents, the rights of the Indian family were less clear cut.

Children found in a state of vagrancy were liable to be declared orphans and placed indefinitely in the state asylum. Chellumbay's son, in her words, 'was taken up by police as having had no parents and was condemned by the Magistrate to fifteen days imprisonment and after the expiration of this time was sent to the Powder Mills'.[42]

It was not unusual for children to be engaged in estate labour, doing weeding jobs for example, from the age of 7 or 8. By the age of 12 or 13, young boys could be on fully fledged indenture contracts and subject to penal sanctions along with their adult co-workers. Gookur's son, placed in the service of Mr Hardy from the age of 8, completely disappeared some years later. Gookur heard that the boy had been taken to the Seychelles without his consent, and asked the Protector to look into the matter.[43] When such child workers defaulted, or were sentenced for other misdemeanours, they could be confined in reformatories and kept there for lengthy periods. Little sympathy was evinced for parents' demands for their return. When 14-year-old Veerasamy, a servant of Madame Bestel in Mauritius, ran away to his uncle's house after being struck by her, the Magistrate condemned him to two years' imprisonment.[44] The criminalization of Indian children by the colonial state thus effectively deprived parents of any rights over their offspring.

In 1872 Ramalingum and Allamel petitioned for their son's release from the Government Reformatory in Mauritius, where he had been incarcerated for a period of five years following his condemnation for a 'petty larceny':

The humble Petition of Ramalingum no. 109,868, Barber and his wife Allamel both of Rose Hill.

Respectfully sheweth:
    That on or about the twelfth day of May, of last year (1871) your Petitioner's son, named Ramen, aged eleven years; was condemned before the District Magistrate of Port Louis to three months imprisonment for a certain petty larceny, committed to the prejudice of Revd. Boswell, and at the end of his imprisonment, was sent to the Reformatory school, for five years. That such steps were then carefully taken by the aforesaid Magistrate, as there is no doubt that he was not aware, that the boy had parents.
    That whereas Petitioners being in good positions and possessing the means of bringing up their children, Humbly pray that your Honor, will be pleased to order and authorize, (if it is in your Honor's power) that the said Ramen their son, be given over to them.
    Petitioners, knowing your Honor's kindness trust, that in case this their application is not of your resort; that you will be pleased to advise them, the way to follow, to get back their child, in order to be brought up by them.
    And Petitioners as in duty bound. will ever pray.

sign. Ramalingum   *mark X Allamel.*[45]

The Inspector of that institution subsequently informed the Protector that their son Ramen was the celebrated 'Cute Boy' mentioned in the island's *Commercial*

Gazette 'who so cleverly imposed upon the Reverend Boswell'. Apparently Ramen had met Boswell in Port Louis and claimed to know him. Boswell asked the boy to carry some boots he had purchased to his home, but Ramen took the boots back to the shop, stating that Boswell had changed his mind, and reclaimed the money, which he kept. The Reformatory Inspector reported that the boy's conduct had not been good whilst in that institution's care, but in support of this could only remember an incident when Ramen was caned for 'maliciously destroying plants'. He further suggested that the father, Fagin-like, might be claiming his son so as to put him to further use as a thief, and proposed an enquiry into Ramalingum's circumstances (Ramalingum is shown in Figure 4.2). He refused to recommend Ramen's release.[46]

When a married couple disputed the custody of a child, there was not, as today, any inclination to accord the mother preferential rights in the interest of the child. Indian women were therefore required to have recourse to courts of law or the ear of the Protector to gain custody of their children. Jeelea claimed that ill-treatment by her husband Boodhun had forced her to leave him, and asked the Protector to restore her son:

The Humble Petition of Jeelea, female immigrant of 1862 from Calcutta.

Respectfully sheweth:
   That Petitioner has a natural male child 2 and half years old by one Boodhun a laborer in the District of Moka, in the employ of Mr. Corvier.
   That Petitioner through ill-treatment now no longer lives with the said 'Boodhun' and is desirous of having her child restored to her.
   Petitioner therefore appeals to your goodness to have an order sent through the police or other channel, to cause the child to be brought before you and restore him to his mother. Petitioner annexes the certificate of declaration of birth, made in the District of Moka; as a proof of her statement that she is really the mother of the child in question. Petitioner ventures to hope that this prayer will be granted for which as in duty bound she will ever pray.

Jeelea X her mark.[47]

The case was sent to a senior judge and his comment was as follows:

The father has acknowledged the child; this is shown by the Certificate of Birth – he has therefore quite as much right to keep the child as the mother may have. Nothing short of a judgment of the Supreme Court could authorise the taking away of the child from her father. The mother is at liberty to go before the Court and take the usual steps to obtain that judgment.[48]

Whilst disputes over childcare have a contemporary ring, nineteenth-century opinions certainly did not favour maternal upbringing, but instead rarely contested the father's right to retain the child.

On the other hand, the lack of an extended family network amongst the early Indian settlers overseas meant that in many cases fathers were simply unable to bring up children on their own. As the petition of Cathan shows, it was current practice, when a man had lost his wife, to give up his offspring to another couple who were more able to look after them:

The humble Petition of Cathan no. 136461 a laborer of the Mount Estate of the District of Pamplemousses.

Respectfully sheweth:
   That your Petitioner has got a male child named Puneandee was born to him on the 19.9.70.

Figure 4.2 Ramalingum migrated to Mauritius in 1852 as a 20-year-old. He was listed as a malabar from Palamcotil. His photograph was taken in 1881. Source: PE 38 and PG 24.

That the said Cathan wishes to give his child Puneandee as an adopted child to one Vyapooree no. 154691 a laborer in the service Esperance Estate of this District, he being a friend of your Petitioner.

That your Petitioner has lost his wife and is unable to take care of his said child on account of his situation as laborer.

That your Petitioner prays your honor may be pleased to take his poor Petitioner into your favourable consideration and to grant the said child for adoption to the said Vyapooree.

And your Petitioner in duty bound shall ever pray

Cathan's X mark.[49]

This represented a kind of *de facto* adoption scheme, often unrecognized by officialdom; but in this case Cathan sought to make this a legal transfer of his son to his friend Vyapooree. Both men were Malabars from Thanjavur; they were of a similar age and had arrived in Mauritius one year apart, in 1854 and 1855 respectively.[50] Cathan is pictured in Figure 4.3. The petitions of Cathan and others like him underscore the difficulties of maintaining a family life in the migrant situation. The response of Indians was to establish networks amongst themselves for the care of their children.

Cathan's caution in seeking official recognition of his adoption plans was wise, if the case of Burthee is considered. She petitioned the Protector in 1875 about her young relation Bugmaneea, with whose care she had been entrusted following, she said, the departure of the girl's parents for India three years before. When the girl trespassed on some land while searching for fodder, the guardian of the property detained her, and kept her as his servant. Burthee demanded that the girl be returned to her home, and asked to be appointed Bugmaneea's legal guardian herself:

The humble Petition of Burthee, Indian woman of Rose Hill aforesaid, coco keeper.

Respectfully sheweth:
That for upwards of three years Petitioner has been taking care and charge of the Indian girl Bugmaneea, a relation of her, and the natural daughter of Pudaruth, No. 151,669, and Sooloomeea no. 151,926, who entrusted the said girl to Petitioner at their departure for India. That up until the 17th inst. the said Bugmaneea had remained with Petitioner, and that, on that very day the said girl Bugmaneea who had gone on a neighbouring ground belonging to M. Colin for some grass for the feeding of the cows, was arrested and brought before Mr David Danielle, guardian of the said land who, instead of bringing the said Bugmaneea before the competent authority, either for trespass or larceny of grass frightened and tampered with her by taking her as servant without any order or authority, which injunction she no doubt indirectly accepted.

That whereas the said Bugmaneea is still at Mr Danielle's, and that for the reasons above explained, Petitioner humbly prays that you will be so kind to take into consideration the circumstances, ie the length of time she gave for the bringing up of the said girl and the trouble she had, as well as the responsibilities which still rest upon her; will be pleased to order that the said Bugmaneea be ordered to come under Petitioner's roof; and at the same time, the Petitioner be appointed guardian of the said girl, in virtue of the powers vested in your Honor in such case, made and provided.

And Petitioner, as in duty bound, will ever pray

Burthee Canadjee.[51]

Unfortunately for Burthee the persons she mentioned as the girl's parents were shown to have both died in Mauritius much earlier: Pudaruth in Pample-mousses in 1860 and Sooloomea in 1862. The couple, both of the Gowala caste from Auzimghur, had arrived together in 1855.[52] Perhaps the falsehood in Burthee's petition was simply designed to make her case stronger; perhaps she was opportunistically seeking to benefit from marrying off Bugmaneea. In any event, the Immigration Office used the discrepancy to minute boldly: 'The girl Bugmaneea given to the charge of Mr Daniel'.[53]

Figure 4.3 Cathan embarked for Mauritius at Madras in June 1854. He was then a 25-year-old from Tanjore. His photograph was taken in 1883. Source: PG 28.

One effect of migration was that relatively large numbers of youngsters were without older relatives to care for them on account of death or abandonment, since many children arrived with only one accompanying parent. It was a common resort of young Indian men to apply for brides from amongst girls placed in the Orphan Asylum or Government Reformatory. The standards and ideology of such institutions do not make it difficult to imagine that early marriage was considered by some inmates preferable to a continuing residence therein. To remove them from the Asylum, however, necessitated the approval of the Protector, and as long as the young women remained there, opportunities for courtship were limited. In this context, one can but sympathize with the heartfelt plea of Boodoo who feared that his Jessie might be sent elsewhere, all the while waiting hopefully for the Protector to agree a date for the marriage:

Most respected and honored Sir,

I am hereby begging your honor to let the girl named Jessie remain in the Orphan asylum until you appoint a day for the settlement of my wedding.
Because if she is sent afar off, your poor servant will be in trouble.

Your most obedient servant

Boodoo (Pion).[54]

Indians were frequently unable to interact with the authorities as clearly and consistently as the latter deemed proper; in such cases they were inevitably more ready to believe the word of a European, such as Mr Daniel. Despite the eloquence of many of the petitions addressed to the Immigration Office, in family matters the Protector and his staff were rarely disposed to intervene or able to resolve issues which by and large were the symptoms of massive displacement of a people, and their grafting onto the alien culture of another. Without the sanction of traditional authorities to regulate the behaviour of family and kin, Indians turned to the Protector of Immigrants in the several colonies for guidance; the rudimentary justice he dispensed did little to disperse a growing sense of mutual incomprehension and distrust. Increasingly, Indians looked to senior members of their own community to regulate conduct, and relied on British officials only to give their decisions the force of law.

The Pull of Home and Family: Migrants' Efforts to return

Indentured migration, whether undertaken for gain or necessity, presupposed a departure from home and a separation from family and environment. If the concern for the welfare of relatives was a major factor in the decision of many to emigrate, the desire to rejoin loved ones constituted a strong pull towards India once contracts had expired. For those who had gained little from the indenture experience, and whose age and infirmities had lessened their usefulness in the eyes of colonial masters, the return to India came to represent a haven of security, where family and kin would support them in their twilight years.

Indentured migrants were entitled to a free return passage to India on the completion of their terms of service, and many took advantage of this either to return permanently, or simply to visit relatives and perhaps even persuade family members to return overseas with them. The financial drain which the free passages represented for Mauritius eventually persuaded the authorities to discontinue the practice in the mid-1850s, and henceforth only those who could pay their way were able to go back.[55]

The position of women without providers was even more insecure than that of elderly men who were unable to work. Carpayee was one of many women rendered unable even to support herself as a result of the death of her husband. In the overseas context, a network of relatives able to sustain the old and widowed was missing. As a result, women like Carpayee sought to return to India, where relatives could be found to look after her:

> *The humble Petition of Carpayee no. 253,427, Indian woman without profession most respectfully sheweth:*
>
> *That Petitioner is the widow of one Moothoo, no. 253,426, who died in this district in the Chebel Estate on the sixth day of July one thousand eight hundred and sixty five (1865) by committing suicide.*
> *That when the declaration of death of the said Moothoo no. 253,426 was made to the Officer of the Civil Status of this District his name was taken down as Mootoo without number (this perhaps in the absence of the ticket which the Police had not then in hands).*
> *That whereas Petitioner has been sickly for the last three years and having no one to support her here; would wish to return to her native country where she has relations.*
> *Petitioner therefore humbly prays that you may be pleased to look into her papers and extract of death of the said Moothoo no. 253,426 in order to ascertain that he was the same who was declared under the name of Mootoo; and further be pleased to allow her to proceed to India.*
> *And Petitioner as in duty bound, will ever pray*
> *Carpayee no. 253,427 X her mark.*[56]

Carpayee's immigration entry did not record the date of her departure, so we do not know if her request was granted.[57] Her situation was doubly distressing because of the manner in which her husband had met his death. Suicide and, in particular, its frequency amongst indentured labourers was a cause of some disquiet for British administrators in the last quarter of the nineteenth century.[58] Officially the motives were ascribed most commonly to jealousy and disputes with friends. In practice, individual case histories reveal frustration with a penal labour system which some felt they would never escape, disappointment at the conditions and prospects, humiliation at beatings endured or menial work forced upon them, as well as the inevitable disputes over women which were a feature of early estate life before the onset of large-scale family migration.

Where the prospective returnee was not evidently disabled by age or infirmity, the petitioner was obliged to offer other reasons for the granting of a gratuitous passage. Beeharry mentioned that he had heard of the death of some relatives, and the desire to see those still living had prompted his return. He claimed that the money he had saved had been expended as a result of sickness, and even pleaded to be given work on the ship as a means of paying his passage:

Sir,

> *I humbly beg your honor to lay a few lines of my humble petition, which sheweth:*
>
> *The undersigned Indian, old, have been in Mauritius from since many years. And all the monies which I earned had been lost by miseries, which is the cause of it I wish to relate before my Protector. Since many month your Petitioner had been laid with sickness and unable for his employ; the money which I have kept to return to my country, I expended and now it is very hardship for me to return to India without money. I had not any sum to pay my passage and go to India, I was not intended to go to India, but just two days ago I have heard that my relations had been lost many of them so I wish to go there.*
>
> *I beg to my protector to let me have any work on the Cooly's ship which is going to India then I can be able to go there with the working class – But if I had any amount then I would pay the passage – But if it please to your Protectorship to have the passage from me then let your poor and helpless Petitioner have any duty in your department till I have earned to pay the passage – while I have caught with illness your Petitioner not have found any situation for his living – the department where I was employed, in my stead a new person has been placed while I lay with a very long time of absence on account of my ill health therefore begging to your protectorship to grant a work on the vessel with the cooly; with work I may return to India to see the relation and parents where I was born.*
>
> *Your Petitioner begs ten times ten and hopes your Petitioner will be favoured with this request, not a person or house is now for your Petitioner's living perhaps if the police should caught to your Petitioner without employ he should be counted as vagabond – praying to your honor to grant this.*

Beeharry.[59]

The Immigration Department was not often prepared to countenance such requests, and in the case of Beeharry bluntly declared 'He appears to be a strong, able-bodied young man'.[60]

Lack of money was not the only impediment to the return of indentured labourers. In many cases, such as that of Potun, unresolved disputes, employers' claims, even the intervention of an abandoned spouse, could all forestall a departure date. Poonoosamy, who wished to return to India with his younger brother, first had to secure his release from the Government Reformatory. Kisnasamy had been arrested as a vagrant in Port Louis at the tender age of 10, indicating again the early inclusion of young immigrants in colonial labour requirements. The brothers asserted that they felt the need to look after their widowed mother as a motive for their return, and declared Kisnasamy's conduct whilst interned to have been good. A petition was drawn up for the Governor of the island in the name of Kisnasamy:

The humble Petition of Kisnasamy an Indian boy, now residing in the Asylum of Riviere des Callabasses

Most respectfully sheweth

That your Petitioner is a Native of Cattoccopeun in India, and came to this Colony when quite a child, and that he is now about twelve years old.

That eighteen months ago, that is, a few days before the Christmas of 1869, your Petitioner, who was then out of employ, was arrested and brought before the Stipendiary Magistrate of Port Louis under the Charge of Vagrancy, and after an enquiry into the then destitute state and inability of your Petitioner of earning his living, the Stipendiary Magistrate of Port Louis sent him to the Asylum of Callabasses, to be kept therein, during the space of four years.

That your Petitioner believes he has won the good will of the Managers of the Asylum by his behaviour and good conduct, ever since he became an inmate of the place.

That your Petitioner's eldest brother, by name Poonoosamy, now in the employ of Mr. Ollivier Trader, is on the eve of leaving the Mauritius and going back to India and has expressed the desire of taking your Petitioner thither with him.

That your Petitioner hopes, that Your Excellency, under such circumstances will make use of the power of pardoning which has been entrusted in his hands, put a stop to his detention, and allow him to go back with his brother, to his native place, to fulfil his duties near his widowed mother, who stands in great need of the presence and assistance of her absent children.

And as in duty bound Your Petitioner will ever pray

signed Edmund Edwards
for the Petitioner.[61]

The Protector, having established that the boy was not in the Asylum, as the petition stated, but in the Reformatory, called for a police report. The Inspector General reviewed the case in these terms:

the boy Kisnasamy was sentenced to 4 years at the Reformatory on the 22nd November 1869, and has since behaved well. He states that he has a brother named Poonoosamy in Port Louis, who is returning to India. I beg to recommend the boy's release for the purpose of accompanying his brother, provided that the Protector of Immigrants will undertake to see that he is really shipped off, and will apply for him in writing prior to his brother's leaving.[62]

As in the case of other children whose families petitioned for their release, there is no hint in this report that the conviction for vagrancy of such a young boy was to be regretted. Rather, the Inspector was concerned to ensure that Kisnasamy would not be allowed to remain in Mauritius.

Letters from Relatives Left Behind

For families in India who had received no news, or who had lost contact with a migrant, the indenture experience was lived as a time of painful isolation and incertitude, and sometimes increasing penury. As the letters collected here testify, some relatives went years, even decades, without hearing from their loved ones, hoping all the time for their return. They went to great lengths to trace the missing persons, and the documents in this section derive primarily from appeals made to officials in India and overseas, connected with emigration, to reunite such families. The experiences of relatives separated by indenture were various; while some had precise information as to the whereabouts of migrants, others barely knew to which colony they should apply for assistance.

Bihari Das was one of those unfortunate individuals whose relative had simply disappeared, leaving no idea as to his whereabouts, even of his continuing survival. Bihari was not even aware that his brother had gone abroad, and his fears that Bishnath Lal might have been poisoned and killed indicate the trauma of ignorance which many must have shared:

> *About 8 or 9 years ago in the month of June my younger brother Bishnath Lal was enticed away from my house by Ram Gobind Rae. I do not know where he took him to. I have been looking for Bishnath Lal ever since. This year in February, Ram Gobind Rae was met by me in the village. I asked him what he had done with my brother. Ram Gobind Rae said he had been to Bombay and my brother was there. I asked him to tell me the exact place so that I might send a letter to Bombay. Then he told me my brother was not in Bombay but had gone to Mauritius. I wrote a letter (produced and forwarded herewith) to my brother – it came back. Again I made enquiries from Ram Gobind – he said Bishnath was not at Mauritius – at last he refused to give any explicit answer. I suspected something was wrong and that perhaps Ram Gobind had poisoned my brother and taken whatever money he had, for Ram Gobind brought a lot of silver and gold coin home with him. When my brother went away he was 10 or 12 years old – now he will be 20 or 21. I made no report to the Police when my brother disappeared. As Ram Gobind had gone I came to the conclusion that they had gone together.* [63]

It was only Bihari's meeting with Ram Gobind Rae, who had disappeared at the same time, which revealed the likely whereabouts of his brother and enabled him to begin the search. His letter to his sibling in Mauritius was, however, returned unclaimed, and at this point he sought the help of a local Magistrate. W. Irvine obtained the following statement from Ram Gobind Rae:

> *Eight or nine years ago Bishnath Lal, brother of Bihari Lal went with me to Mauritius. I and two others went viz. Bishnath Lal and Poordil Moosulman and I – a fourth man Mirza Moosulman remained behind in Calcutta. When we reached the Mauritius we separated and entered into service. I was enlisted in the Police (character certificate shown – copy annexed) Bishnath entered into the service of some gentleman. Three or four months afterwards I met him and as long as I remained on the island I saw him every two or three months. Three years ago I became ill. I asked Bishnath if he would go home and he refused. I got my discharge and came away. Bishnath stopped behind in Mauritius. I have been at home from a year to eighteen months. I started from Calcutta in Asarh (July) nine years ago (1861) and arrived at Mauritius in Bhadwan (August–September). I do not know the name of the ship. Three days after I arrived I was enlisted in the Police and stationed at 'Labesis' (doubtful pronunciation W.I.) It is eight miles north of Port Louis on the sea-board. Serjeant Steeman was the officer in charge. Bishnath was in service at a place 6 miles to the northeast of the island – the owner's*

name was Monsieur 'Hoolsan' (the man's pronunciation is imitated as closely as possible - W.I.).[64]

The Magistrate then wrote to the Protector at Bihari's request, forwarding the statements of Das and Ram Gobind Rae. He also annexed the discharge certificate of Rae, who had been employed in the Mauritian Police Force. He had been a constable from 1862 to 1868 and was given a good character recommendation.[65]

Bihari's chance of finding his brother was limited by his lack of information of Bishnath's whereabouts in Mauritius, or his all important immigrant number, and it is doubtful if the Immigration Office would have been able to help him. The attempts to trace migrant relatives from the scantiest information often gave rise to heartfelt letters such as that addressed by N. Venkatasami to the 'Agent of Emigrants' in Mauritius. Unsure whether his brother was alive or dead, the writer had obviously been clutching at any information he could obtain. Thus he had heard that some returnees, one of whom had a name similar to that of his brother, had died of cholera on the way back to Masulipatam. The man had left behind a son and Venkatasami had obviously been to see the boy because he thought he detected a family resemblance. It is easy to imagine the emotion the brother experienced, not knowing if the child he saw was his own nephew or not. He consequently sought confirmation from the Mauritius Immigration Office:

Sir,

In 1853–54 myself and my brother Nalayapala Ramasawmi alias Bapanayya here in the employ of the Department of Works under Captain Tullard in the village of Chebrolu of district Kistna of Madras Presidency, when my brother the said Ramasawmi alias Bapanayya entrusted himself as a cook for the Mauritius. My brother took along with him a certain woman named Lakshmibayama with a daughter who was born to him of that woman.

I subsequently heard that my brother along with some 63 or so embarked from Madras; at Madras, I was informed by one Jeerdandaji of Russelcondal that my brother was employed in the sugar cane plantation of one Mr Noole of Mauritius. My brother not having kept up a correspondence I lost sight of him altogether.

In 1884 several coolies from the Mauritius disembarked at Madras and of these some were making their way home towards the Kistna district when one Ramasami and his wife Gonudana both died of cholera in the Buckingam Canal; as I have reasons to believe that the deceased is my brother I beg to enquire if you can by any means obtain for me the least information you can about my brother.

The deceased was coming home to Masulipatam, he had transferred his bank assets to this station to a son whom he has left behind resembles us. I shall therefore esteem it a great favour if you can obtain from any records any information relative to my brother, or point out to me from where I can obtain the information asked for.

Begging you will you do me the favour of obtaining me this information and if my brother be there of giving him the enclosed letter.

Please reply giving particulars to the address given below.

I am yours imploringly

Nalayapala Venkatasami.[66]

In case it was not his brother who had returned and died *en route*, he enclosed a letter for his sibling, which has unfortunately been lost. In June 1885 enquiries were made for the brother, but on the basis of the scant information given, the man could not be found, and the familiar reply went back that 'careful searches have been made but that no traces can be found, of the persons referred to in this letter in the books of the office'.[67]

The Protector was also obliged to inform Chennapah, who was searching for a brother, that:

> with the view of finding the name of Lakekannaya amongst the coolies that arrived in this colony at the end of last year, searches have been made in this office but I regret to say unsuccessfully. Further searches can however be made if you will obtain from our Agent at Madras the name of the Vessel in which your brother was embarked.[68]

However, it seems clear that Chennapah did not give up, for four years later he was reapplying for information respecting his brother. On this occasion the relative's name was spelt Masoomannah, and it is likely that the difficulties Chennapah experienced were at least in part related to the problems of transcribing his brother's name. The situation was further complicated by the fact that the brother was stated to have emigrated under the name 'Patero'. Chennapah sent on this occasion two letters to Mauritius: the first was addressed to the 'Secretary of Transamigration':

> *Honoured Sir,*
>
> *I Chennappa brother of Masoomannah respectfully beg to state that my brother who left Kurnool and came down to that country but he is not writing letters to me about his health for which we are exceedingly sorry in order to know his welfair. Requesting to let me know whether he is there or not. He is called here by the name for Masoomannah and there as Patero.*
>
> *I beg to remain Respected Sir,*
> *Your most obedient servant,*
>
> *Chennappa.*

The second was addressed to his brother. This letter is a simple but very evocative document. Chennapah stresses that the fact that his brother has not been able to send any money is not important: he seems concerned that Masoomannah may not be communicating because he is ashamed not to have money to send. Chennapah wishes to assure his brother that the family is only concerned to know that he is well. As is usually the case in letters between migrants and their families, the situation of family property in land is relayed, and relatives are mentioned:

Dear brother,

We are exceedingly sorry for not knowing your health from a very long time since your departure from Kurnool. Even if you not send us anything, we do not care about that but only thing what we wanted is to receive letter from you that is our main object. The children are all doing well. After you left Kurnool two children born, one is male and the other is female. The land what you have given to me is not ploughed being no rain. The Madiga which is in Kurnool is not rented. Thippiah is troubling me very much. He is going to take back the land. Besannah also is very anxious to see you.

My best compliments to you. My wife convey best compliments to you. Children send their kisses to you.

Your obedient Brother

Chennappa.[69]

On this occasion the clerks at the Immigration Office found that one Musalanna, No. 425,280, father's name Achanna, mother's name N. Venkatamana, had arrived from Kurnool, Madras, per *Istria* on 2 October 1903. He was then aged 25, a Telugu, and was described as having a scar below his left eyebrow. He was allotted to La Barraque Estate at Grand Port on 15 October 1903. The manager of that estate was accordingly written to and instructed to ask the labourer concerned whether he had a brother named Chennapah residing at Kurnool and other relatives named Thippiah and Besannah.[70] Unfortunately the answer came back from La Barraque that the man did not know the people mentioned in the letter. The reply was sent to Chennapah that insufficient information had been provided to enable his brother to be traced and advising him to apply to the Mauritius Government Emigration Agent at Madras, who might be in a position to 'let you have full particulars as to the name, ship number and date of your brother's emigration'.[71] Chennapah's quest was destined to continue. Musalanna died in Mauritius in 1923: he is shown in Figure 4.4.

Mhamji was luckier, because the numbers of her son and nephew could be traced. She had waited more than a decade to hear news from them before, in her turn, soliciting help from the Magistrate of Ratnagiri in western India. She wished her relatives in Mauritius to be informed that the family in India was well, and asked, in her old age, to be given the chance to meet her only son again. The translation of her petition read:

My son Babajiraw Lal Dowlatraw Surve and my nephew Jujyabarawbin Dhakajiraw Surve and Ermajirawbin Putlajiraw Surve went from Bombay about 13 or 14 years ago, in order to earn their livelihood. They then migrated to the island of Mauritius. I have patiently waited till now, expecting that they would return; but I have heard nothing from them, since their departure.

I therefore pray that you will out of charity, intimate to them and well being of all the members of the family here and request the authorities there to advise them to return to their country. I also pray that I may be favoured with information as to how they are doing. I have now grown very old, and if you will kindly bring about their (i.e. my son's and nephew's) meeting with me, but for ever so short a time, I shall be under ever lasting obligations to you. Babaji is my only son, and I earnestly hope that you will arrange for their return.[72]

The Magistrate forwarded her petition to Mauritius, explaining that she was 'a poor old woman whose only son went to Mauritius some years ago', and stating that 'any information would be gratefully received'.[73] The Immigration Department found that her son had arrived in the company of two male relatives: Jeejaba, Oomajee and Babajee, all from Ratnagiri, on the *Hyderee* in 1860. Babajee had been listed as only 13 years old at the time, Oomajee was 14, and Jeejaba was 30.[74] There was no trace of their tickets after 1865, when they were engaged to Daruty & Co. It was subsequently discovered that they were afterwards engaged to Dubois & Co., L'Unite, Flacq, where the current

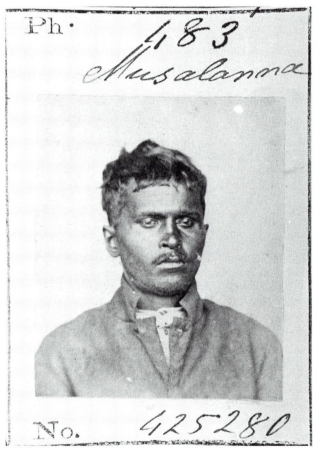

Figure 4.4 Musalanna came to Mauritius in 1903 as a 25-year-old. He was a Telegu and is listed as 1m 55 tall. He died in 1923 at Grand Port, Mauritius. This photograph was taken in 1911. Source: PE 153 and PG 51.

manager, F. Chardoillet, was contacted. Four months after the enquiry was received, the Protector in Mauritius was able to update the Collector at Ratnigiri:

> All three men were still living in Mauritius, and he reported none of them are married but Oomajee is living with a woman by whom he has five children. They would have returned to India but lost all that they had in the hurricane of March last and they wish to remain until they have saved something. They are living in the district of Black River and are market gardeners. I enclose the photographs of these men which I have had taken and a letter which they have written to their friends.[75]

It is easy to imagine the mixture of curiosity and joy which Mhamji must have felt as she opened the packet and looked at the photographs of boys who had grown into men since she had last laid eyes on them. It is unlikely that Babajee ever returned to meet his mother, however. Their entries in the Immigration Register reveal that all three men were still in Mauritius at the time of their deaths: Jeejaba died at Savanne in November 1889, Oomajee at Quartier Militaire on 16 June 1907, and Babajee at Black River on 25 April 1892.

The family networks of migrants who went to Mauritius were very important in the re-establishment of links between relatives in India and overseas. The brother of Narayna had not seen the latter for thirty-five years, and was finally given information as to his whereabouts by some relatives who had also been in Mauritius. These persons had seen Narayna eighteen months earlier and were able to report that he was living in a place which they transcribed as 'Rozwayal attached to Maipur police about 30 miles from upper town and that he was then serving as a cooly under Mr Galley contractor (tikkabund) of that place'. The brother had further been informed that 'is brother's wife Jaiyalee and her sons Kolander, Salagun and Govinden are said to live in Pitherboth ... They are working as coolies'. The brother, whose name is not given, accordingly went to the local Collector at Tanjore to request further information concerning the man whom he described as 'Narayna Salagan joint Pattadar no. 58 of Panaveli Village, Tanjore taluq Tanjore district'. In cases where such a long time period had elapsed between the migration and the enquiry, it was usually very difficult for Mauritian officials to pinpoint the current location of the migrant, and we do not know the results of this search, but certainly the information of Narayna's relatives must have aided his brother's quest.[76]

Even in the early twentieth century, when the last trickles of immigrants were arriving in Mauritius and communications should have been better, it was still possible for relatives in India to lose sight of their loved ones. In 1905 the Protector of Emigrants at Madras forwarded the translation of a Tamil petition received from one Muthealoo Maistry, and requested that his opposite number in Mauritius would 'be so good as to institute enquiries and let me know the correct address and any other particulars of the Emigrant Dorasami Son of Cuppen referred to. He emigrated to Mauritius per S.S. Istria on the 29th April

1904'.[77] His number on the ship was 145. The Tamil letter which Cuppen wrote to his son Gengen was not translated as such, but rather summarized and rewritten in the form of a plea for his whereabouts by another individual called Muthealu Maistry, conceivably the recruiter of Dorasami, and no doubt the man called Muthealoo above. The result is that the document actually transcribed presumably bears little resemblance to the original. The transcription is as follows:

> *In what village are you; please inform me. He left on Sunday the 17th April 1904. His father's name is Kuppu Maistry and mother's name is Sali Ammall. He has given out his name as Dorasami. He is a Washerman by caste. His age is 18. Complexion dark. Has a twisted silver wire on his leg. Prays for information as to his correct address and any other particulars about him. He emigrated to Mauritius.*

The Protector of Immigrants was able to communicate the following information to the Protector of Emigrants, at Madras:

> – Name Dorasami; father's name: Cuppen; mother's name: Salli; age, 18 years; arrived per S.S. Itria from Madras on 14th May 1904 and engaged 'Bel Air' Estate, district of Savanne for 5 years from 20.5.04 – Immigration number: 425769.
> – Dorasami is still working on the above Estate, and any letter intended for him may be sent thro' this office or direct to him, addressed as under:

> To Dorasami No. 425769
> c/o The Manager, Bel Air Estate,
> Riviere des Anguilles Post Office,
> Mauritius.

Dorasami's picture has been retrieved from the Immigration Archives (Figure 4.5). At this stage, therefore, the Mauritian state had obviously adopted a stylized format through which immigrants could receive their letters.

By this period relatives were usually well aware of the nature of the work and the duration of the engagement of migrants in Mauritius. However, when loved ones failed to return at the end of the stipulated time, worried relatives continued to petition for information. Thus in 1908 the Calcutta Agent of the Mauritian Government was informed by the Political Agent of the Eastern Rajputana States that the relatives of one Goberdhan were anxious to know why he had not returned to India on the expiry of his contract. He had migrated on the steamship *Wardha* in 1902. The family wanted to know whether he was alive and well; and if so, to have him instructed to write to his relatives. In this case Goberdhan's address was given as c/o Monsieur Degaye at the Establishments Devale Cent Garlette, Station Cluny, District Grand Porte. The spelling mistakes were minor and the address was therefore much more intelligible.[78]

In reply, the Protector explained that Goberdhan, No. 423,824, had, after the expiry of his five-year agreement, contracted another engagement for one year with Cent Gaulettes Estate on 6 March 1908.[79] A letter was addressed to the Manager of that estate asking him to communicate to Goberdhan the gist of the letter received from the Emigration Agent at Calcutta.[80] The Immigration Office was informed that Gobardhan had promised to write to his relatives in India, and the Emigration Agent at Calcutta was told on 15 June 1908 that the man was well and would be in touch with his relatives. However, Gobardhan, whose immigration register records him as being of the Jat caste from Bharatpur, never went back to India: he died in Mauritius in 1934.[81]

C. Ragooputty Naidu did not need to rely on luck to determine the whereabouts of his son, and he also had the means to pay for his return. He asked the Emigration Agent at Madras 'to obtain the release of his son from the remainder of his industrial residence in the Mauritius and to send him back by the first return emigrant ship that may be leaving the island'.[82] He was prepared to pay a great deal of money to achieve this, and left Rs200 with the Agent for the purpose. He provided precise details, including his son's immigrant number, to

Figure 4.5 Dorasami arrived in Mauritius in 1904 as an 18-year-old from Madras. Source: PE 153 and PG 48.

assist the search, in an original memo preserved in the archives. The information therein provides an interesting insight into the socio-economic background of C.R. Kistnasamy Naidu, the departed son. He was by no means from a poor background: his father was a brass-posts merchant at Coimbatoor, and his brother was employed as a draughtsman. One can only speculate as to what caused Kistnasamy to leave for Mauritius, and to the regret which had perhaps led him to provide his father with details of his whereabouts. Kistnasamy's Immigration entry at Mauritius reveals that he had arrived in Mauritius in July 1874 at the age of 20 and had been employed in Savanne. For Kistnasamy, no doubt because of his father's means and prompt action, the length of the stay in Mauritius was brief. He is listed as returning to India in April 1876.[83]

The discovery of correspondence concerning migrants written by their relatives in India demonstrates the attempts made by these latter to rescue their family members from disagreeable working and living conditions in Mauritius. The actions of such relatives, often stimulated by letters from migrants or word sent through returnees of their desire to come home, thus represented an avenue of escape for those who had been deceived into emigrating or regretted their decision to go overseas.

Mr Pillay's letter to the Protector, written in March 1885, is another example of a worried father's attempt to remove his son from his unhappy situation in Mauritius. The writer had learnt that his son, who had disappeared from home six months earlier, was in Mauritius. Obviously the boy, like Kistnasamy Naidu, was not an ordinary labour migrant: his father mentioned his education and lack of experience of manual work, and was concerned that his son might attempt suicide. He was aware that he would be required to take some steps, in the form of a payment, to free Mootoosawmy from his contractual obligations and in the meantime asked that his son be given work more suitable to him:

Honoured Sir,

I, the undersigned beg to bring the following few lines for your honour's merciful consideration – My eldest son, one 'Mootoosawmy' who I hear from a friend of mine that came from Mauritius is employed under Mr Belzim and Harel of Trianon Estate in the District of Plaines Wilhems or Rose Hills and is said to have been admitted on the 24th November 1884, has a fair knowledge of English and Tamil.

He disappeared from his home and relatives on the 18th September last, and I have been searching for him in vain till at last I heard his whereabouts. I learn that the work he is now engaged upon is a hard one and not suited to his taste. Having been from his infancy used to no hard work of any kind he would naturally find his present work anything but pleasant. I am afraid that the hard work, separation from home and the suffering he is undergoing now would induce him in an evil hour to put an end to his life. The loss that he would thus entail perhaps on his employers would be one of many but that on his parents would be long standing and inseparable. The domestic affliction attending on the loss of a son to his parents is too well known to need any mention on my part.

Having thus entered but briefly on his present temperament I appeal to your Honor to give him some work that would benefit his education and taste till such time as I would

be able to procure his passage money and send it to him. This I need scarcely assure your
honor would be a great relief to me from my present affliction. I request further that your
Honor would also be pleased to communicate to me the means that I have to employ to
free him from his work and then enable him to return to his parents.
In return for this act of generosity all that a poor man like me is capable of doing is to pray
for your Honor's prosperity and long life.

I beg to remain
Honoured Sir,
Your most obedient servant
Mr Annudanada Pillay
alias Mooniasawmy Pillay
residing no. 12 Fond Street
Poodoopet Madras.[84]

On enquiry, the Protector's office found that the son of the petitioner had been given immigrant number 399,783 and was engaged to 'Trianon' Estate for five years from 24 November 1884. Evidently, Mootoosawmy was called into the Office to give evidence, for on 18 May 1885 he made a statement as follows:

I was a school master of the 3rd class in a mission school in Madras, and have not done
any agricultural work. I am not able to do the work required of me at Trianon, which is
to work in the fields. I would like to have my engagement cancelled as I wish to return to
India to my friends.

We do not know why an educated individual like Mootoosawmy disappeared from his home in this sudden fashion and turned up in Mauritius. What is certain is that recruiters continued to take advantage of persons who, as the result of misguided ambitions or personal problems, sought to leave their homes. Mootoosawmy was one of the lucky ones who, through the information given by returnees and the actions of relatives, was able to secure some kind of redress. The stories of persons like Mootoosawmy reveal once again the crucial role performed by returnees who were able to alert relatives to the plight of unhappy migrants.

Even those with lesser means were prepared to sacrifice their meagre wage to be reunited with loved ones. In 1868 the Emigration Agent at Madras had written to the Protector about Gopal Nandu. He was a pensioned Jemadar of the Madras Native Army who had complained that his only daughter had emigrated to Mauritius with her husband, a bricklayer, without his consent in 1862, aged 20. Her husband had since died and Nandu had heard that his daughter 'has occasionally to beg her bread at Mauritius – her means of living being precarious'. The Jemadar, reported the Agent, 'a very respectable man and deeply affected with the accounts he has received of his daughter begs of me to intercede with the Mauritian Government to send his daughter back to him'. He was prepared to pay R2 a month out of his pension of Rs8 a month for her passage back.[85]

Baboo Bhicajee was not even obliged to pay for the passage back to India of his nephew. The Mauritian government had written him a letter stating that the boy would be given a free passage to Bombay if Baboo would declare his willingness to receive him. Perhaps the boy was an orphan and the government had been informed of the existence of relatives in India who could look after him. At any rate, Bhicajee provided the necessary letter:

> *I Baboo Bhicajee (sepoy) employed at the Bombay Custom House in the Preventive Service am the Uncle of the boy named Ramchunder Sonoo who is at Mauritius – and as there is no one to look after him I would feel obliged if the Protector of Immigrants at Mauritius would send the above named boy to Bombay whom I shall receive with greatest pleasure and shall always pray to God for the Protectors of Emigrants of Mauritius and Bombay, for their long life and prosperity.*[86]

Ballaram had only been in Mauritius one year when his relatives applied to have him sent home, and paid for his return passage. Accordingly the Protector requested 'that a circular may be sent to Magistrates to forward the man to this office should he appear before any of them'.[87] Perhaps the message never got to Ballaram, because he certainly did not make it back to India within the next couple of years. It is rarely made clear in the correspondence which passed between the Agencies in India and the Immigration Office in Mauritius why such migrants failed to return. Were they tied into long contracts on estates and unable to gain approval to return, or had they simply formed new ties in Mauritius, or taken on new responsibilities, which made them reluctant to leave property and people and go back to India? Relatives waited for many months before finally receiving news or, as in this case, giving up after two years. Having sent Rs30 to pay for his return passage in 1849, Ballaram's friends later requested their money back. In the Agent's words:

> in consequence of Ballaram's non arrival from the Mauritius where he had emigrated, his friends have solicited me to request the favor of your returning by the first opportunity the sum of (30) thirty Rupees which was sent to you to pay for Ballaram's return passage.[88]

Many letters from relatives requesting the release of migrants and their return to India could not be acted upon because the Indianization of Mauritian place names in letters that were translated one or more times and re-transcribed meant that they were unrecognizable, and the information given about the individuals they concerned was too scanty. This was the fate of Huldar's petition concerning his brother Beeharry, who had migrated to Mauritius. Beeharry had written to Huldar telling him that he wished to return to India, but Huldar's account of his brother's whereabouts could not be understood. In his petition to the Mauritius agent at Calcutta, Hulder had written:

> *That your poor petitioner has about three months ago heard from his brother Behary son of Futteh mea, from Mauritius to say that he, your poor petitioner's brother, is there and*

also his son in Mayapur Kurtee on estate of Monsieur Kurby, he has been there for nearly 30 years and is anxious to return to India not being able to support himself and family with the income of his son, as he himself is unfit for manual labor, his right arm being paralysed.

That your poor petitioner thereby prays that your honor will be graciously pleased to grant his brother and also his son a free passage to Calcutta as he has not got money for passage and for which act of kindness your petitioner as in duty bound shall ever pray.[89]

The Protector minuted:

the information given from India about this man is so meagre that we cannot find him. . . . I would suggest that the Agent Mr Warner, be asked to request Huldar to write to Beeharry from India and tell him to call at this office and we shall see what we can do. Beeharry's letter to Huldar gives perhaps his proper address.[90]

In other cases, it was only after migrants had produced the evidence of communications received from relatives in India that employers could be prevailed upon to release workers from their engagements. At least, as the example of Chinapien shows, the Protector was generally favourable to such requests. In 1882, that officer wrote to the Manager of the Riche Bois Estate in Savanne, stating:

The bearer Chinapien no. 371,628, an engaged laborer of Riche Bois Estate for a year from 18 July 1882, has produced a letter at this office with the postmark of India thereon and which is addressed to him. From a translation which I have had made of this letter, it appears that his father has died recently and his mother is left alone with a small child who is unable to cultivate the land belonging to them so as to provide for their wants. In these circumstances, she has written to the bearer to come and join her.

Chinapien states that you refuse to cancel his engagement so as to enable him to comply with his mother's request.

The Protector is sure that now you are in possession of the facts of the bearer's case, you will make no objection to discharge him from his contract with you.[91]

The Immigration entry of Chinapien reveals that he had arrived from Madras in 1874 as a 19-year-old. His family, of the Vannien caste, lived in north Arcot. The register does not record whether he returned to India, but his photograph, taken in the same year as he made this request, is reproduced as Figure 4.6.[92]

Ramnarain Agarwalla, another migrant in Mauritius, might have been very glad of a good deed he performed years before in India, if the substance of James Haly's letter ever reached him. Haly, a tea planter in Assam, wrote to the Protector at Mauritius on behalf of one Shankar Das Agarwalla. This latter, a businessman operating in Assam, was anxious to trace Ramnarain because he had once been helped out of a great difficulty by the latter. Ramnarain had gone to Mauritius from Calcutta in 1869, his description was given in the letter and his whereabouts asked for, so that Shankar, should he need it, could assist him in turn.[93]

For persistence, however, few could rival Peary Mohun Ghose, whose repeated efforts to induce his brother to return to Calcutta generated a considerable correspondence in the Immigration Office files. The Protector informed the Calcutta Agent in December 1879, on Peary's behalf, that his brother Heeroo, No. 335,805, had arrived in June 1868 on a five-year engagement to the Hermitage Estate, Moka. He had subsequently engaged on the Valetta Estate. The Protector reported that Heeroo was well:

and begs me to state that he did not write to his brother in India because he had nothing important to communicate or any money to send to him and further that he did not know his address and for the present has no desire to return to India.[94]

Figure 4.6 Chinapien boarded the '*Reigate*' at Madras in June 1874. He was then 19 years old, a Vannien of north Arcot. He engaged with Mr Hewetson of Savanne. This photograph was taken in 1882. Source: PE 121 and PG 27.

Heeroo did, however, send a letter for his brother. Undeterred, Peary evidently went again to the Emigration Agent, because that official penned a further letter to the Mauritian Protector on 2 October 1880. This letter was one of a series enclosing correspondence in Ghose's native Bengali for his brother Heeroo, and asking the Protector at Mauritius to persuade Heeroo to return to his wife and other relatives.[95]

The Agent also enclosed a petition Peary had addressed to him. It stated that Heeroo had left without informing his relatives, simply because he wished to see the world. Peary stressed the foolhardiness of his younger brother, who had left his wife behind, which for a Hindu woman, he pointed out, represented a particular hardship. The separation was also difficult for Peary himself to bear, the latter confided:

Sir,

With reference to your no 2 dated 3rd January 1880, to the address of the Protector of Emigrants, Calcutta (copy enclosed for your reference) I most humbly beg to submit the following grievances and from the pitiful nature of my case solicit, that my prayers may be heard.

My brother Heeroo, as named in your letter quoted above, and who is now residing at Mauritius, has left his motherland, quite unknown to his friends and relatives, and with no other apparent cause than the desire of an unfortunate sejourn to some distant countries in the world – In the folly of his youth he has not only left some of his nearest and dearest relatives to mourn his separation for the last twelve years, but a wife without any issue and solely dependent on him – I believe it is already known to you that a Hindoo woman however secluded from all worldly enjoyments has only one consolation in life, ie the company of her husband and she must be a most wretched woman in the universe who, while her husband is alive, is thus deprived of his companionship for ever in the world.

Moreover bound with the link of nature and as an elder brother of Heeroo and sole guardian to the members of his family, myself am not a less sufferer for the loss of an only brother, and it is difficult to express adequately in words, to what a painful position I am placed, forever being separated from a brother, born of the same parents, and nourished from the bosom of a same mother.

Under the circumstances stated above and considering the surrowful position to which the wife of Heeroo is placed in this world, I solicit the favor of your issuing necessary orders to the authorities at Mauritius to induce my brother Heeroo to return to his native land and thus put an end to all the mortifying agonies of a loving wife and a beloved brother.

I take this opportunity to add that if my brother refuses to return home on the plea of debt I shall be glad to deposit or remit any amount that may be required for his such return to India.

I beg also to be furnished with the right direction of Heeroo at Mauritius as the one already given by him in his vernacular letter received with yours under reference, has probably been changed since, some registered letters, posted by me, failed to reach his present destination in Mauritius.

Signature of Peary Mohun Ghose
10, Boloram Dey's street

Jorasanko, Calcutta.

P.S. *You are requested to see that this letter written in Bengali is delivered to Heeroo.*[96]

The Immigration Department at Mauritius replied in November 1880 that Heeroo was still an engaged laborer of Valetta Estate in the district of Moka. He had engaged for a year from 29 April 1880. Heeroo had promised that at the beginning of the next year he would have his contract cancelled and go to India. With regard to money that he might require, he stated that he would write direct to his brother, whose address had been given to him in writing. Lastly, the Protector reported, 'he appears in good health'.

In January 1881 Peary sent another Bengali letter to be given to Heeroo, and the Agent informed the authorities in Mauritius:

if Heeroo can be induced to fulfil his promise and return to India Peary M. Ghose will be greatly pleased and in this hope and expectation he has deposited in this office Rs50 to defray the cost of Heeroo's return passage to Calcutta, and out of this sum the passage money will be paid to the master of the ship which may bring him to Calcutta.[97]

The Department subsequently minuted:

Heeroo presented himself here today. His engagement with Valetta estate expires on the 29 April next. He states that he will leave for India in the next vessel chartered for the conveyance of coolies. He will pay for his own passage. He will call here in 3 weeks time to see when a ship is likely to be ready.[98]

The Register entry for Heeroo does not report whether this Bengali from Burdwan, who had arrived in Mauritius at the age of 20 thirteen years previously, did indeed return that year. One suspects that he might have done, for no more visits of Peary Ghose to the Calcutta Agent are recorded.[99] Once again, this correspondence reveals that among the young men arriving at Mauritius in the mid-nineteenth century were some, by no means from poor and starving families, whose migrations had been shaped less by necessity than by curiosity, or perhaps bad advice, and who were urged home by anxious families in India. In these and other cases, the literacy of migrants meant that regular contact was the norm not the exception. In the case of Peary, it was an unnotified change of address, rather than the culmination of long years of patient waiting for news, which had prompted the recourse to the Agent.

Peary, in his petition, had highlighted a problem which is a particular feature of the correspondence from India. Women whose male relatives had left faced special hardships without them, and their letters pleading for the return of husbands and sons make emotional reading. Saeed ul Nisa Begum spoke of the 'mournful state' in which she had been placed by her husband's emigration. At first taking refuge with her parents, they at last sent her to her father-in-law's house with her son, but her fear that he would do little for her prompted the Begum to address a petition to the Protector:

Most Respected Sir,

I the undersigned Saeed ul Nisa Begum residing at No. 18 Tanappah Chetty Street, Triplicane, Madras, most respectfully beg leave that these few humble lines, setting forth my mournful state, will move your honor's clemency towards me, an unfortunate female, having a boy to support, as it is in your honor's power to grant me the assistance I solicit at your honor's hands.

My husband named Yakoob Hoossain left me and went to Mauritius or Bourbon, as an emigrant in the Mahomedan month of Ramzan which commenced from 25th November to 23rd December of that year. My husband's father gave me no aid, and I staid with my parents at Sydapet village 6 miles from Madras, but having a large family of their own, they now tell me to go away to Mysore to my father-in-law. I do not like to go there, as I fear my father-in-law will not protect me. I therefore enclose a letter to my husband, which you will graciously give to him, as you have the means of knowing his residence.

I humbly beg to enclose a paper to identify my husband, beseeching the favour of a reply addressed to me, a poor female, and praying for your honor's long life and prosperity.

I beg to remain Honored Sir,
Your most obedient and humble servant
Saeed ul Nisa Begum.[100]

With it she enclosed a letter in Urdu for her husband (Figure 4.7), and a minute description of him to aid the search:

Statement of identification of Emigrant Yakoob Hoosain

1	Name	Yakoob Hoossain
2	Size	6 feet – Thin made.
3	Face	Oval
4	Eyes	Large – Squinting.
5	Colour of body	Bomboo
6	Colour of hair	Black
7	Mustaches	Small
8	Beard and whiskers on the Chin and Cheek	Hairs apart
9	Chest	Narrow
10	Hands	Long
11	Palm of Hands	Broad
12	Fingers	Long
13	Legs	Long
14	Feet	Broad and Long
15	Vernacular	Hindustanee which he can read and write as also English and Tamil
16	Birth place	Madras
17	Father's name	Goolam Dustagheer Sahib. Sub Inspector of Police in the Town of Mysore. Presidency of Madras.

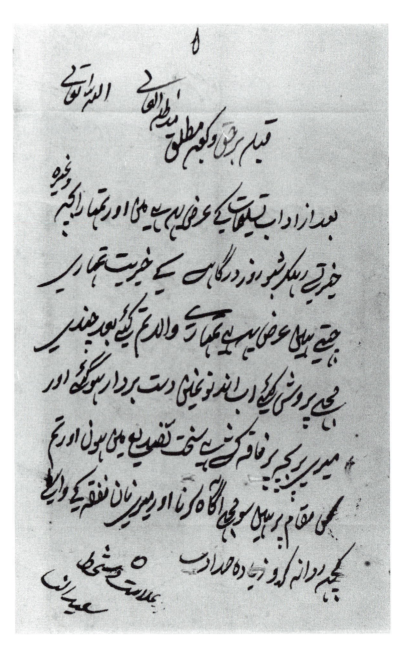

Figure 4.7 Letter (in Urdu) from Saeed ul Nisa Begum to her husband in Mauritius. Source: PA 22.

The authorities at Mauritius evidently could not trace her husband, for the letter lies unclaimed in the archives. Its translation reveals her formal and brief greetings to him and relays her distress and a request for money:

Respected sir,

After greetings this is to say that I and your child are well and we pray for your safety. This is also to say that after your departure your father looked after us for a while but has now relinquished that responsibility and my child is starving. I feel very distressed. Let me know of your whereabouts and send me something for my day to day living expenses. Goodbye. [101]

Her fussily precise description of Yakoob Hoossain in her petition to the Protector again reveals a man of some learning – an ability to read and write Hindustani, English and Tamil – and of a reasonably well-to-do background, his father being Sub-inspector of Police at Mysore. She was probably not literate – a signature on the letter suggests that a scribe had written it on her behalf.

The existence of such correspondence is evidence that indentured migrants could and did retain contact with relatives on a far greater scale than slaves would have been able to achieve, and that the temporary character of indenture allowed those overseas to retain a hope for a life plan which very often incorporated a vision of return. At the same time, the number who achieved this return, or who retained contact with relatives, was always to be a minority of the indentured masses. Contemporary observers reported on the unfortunate circumstances of those who waited without news:

I found wives who had long supposed their husbands dead of starvation and who only learnt through me that the husband had emigrated; parents who had given up their children as lost . . . other wives who knew their husbands had emigrated, but had vainly waited for news, and knew not whether the emigrant was alive or dead. [102]

Folksongs from India record the despair of the women left behind:

All my friends have become mothers,
and I remain lonely and childless
Again and again I pleaded with you not to go East.
For there live women who will win your heart.
For twelve years you haven't written a word:
How shall I spend the days of chait?

Happy is that woman's lot
Whose husband is at home.
Wretched is my fate
Whose husband has gone away.

Absence with its flame
Tortures me each day . . .

The sun is cruel and bright,
A lot of work still to be done.
People have returned to their homes
Yet no call for meals has come for me.
Here, in these lonely fields,
I, the unfortunate, alone work,
My lord being in a distant land,
who will tell me 'Thy lord has come'
The day of thy happiness has dawned'.

From the east came the rail, from the west came the ship,
And took my beloved one away.
The rail has become my sawat
Which took my beloved one away
The rail is not my enemy, nor the ship,
O! It is money which is the real enemy.
It takes my beloved one from place to place,
Money is the enemy.[103]

There are still today ex-indentured workers in Fiji and the Caribbean who receive letters from families left behind in India. Jaipal Chamar left Basti in 1912 for Jamaica, where he spent five years as an indentured labourer, and later settled in Kingston. In 1954 at the age of 66, Jaipal re-established links with his family in India and discovered the existence of a son born after his departure. The boy, Ayodhya Das, wrote the following letters to Jaipal in Jamaica:

Respected father,
You will be surprised to know that a son whom you might not have seen is replying from this side. I was about to born when you left this place. We were two brothers. Our mother looked after us anyhow and we came to Calcutta for service. Fifteen years ago my brother Dwarika passed away and left me alone, unlucky in this world.

Jaipal sent greetings to his former acquaintances in the village and asked after his wife. The son replied in words which indicate his longing to meet a father he had never seen:

Whenever your letter comes I wish I had wings
And could fly away to see you.
Your destitute sister has no one and
I am looking after her
She has gone blind crying for you.
She now lives only with the hope of
seeing her brother's face.
And my mother after receiving your first letter
cried for ten days and died.[104]

The indenture process was thus a decisive break with the past whilst at one and the same time India remained a constant focal point and source of sustenance.

Notes

1. Tinker, 1977: 5. See Reddock, 1985: 84–5, for a view of Indian women enjoying sexual freedom on Trinidad plantations; Emmer, 1985: 247, for a depiction of women as escaping oppressive social relationships in India, and Beall, 1991: 89–116, for a description of 'super-exploited' women in Natal.
2. Kelly, 1992: 246–67; Mohapatra, 1992.
3. For a further discussion of these issues see Carter, 1995: 57–112.
4. See Carter, 1992b: 11.
5. CO 169/11 Ordinance 3 of 1856.
6. :214–15.
7. See for example PA 43 Lachmee to Protector, 29 Oct. 1880.
8. The PD series held at the Folk Museum of Indian Immigration, Mahatma Gandhi Institute, Moka, Mauritius, is a collection of such marriage certificates, generally issued to emigrants at the ports of departure and carried aboard ship to be maintained at the Immigration Office in Port Louis. Lal (1983) interprets family data from Fiji Emigration Passes but Bhana and Bhana (1991) offers no comparable data for Natal.
9. PA 26 Petition of Jhowry, 22 Feb. 1875.
10. Jhowry had arrived as a 26-year-old in 1860, according to the immigration register. He was of the Kahar caste from Gaya and died in Port Louis, PE 91. In describing Deeleea as an 'old female immigrant' in the petition he was simply adopting the contemporary practice in Mauritius of distinguishing those 'new' immigrants still under service of indenture – that is, having spent less than five or ten years in Mauritius – from those who were no longer obliged to undertake plantation work, and were given a special pass as old immigrants.
11. PA 26 Petition of Carpanen, Immigration Department Note, n.d.
12. A Hindu widow or abandoned woman would not only have been economically in a disadvantaged position, but might also have been socially ostracized. The position of widows was gradually ameliorated over the course of the nineteenth century under the influence of various reform movements. See O'Hanlon, 1994.
13. PA 22 Petition of Kurmally, 30 Nov. 1874.
14. See the Royal Commissioners' Report, Case E28, p. 285, for example.
15. PE 107B immigration register of Kumally.
16. See Carter, 1995: 94, for yearly figures of women claimed by relatives in this manner.
17. PA 22 Petition of Boodun, 5 Feb. 1874.
18. See, for example, Jayawardena's comments on marriage patterns in Fiji, in Mishra, 1979: 62.
19. Carter, 1995: 245–8.
20. PA 26 Petition of Rutnag, n.d.
21. Adamson, 1972: 157.
22. Beall, 1991: 109. For a detailed discussion and more examples of wife-murder under indenture see Carter, 1994: 57–112.
23. Lal, 1985b: 142.

24. PE 105, Madras, Feb.–Nov. 1864.
25. PA 43 Petition of Vencatachellum Appoo, 23 Aug. 1880. Appoo had arrived as an 18-year-old from Tanjore in 1864.
26. PA 43 Immigration Department Report, 1/9/1880.
27. PA 43 Petition of Lutchmee, 27 Oct. 1880.
28. PA 43 Immigration Department Note, n.d.
29. PE 92B Register of Immigrants 'Mariner', Aug. 1861.
30. PA 43 Petition of Reshmee, 23 Apr. 1880.
31. PA 43, District Magistrate's Report on Case of Reshmee, 26.4.80.
32. PE 117 Register of Immigrants per 'Allumghier', 1868.
33. : 214.
34. Sanadhya, quoted in the *Fiji Sun*, Friday 23 Mar. 1979, p. 9, and retold in Lal, 1985a.
35. Beall, 1991: 106. For Bibee's story see Carter, 1994: 41–2.
36. Lal, 1983: 112–14.
37. Mesthrie, 1991: 205–6.
38. PA 43 Petition of Jeeachee, 15 Mar. 1880.
39. PA 43 Immigration Department Note, n.d.
40. See for example PA 26 Petition of Nusseebun, who demanded the restitution of a girl to his house.
41. PA 26 Petition of Arnaselum, 20 Feb. 1875.
42. PA 14 Chellumbay to Protector, 7 Oct. 1872. The Powder Mills was the site of an Indian Orphan Asylum set up during the time of Governor Barkly in Mauritius.
43. PA 14 Gookur to Protector, 12 Sep. 1872.
44. PL 79 Petition of Nagen and Camatchee, 8 Sep. 1868.
45. PA 14 Petition of Ramalingum and Allamel, 24 May 1872.
46. PA 14 Inspector, Government Reformatory, to Beyts, 26 Jan. 1872.
47. PA 14 Petition of Jeelea, 2 Oct. 1872.
48. PA 14 Procuror General's Note, 2 Oct. 1872.
49. PA 14 Petition of Cathan, 15 Oct. 1873.
50. PE 45 'Diana', 1854; PE 51 'Lord Hungerford', 1855.
51. PA 26 Petition of Burthee Canadjee, 21 May 1875.
52. PE 50 Immigration Register for the 'Nusser Musjeet', 1855.
53. PA 26 Petition of Burthee, 21.6.1875; Immigration Department Note, n.d.
54. PA 26 Petition of Boodoo, 27 Dec. 1875.
55. CO 167/339 Higginson to Pakington, 3 Dec. 1852, and Colonial Office minutes; CO 167/344 Higginson to Pakington, 25 Apr. 1853, Newcastle to Higginson, 30 July 1853.
56. PA 26 Petition of Carpayee, 25 Aug. 1875.
57. PE 82 'Walter Maurice', 1859.
58. Parliamentary Papers 1875 (C1118) Gordon to Kimberley, 11 Sep. 1871.
59. PA 22 Petition of Beeharry, 26 May 1874.
60. PA 22, Immigration Department Note, n.d.
61. PA 11 Petition of Kisnasamy, 5 July 1871.
62. PA 11 Note of Beyts, 19-7-71; Acting Inspector General of Police 3-8-71. This was approved by a note of A. G. 7-8-71.
63. PA 10 Statement of Bihari Das.
64. PA 10 Statement of Ram Gobind Rae.

65. PA 10 W. Irvine to Superintendent of Indian Immigrants, Mauritius, 5 Nov. 1870; O'Brien, Discharge Certificate, 3 Dec. 1868.
66. PA 68 Nalayapala Venkatasami to the Agent of Emigrants, 5 Apr. 1885.
67. PA 68 Immigration Office note, 10.6.1885.
68. PL 54 Protector to Chennapah, 9 Sep. 1903.
69. PL 24 Letters of Chennappa, 23 Aug. 1907.
70. PL 24 Protector to the Manager, La Barraque, 18 Sep. 1907.
71. PL 24 Protector to Chennapah, 16 July 1907.
72. PA 22 Translation of a petition addressed to the Magistrate of Ratnagiri by a woman named Mhamji known as Dowlatraw Surve inhabitant of Kumbharkham budrukh and Sangmeshwan taluka of the Ratnagiri collectorate, 21 July 1874.
73. PA 22 J. Elphinstone, Collector at Ratnagiri, to Chief Commissioner of Emigration, Mauritius, 25 Aug. 1874.
74. PE 86 'Hyderee', 1860.
75. PB 19 Protector to Collector, Ratnagiri, Bombay, 12 Nov. 1874.
76. PA 67 Deputy Collector, Tanjore, to Colonial Agent Mauritius at Madras, 2 Oct. 1885.
77. PL 14 Protector of Emigrants, Madras, to Protector of Immigrants, Mauritius, 2 Feb. 1905.
78. PL 29 Emigration Agent, Calcutta, to Protector of Immigrants, 22 Apr. 1908.
79. PL 29 Immigration Department Departmental Minute Paper, 1.6.1908.
80. PL 29 Protector to the Manager, Cent Gaulettes Estate, 5/6/1908.
81. PE 241 Immigration Register for the 'Wardha', 1902.
82. PA 24 Emigration Agent, Madras to Protector, Mauritius, 28 Oct. 1875.
83. PE 121 'Latona' 1255, 18 July 1874. The Immigration Register records that Kistnasamy was of the Vellala caste from Vellore, arriving in 1874 and leaving in 1876.
84. PA 68 A. Pillay to Protector of Immigrants, 26 Mar. 1885.
85. PL 79 Emigration Agent, Madras, to Protector, 5 Aug. 1868.
86. PA 54 Protector of Emigrants, Calcutta, to Protector of Immigrants, Mauritius, 24 May 1883; encl. Letter of Baboo Bhicajee, Bombay, 3 May 1883.
87. PL 32 Protector to Colonial Secretary, 3 Nov. 1849.
88. PL 33 Emigration Agent, Calcutta to Protector of Emigrants, Mauritius, 1851.
89. PL 44 Huldar to O. Warner, Esq., Immigration Agent, Mauritius Government, Calcutta, 30 July 1886.
90. PL 45 Immigration Office note, 29.9.1886.
91. PL 46 Chief Clerk, Immigration Department, to the Manager, Riche Bois Estate, Savanne, 6 Sep. 1882.
92. PE 121 Immigration Register for 'Reigate', 1874.
93. PA 36 J. Haly to Protector, Mauritius, 9 Dec. 1876.
94. PL 43 Protector to Emigration Agent, Calcutta, 1 Dec. 1879.
95. PA 42 C. Eales, Emigration Agent, Calcutta, to Protector, Mauritius, 2 Oct. 1880.
96. PA 42 Peary to the Emigration Agent, 1 Oct. 1880.
97. Eales to Protector, 6 Jan. 1881.
98. PA 42 Immigration Department Note, 14-2-81.
99. PE 117 'Calliope' 1170, June 1868. The register records that Heeroo was of the Gowalla caste, which seems unlikely, given the family name of Ghose.
100. PA 22 Petition of Nisa Begum, 13 Jan. 1875.

101. PA 22 Saeed ul Nisa Begum to Yakoob Hussain.
102. Pitcher Report, p. 3.
103. *Uttar Pradesh Ke Lak Geet*, 1971: 46; Elwin and Hivale, 1935; Elwin, 1946: 435; Majumdar, 1946: 29, quoted in Lal, 1983: 113–14, and Lal, 1980: 67.
104. These letters are quoted in Samaroo, 1987b: 43–4.

CHAPTER FIVE

New horizons: the world beyond indenture

Contemporary accounts of the coolie lines and historical analyses of indenture have tended to depict a mode of living and a status for the Indian overseas which comes across as fundamentally static. It is true that for some the girmit years lasted a lifetime, but the contract could also represent a lifeline for a family in India in receipt of a remittance, whilst its completion could signal a new beginning for an old immigrant. The journey across the kala pani certainly marked a break with the past; it also created a class of new providers, some of whom would become property owners overseas, and the founders of new settlements.

New Providers: Relatives and Remittances

Correspondence between families in India and their relatives overseas was undertaken not simply in a desire for news but, as the letters of women in particular show, to request financial support. The letters collected in this section reveal that, for their part, the overseas Indians evinced a great sense of responsibility for the maintenance of their families back home. Despite the distance and the often lengthy periods of separation, the correspondence sent back by Indians working overseas reveals a strong tie with and closeness to the relatives left behind, and a continuing involvement in family problems and celebrations. Of course, the rarity of such documents is a function of their very personal nature. In most cases, letters between migrants and their families only found their way into the archives when the contact had been lost; a testimony to the constraints imposed on such communication by the indenture experience itself.

Indentured labourers who managed to save some money found many ways of providing for their relatives overseas. Remittances were sent through the official channels, but friends and co-villagers returning to India also constituted an important means of maintaining contact with home and passing funds onto the family. Returnees could equally be the bearers of bad tidings, informing relatives of deaths among the overseas migrants. The curator of vacant estates in the colonies was charged with the sale of assets possessed by such individuals and transmitting the money to relatives in India. A further function of returnees was to advise family members of claims they may have had to such funds when the colonial authorities had failed to trace them.

The letters between Sheoraj Tewary of Sultanpur and his brother Ganesh in Mauritius were passed onto the Immigration Department and filed there only when a registered letter sent by Ganesh failed to enclose the bank draft mentioned therein. Sheoraj went to see the local Commissioner, Walter Wells, who was in charge of the registration of emigrants for Sultanpur. He complained that a letter carrier had brought him the registered letter and taken a receipt, and that although the letter stated a bill or draft of Rs200 was enclosed, he had not found it. Sheoraj believed that the draft had possibly been sent to the Calcutta Treasury, because the previous year he had received a Rs100 draft from the same brother. He had been unable to get it cashed at the District Treasury, so he had given it to a mahajan on payment of Rs5. Wells commented: 'This shows how easily a theft and fraud may have been committed in this case'. The Commissioner asked Sheoraj to write a letter to his brother, but since the whereabouts of Ganesh was unknown, Wells forwarded the original letter and envelope from Mauritius to the Emigration Agent at Calcutta, asking the authorities there to try and trace the brother. Wells asked the Agent to make every possible enquiry, 'as the loss of Rs200 in this way, if it be lost, will be most serious to the parties concerned, and not likely to bring credit to the Post Office here, or the authorities at Mauritius'.[1]

The Agent established that the original letter was registered on 22 April at Mare d'Albert, and forwarded it to the Mauritian authorities, together with a letter from Sheoraj for his brother if traced.[2] The letter from Ganesh offers an inkling of the relationship which families maintained despite separation:

After the usual ceremonious expressions, and wishing blessing and good health to persons named in the original, the writer represents:

I have received the letter you sent, and I am much pleased to learn your welfare, but you stated nothing in that letter about the money I sent you before along with my own, this gave me much pains in my heart. The money was sent you by Ramsurup Missa relative of the people of Sajrampur, which you stated you did not receive. You better make a search for the house of Ajudhia Singla of Galal in Kodaimisser Kapurva near Sagrampur and take Rs20 from Ramsurup positively. My uncle Balgobind you had written me before that you were in hard circumstances. At the very sight of your letter I sent you money accordingly and told you not to expend the money uselessly and to purchase cows, bullocks and provisions if possible. I also told you to send you another Hundi that you may pay off the debt if you have any. I hope you will send me a letter quickly. I will send you as much money as you require but you better not expend it uselessly. You should give me information about the money you require through Juggu. I have learnt what you wrote about the marriage of your daughter. Kalka Misser is alive, you should settle according to his advice. Try if you can make arrangements for the marriage of Sheeraj and let me know the result through a letter. I will go after two months. I have learnt the number (of the village) is going to be made in the name of Bishnath. It is advisable to go.

I will see you all. my experience is not imperfect. I will pay all expenses. Look to the value of the case. I have despatched a Hundi of Rs200 to Sultanpur. The Hundi was enclosed in a letter. Go to Chandan and ask from Ramnath Misser where Ramsarup resided. He will tell you. Bring the money by Ganesh. I have paid off what I owed to Kalka Misser. Kali Beehin Zemindavi of Sukhana did not pay me Rs2 she owed me. Do not fear I will take that sum from her anyway how. I have neither father nor mother. I got no further information. I will send you money as soon as I will receive a letter from you. I have purchased land. People wish to purchase the same from me, but I will not sell it. If you tell me, I will sell that land for travelling expenses. Try to get the number of the village for Sheoraj. Ram Sochit is not here. Rs200.

    Ganesh Tiwari offers prayers for Babu Singbali Singla and Amres Singh. You should send me a correct account of what you will have to pay in future and I will send you the amount accordingly. You my uncle Balgobind, you are a worthy man and you should be a well-wisher of the whole family. Through your bounty I have heard Serimal Bhagwat for 7 days. Do not lose the case for money. Be contented. Do not let the case be spoilt. Get the letter written by a good writer. Write in your letter the sum of money you receive from me.[3]

The letter gives few details of Ganesh's life in Mauritius; the only important event he mentions is the acquisition of some land and his unwillingness to sell it unless the family at home has need of money. He, offers the tantalizing 'my experience has not been imperfect' but does not enlarge upon it. His main concern in the letter is with the issues confronting his family back home. He offers advice about an arranged marriage and cautions his uncle to spend the money he has sent wisely. Throughout there is a sense of his feeling of responsibility for and closeness to his family in India. He is concerned about debts, and worried that the money he has sent is not being received. He looks forward to his prospective return. There are also a number of references to individuals both in India and Mauritius, and it is clear that a letter to one family also sought to convey news for other families wishing to hear from relatives in Mauritius, or believed to be so, and sending greetings from the latter in return. Ganesh has evidently used the services of returnees to forward money on occasions, instructing his relatives to apply to neighbouring villages for the same. He writes of his frustration at not hearing from them more regularly and asks them to have their letters written by a good writer.

Sheoraj's reply is even more prosaic, evidently written only to explain the circumstances of the missing draft:

My dear brother

I have received your registered letter, in which you had written that you sent Rs200 in my name in the Sultanpore treasury but in the letter there was no cheque. I send a case against the dock peon; but the office of the Court, after some inquiry from the peon, ordered me to get a letter from you whether you had sent the cheque in the latter or not, or you had forgotten to send it at the time of shutting the envelope.

    Please inform me of this very soon in English the no. of the cheque and the place from which you had sent the money and the place here payable.

Yours affectionately,
Shew Raj Tewary, son of Bal Govind
Village Gal Baha, Zillah Saltanpore.[4]

One is left with the sense that the onus of responsibility lay on Ganesh to provide for and maintain contact with the family at home. In this respect his migration seems to be considered by both himself and his relatives to be but a temporary sojourn in the interest of amassing funds for the family's welfare.

The letter sent by Kulup and Sahadewo to Dwarika Rao and his family shares many of the same features as that of Ganesh. The letter opens with traditional greetings for all family members, reports that the writers are well and expresses a desire to hear the news from family members in India. The important information in the letter is the fact that money has been sent back by means of returning emigrants and that no information has been received as to whether the money reached Dwarika and the family. Once again the importance of writing to the correct address is stressed, and the name of the estate and employer given:

To, Dwarikarawoothoo and his sons and daughters. Kaleph Babooji's Salam to Mother. Salam to Teeluck uncle. Salam to brothers Goorbarry, Mannoo and Pooley. Salam to three brothers' wives. Blessing to Rageeram and Seetaram. Salam for neighbours and acquaintances. Salam for all the elderly people, and, blessing for all the youngsters.

By the grace of Mother, Father, Gungagee and all Dewoothas (or deity) we are quite well. Kulap and Sahadewo are quite well. We all are desirous and waiting to hear about your good health. I have given twenty five rupees in the hand of Rewootee Gourie.

The rupees which were given by both Kulup and Sahadewo in the hands of Gopee Ram, received or not, the letter and 25 rupees given by Kulup and Sahadewo even of this there is no news. One year four months have passed, as yet no news has been received.

If you send letter in future, you must address, thus District Bambou, Wolmar estate, master Challin, to Kulup or Sahadewo.

If spared with life we will meet you all our brethren. Excuse me for the words badly expressed in my letter.

12 Karthik 1285.[5]

The last but one sentence of the letter encapsulates both the longing to return and the recognition that migrants had embarked on a long and perilous mission. This letter had been forwarded to the authorities by Dwarika Rao because his own reply to it had come back. He therefore asked the Agent at Calcutta to obtain the correct address in English of Kulup and Sahadewo.[6]

The problems of communications between migrants and their relatives are underscored by the difficulties experienced at Mauritius in translating the original Hindi letter from Kulup and Sahadewo. Rysingh, a peon in the Immigration Office, said the letter was badly written and he could not decipher it.[7] However, the two men were found; in April 1883 the Emigration Agent at

Calcutta was asked to communicate to Dwarika Rao that their addresses were as follows:

> Kalup Nauth no. 384, 892 and Sahadew no. 384,891, c/o The Manager, Clarens Estate, Black River.[8]

The pictures of these men have been traced in the Immigration Archive at Mauritius (see Figures 5.1a and 5.1b). Both were of the Kurmi caste from the village of Domroa in Bhojpur, Arrah, had arrived together in June 1878, and were engaged to the same estate. Dwarka was Kulup's father, but the son never did return home; despite leaving his wife and family in India, he stayed in Mauritius until his death in 1921.[9]

The few examples of letters which we do have suggest that many indentured labourers were able, through the written medium, to maintain contact. It was only when the communication broke down that the authorities were called in to assist. Thus another Tewary family had kept up a regular correspondence with

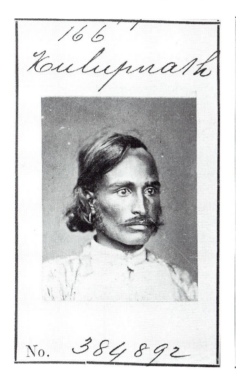 

Figure 5.1(a) and 5.1(b) Kulup and Sahadewo arrived in June 1878. They were both from Arrah, of the Kurmi caste and engaged to a planter in Black River district. Kulup was 28 and had a wife in India, and Sahadewo was 20 years old at that time. They both registered as old immigrants in Mauritius. Kulup died in 1921. Source: PE 131 and PG 28.

one Santo Moharaj at Mauritius. It was only when Jogessur Tewary failed to
hear from his brother Santo for a period of one year that he asked for news. His
letter for Santo was forwarded to the Manager of Beauchamp, Flacq, which was
evidently where Santo had last been heard of.[10]

Many Indian families, however, could not read or write and were therefore
dependent on others to interpret their correspondence. It was also common for
migrants to transmit money or news via other returnees or relatives and
although such means generally constituted effective ways of reaching family
members outside the more cumbersome official channels, the potential for
abuse and treachery was ever present. Rajman Rai had received a regular letter
from Chintuman Singh, at Mauritius. When Rajman died his wife passed on
the letter to Chintuman's brother. However, the middle part of the missive was
missing: only the top and bottom had been forwarded, leaving the brother to
suspect that details about an enclosed remittance had been detached. He
determined to find the whereabouts of Chintuman for himself. The only
information he had was that Chintuman had left more than twenty years earlier
and had stayed some time in Patna before emigrating to Mauritius. In his letter,
however, he had given his address as Rosbel (Rose Belle).[11] The Mauritian
authorities could not find Chintuman and the matter remained unresolved.

Some migrants went to extraordinary lengths to ensure that their remittances
were either paid or returned to them. Chottee Lal took considerable pains to
ensure that his brother had received the sum of Rs50 which he had sent, writing
no fewer than four letters. His story may be taken as representative of the
difficulties inherent in the system. In December 1905 Chottee, a new immigrant, No. 162,016/435,839, expressed a wish to remit Rs40 to his brother
Pandit Chandra Bhall of Behandoor village, Sandillah thanah, in the district of
Hardoi, Lucknow. Chottee was at that time engaged to J. Desplaces of
Curepipe Road. He also sent a letter for his brother.[12] To facilitate this request
the full emigration particulars of Chottee were noted: his caste was described as
'fakir', and he was stated to have left Calcutta on 13 June 1904 aged 21.[13] On
18 December 1905 this remittance was accordingly transmitted to the Indian
authorities, who were asked to ensure that the sum of Rs40 was paid to the
Pandit 'on his showing proof that he is entitled to receive the money'.

Evidently, however, the money was not paid out, because a rather silly error
had been made in Mauritius by which 'the name of the payee had been given as
Pandit . . . it should have been Pandit Chandra Bal'. A further request was made
for the payment of the money and another letter addressed to the Pandit by
Chottee was delivered over. On this occasion the Comptroller, India Treasuries, confirmed that the sum of Rs40 had been paid over.[14]

In January 1907, Chottee Lal sent another remittance of Rs20 to his brother.
Once again, the transaction was not carried out. In July 1907 Chottee accordingly addressed the first of several letters to the Protector, to obtain a reimbursement of the money:

Sir,

*Last year towards the end of August I forwarded to you, through my employer, Mr J
Desplace Rs20 which you had the kindness to send to my brother Chandrabal at Dilla
Hardoye (Bindar) in India. I received a few months ago a notice from the Central Post
Office stating that the man could not be found and that consequently the money had not
been paid and was at my disposal.*

*A few days after I received a letter from my brother in which he told me that he had
applied for the sum at the Post Office in India but had been answered that there was none.
In answer I gave him full instructions as to how he might receive this sum, but I have just
received another letter saying that he has several times applied in vain.*

*Such being the case and considering the long time already elapsed, I wish you to be so
kind as to apply at the General Post Office for the sum and return it to me. I am a poor
immigrant who have but scanty means and I hope you will take my demand into
consideration.*

In expectation of an answer.

I remain, Sir,
Your obedient servant

Chottee Lhal.[15]

Having received no answer, he sent another letter at the beginning of September:

Sir,

*Some time ago I sent you a letter in which I asked you to be so kind as to give orders to
the effect that the money I forwarded last year to my brother, be returned to me, as it was
alleged that the man could not be found.*

*As I have up to now received no answer, I am now obliged to trouble you once more,
for I fear that the letter may have gone astray.*

*As I wrote to you before, I have but scanty means so that an answer would much
oblige.*

Your obedient servant

Chottee Lhal.[16]

Initially the Immigration Office could find no trace of it in their books.
Eventually, a record of the Post Office Order of Rs20 including commission,
made by Moteelall to Chandrabal (through Mr Desplace, Curepipe Road), was
located, but the money had been returned and was therefore still at the disposal
of Chottee. A memorandum was sent to Chottee to this effect. The Protector
was advised that:

There was apparently no record whatever kept in this office of the Rs20 handed in
by Mr Desplaces on behalf of his labourer Chottee no. 425839 for remittance to
his brother Chandrabal in India. The order was not paid to the payee owing
probably to the name of remitter having been incorrectly given; i.e. Moteelal
instead of Chottee.

Chottee was now to be asked, in September 1907, whether he wished the order to be readvised to Calcutta giving the correct names.[17] A letter was accordingly forwarded to Mr J. Desplaces requesting him to inform Chottee that the remittance of Rs20 was still unpaid, and that the money order could be sent back to Calcutta or paid back to him by the General Post Office on production of a receipt. In reply, Chottee sent a third letter explaining that he had no receipt because Mr Desplaces had remitted the money on his behalf:

Sir,

Referring to your memo No. B 893/1282/07 dated August 28.07 I have the honor to tell you that I am not in possession of any receipt from the post office for the money was not directly sent by me but remitted to you *by my employer Monsieur J Desplaces to be kindly transmitted to my brother Chandrabal in India. This was in November 1906. In expectation of an answer and thanking you before hand.*

I am Sir,
Your obedient servant,

Chottee Lhal.[18]

Mr Desplaces himself also called at the Immigration Office in November 1907 and intimated that his labourer Chottee wished to have the money paid back to him, handing in the relevant papers. Later that month, Chottee sent in his fourth letter, asking if anything had been done in his case:

Monsieur,

Il y a quelque temps de cela, mon employeur Mr J Desplace vous remit certains papiers au sujet d'un mandat poste par moi expédié dans l'Inde et qui n'a jamais été payé. Il n'a pas eu depuis le temps d'aller vous voir.
Avez vous pu faire quelque chose pour moi, vous me rendrez un grand service en me le faisant savoir.
Avec mes remerciement anticipés.

Je demeure Monsieur
Votre obeisant serviteur

Chottee Lhal.[19]

In reply, Desplaces was informed again in December that Chottee would need to call at the Office with his receipt. One begins to doubt whether poor Chottee ever saw his Rs20 again, and whether he was not persuaded to find some other means to help out his brother in India! The hapless Chottee is pictured in Figure 5.2.

Of course, such correspondence as can be found in the archives concerning remittance procedure tends to exaggerate its flaws, because documentation was only generated when moneys had gone missing or not been claimed. In Dauhoo's case, at least, the efficacy of the system was demonstrated. A proprietor at L'Escalier in Mauritius, he had sent Rs25 to his sister to be forwarded to Gaya, 'place called Nurhut pargana Hasooa thana gaon palee'. Some time later he received a letter from his sister informing him that she had as yet not got the money. However, the Protector was able to discover that the remittance, which had been made on 13 May 1884, had been paid to the woman in Calcutta on 21 July 1884.[20]

In some cases, migrants went so long without news of their families in India that by the time they came to enquire about the fate of their remittances, some of the recipients were already dead. In May 1899, an immigrant named Bhoyroo, No. 303,397, called at the Protector's office and made the following statement:

I left two brothers in India when I embarked for Mauritius about thirty years ago. Although I have posted several letters to their address, yet I have never heard from them. About 18 years ago I sent a registered letter containing a remittance of fifty rupees to one

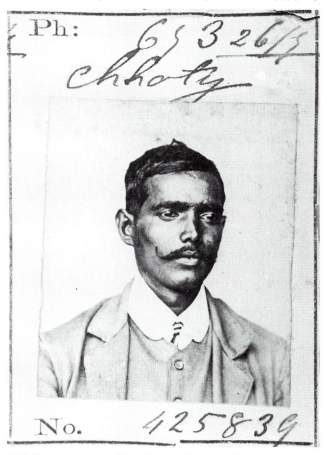

Figure 5.2 Chottee came to Mauritius in 1904 as a 20-year-old. He was of the Thakur caste and originated from Hardoi. The photograph was taken in 1911. Source: PE 151 and PG 51.

> *of them named Sidar. I would wish to be informed whether they are alive or not. Their address at the time was Zillah Hazareebag, Purgana Rampoor, Thana Bogodah. The last time I wrote to my brother named Gunnessee was on the 13 November 1896 and on inquiry at the Post Office at Mauritius in July 1897 I was informed that the letter has been delivered to the Indian Office to the addressee on the 14 December 1896.*

The Protector accordingly wrote to the Emigration Agent at Calcutta, asking him to enquire as to the whereabouts of Bhoyroo's brothers Gunnessi and Sidar; their father's name, he added, was Kakundoo.

In March 1901 the reply was received that information had been obtained by the Deputy Commissioner of Hazaribagh that Sidar, brother of the emigrant Bhoyroo, was still alive, but that Gannessi had died five or six years before. Sodar Kahar, now described more accurately as the father's name, and Luttaha Kahar, Chohna Kahar and Lidna Kahar, the brothers of Gannessi (and presumably of Bhoyroo and Sidar also), were reported to be alive and to be living at Mashipiri, thana Barhi, outpost Barkata. The delay in procuring this information was ascribed to the fact that the name of the thana as given had been incorrect. A memorandum was accordingly sent to Bhoyroo of Grande Rosalie estate informing him of these findings. Thus after thirty years the migrant gained some scant knowledge of his family.[21] Bhoyroo died in Mauritius in 1915, and, since he declared his age as 40 when he had arrived in 1864, this would have made him 91 years old at his death.[22]

When the fears of writers such as Kulup and Sahadewo were realized, and migrants died overseas or on their way home, relatives petitioned the local authorities for the goods left by the deceased relative. Malayen was anxious to claim money left by his elder brother who, returning from Mauritius, had died of cholera on the way to Trichinopoly. Malayen had heard that a cheque was due to him and requested payment of the same by writing from India to the Protector of Immigrants in Mauritius:

> *The humble petition of Malayen youngest brother of the deceased Venathethan, residing at Erraiyoor in the Perambalur taluq of the Trichinopoly district*
>
> *Sheweth*
>
> *That on the way to Trichinopoly, he was attacked by cholera and died at Oolluntoor; at his death bed, he advised to the village moonsiff of that place to give over the money with him and the cheque to his youngest brother Malayen.*
>
> *That officer transmitted the properties of the deceased to the tahsildar who after close enquiry has found out that Malayen is entitled to them he then got the cheque remitted at the Trichinopoly Treasury but he was informed that the money had been remitted or returned at your honor's office. He begs your honor will be good enough to issue order for payment and intimate him of the same.*
> *A copy of which is herein enclosed.*
> *For which act of kindness I shall every pray.*
>
> *His mark*
>
> *(Tamil signature).*[23]

In this case, however, there were competing claims for the money, and Malayen was informed that the amount had been paid to his brother's widow. The untimely end of Malayen's brother is a reminder of the final hazard which awaited time-expired migrants: the return passage and the journey back to the natal village.

Not all relatives anxiously awaited news of their migrant family members. In some cases the journey overseas had been undertaken as an act of defiance or escape, and it was only in death that the fate of such individuals was communicated to their families in India. Parboteea had allegedly eloped with one Biku Rai to Mauritius after the death of her husband, taking a nephew, Bhirgunath Rai, with them. However, on hearing of her death, her brothers, Ootun and Bhorosa Rai, laid claim to her estate. The Calcutta Police report noted caustically: 'the woman having left her home with Biku Rai lost her caste ... (the family) dismembered all connection with her but hearing that she has left some estate have now appeared as heirs'.[24]

Bishnu Upadhia was motivated perhaps more by poverty than by greed in seeking to recover the property of his brother Babooram. He had learnt that his brother had left on his death Rs30, which was in the custody of the Mauritian government. He accordingly petitioned the Protector at Mauritius through the Magistrate of Ghazipur, requesting an enquiry to be made to investigate his claim to that estate:

The humble petition of Bishnu Upadhia
of Zilla Ghazeepore, Pergunnah Koodhu, Mouza Lodepore

Most respectfully sheweth

> *That your poor petitioner has learnt that his brother named Babooram Upadhia who was an emigrant at Mauritius, district Lapoodohar, thanah Naide Lapoodohar Koti or plantation Moosatope died in the month of Bysack 1288 ie the month between April and May of 1881 leaving a deposit of Rs30 under the custody of government.*
>
> *That your poor petitioner therefore prays that such measures may be adopted as will enable your poor petitioner to be a recipient of the money.*
>
> *That your poor petitioner ventures to state moreover that an enquiry may be made by the police authorities of the district of Ghazeepore with a view to ascertain whether or not your poor petitioner is the lawful legatee of the estate.*

and as in duty bound your petitioner will ever pray

s. of Bishnu Upadhia.[25]

Evidently the network of returnees was functioning well enough for Bishnu to have heard of his brother's death, but the Indianization of the Mauritian place names as usual did not make Babooram Upadhia's identification easy. The Immigration Department decided that Lapoodohar was probably meant to be Poudre d'Or, but they could find no person of the name mentioned who had died there during that year. However, a man named Babooram Teebaluck had died on Schoenfeld estate at Poudre d'Or in April 1881. The man's Immigration Register entry listed his village, pargana and zillah as respectively Busdowa, Gurleea and Ghazipur. He had arrived from India in the ship *Gainsborough* in 1873.[26] The notorious inaccuracy in the recording of names at the point of entry was probably responsible for the discrepancy. The case demonstrates the difficulties of deciding upon the claims of relatives given the problems of identifying individuals, although in this case Bishnu's relative had been accurately located. In 1883 a bank draft to the value of 304 rupees, 15 annas and 6 paise was sent to Bishnu in settlement of his claim to the estate of Babooram.[27]

When Daroobibi sought to claim her husband's estate she did so with a very stylish petition and no fewer than eight signatories, including local dignitaries and a priest:

I Daroobibi wife of Balloo mia of Panalja taluka Khed district Ratnagiri in the Presidency of Bombay, India beg you most humbly and respectfully that my husband Balloo Mia was serving there as Police man under your command for about 8 or 9 years and who died there in his duty by twenty two days' fever on 22nd June 1899. Balloo mia left here four men, viz I and my three sons I was maintaining by the money which he used to send monthly from his wages. Now no one here who could help to support me and my sons. I am a poor woman and no means neither estate nor business by which I can live.

My sons are minors i.e. the eldest son is of 14 years old second 11 years and the third 10 years. I most humbly beg you therefore to overlook my poor condition and kindly offer me the fund standing in my husband's name.

I would have come up to you to ask justice from your kind honour but as I am a woman and nothing left with me for the fares of steamship the consequence being that I am unable to do so and therefore your honour will greatly oblige me to give same to my husband's brother Nazirkhan Manoorkhan who is serving there in government's boat who will remit here by post on having paid the amount of fund oblige me to inform with the sum paid to him.

I herewith enclosed my application to Police Patel and a report from him and a copy of power to Nazirkhan Manoorkhan which I trust your honour will find in good order.

I beg to remain Sir
Your most obedient servant

Mark of Daroobibi wife of Balloo mia

Witnesses to the mark
1. *Allykhan Shaboodeen Khan*
2. *Jenanarkhan Budakhan*
3. *Molvi Syed Habibullah (priest of this place)*
4. *Omarkhan Jamalkhan*
5. *Samsarekhan Mamsorkhan*
6. *Talemarkhan Masoodkhan*
7. *Ameerudeen Amroodeen*
8. *Allykhan Saley khan.*[28]

Her petition reveals that hers was one of many families that received regular remittances from relatives serving in Mauritius. Her deceased husband, Balloo Mia, had been a serving police officer in the island. As with others, more than one member of the family was working in Mauritius: she also had a brother-in-law in government employment on the island. Ratnagiri, the coastal district of Maharashtra from where she originated, was one of the most important districts for migration from Bombay to Mauritius.

When letters in the vernacular languages reached the Immigration Office at Mauritius, individuals from the linguistic regions concerned were asked to ascertain to whom the letter was addressed, and if this was not understood, to open it and decipher the contents. Since many of the missives were written by persons transcribing the verbal request of illiterate migrants or their relatives, and who themselves had only a scant knowledge of the written form, many of these communications could not be easily understood. In the case of a letter written in the Telegu language by one Misal Papama of Parowtiporum, Coringhy, to her son Appadoo in Mauritius, two different translations were made. Abdool deciphered the letter as follows:

> That she has received Rs60 from his [*sic*] son Appadoo in October and since that time she has not received any money from him. She is desirous to know whether Appadoo continues sending her, every month, any money: as he promised her to do so when he sent the Rs60 in October.[29]

According to the translation made by Luchmaya, peon of the General Board of Health, however, the letter read: 'that she has heard that her son Appadoo who is in Madras has made a remittance of Rs60 in her favor and that she has not received the money yet'. The letter in the original Telegu is reproduced as Figures 5.3a and 5.3b, and the more literal translation is as follows:

> *We the residents of Parvatiperam in the district of Vishakhapatnam, Cudari Chuncu and Miisala Paramma, inform you, as follows:*
>
> *We came to know through the Collector of Vishakhapatnam that Miisala Appadu sent money to us. But since he had gone from here, only in August he had sent us only Rs60. Since then we do not have any information from him in spite of our writing to him several times. Because of this, his mother is feeling very sad and is facing a lot of problems for day to day living.*
> *Your excellency may kindly call him and enquire into the matter and ask him to send money every month and request him to write two letters per month. He is writing that he is making payment every month. But we have not received any. Since Appadu is not giving any reply, we are writing to you.*
>
> *September 31, 1885*
>
> *Chenchu (Vralu).*[30]

In any case, the Protector was unable to help the woman contact her son because they could not understand his address. He did check the number of remittances she had received, however, and minuted:

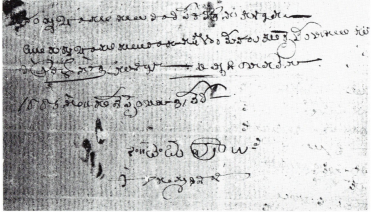

Figs 5.3(a) & 5.3(b) Letter (in Telegu) from Chenchu and Misal.
Source: PL 48

I submit the writer be informed that the address of her son Appadoo not being properly given her letter cannot be sent to him and that she be informed that he has made no remittance to her through this office. Search has been made as far back as June 1884.[31]

In 1886 the Protector at Mauritius received an enquiry about one Ajudhia Sing, said to have died on the island. A petition had been presented at the Benares Court by Ramjing Sing to the effect that intimation had reached him that his brother Ajudhia Sing, son of Boijnath Sing, had died at Rusknar Lutrony in the colony of Mauritius. He requested that the property left by his deceased brother might be made over to him, that he might perform the funeral ceremonies of the deceased and support his widow. The Magistrate therefore wrote to ascertain whether Ajudhia Sing was really dead and had left any estate behind him in the colony. Eventually, in October 1891, the sum of 205 rupees, 1 anna and 9 paise was received in part payment of the vacant estate of Adjudya Singh, No. 10,108. This immigrant must have come to Mauritius in the 1840s, judging by his number, and in this case at least, his family had gained some pecuniary benefit from the migration. One cannot help wondering, nevertheless, about the situation of his wife and whether she had remained all the intervening years separate from her husband, since she was obviously resident in India at the time of his death.[32]

Payments made for the estate left by deceased migrants could be complicated if there were competing claims in Mauritius and India. The authorities tried to deal with this by awarding only part of the sum left by an individual to any heirs in the island, and notifying the Indian government of the death to ascertain whether other heirs would come forward from that country. Eventually, in the event of no further claims, the whole of the estate would be paid to the heirs in Mauritius. When Chakkan, No. 408,253, died, his brother Goordin, also in Mauritius, managed to acquire the entire estate in this way. It was not until an heir in India, one Karia, made enquiries concerning Chakkan that the Mauritian Curator of Vacant Estates realized that Goordin had acted fraudulently. Chakkan had evidently died in 1899, because enquiries concerning any Indian heirs were made to the Emigration Agent in October 1899. However, it took two years for the answer to come back that Chakkan did indeed have an heir, by which time Goordin had already claimed the estate. In fact it was not until May 1901 that Karia, the brother of Chakkan, had been alerted by the Magistrate of Basti as to his claim for the estate, and had acquired a Succession Certificate, which, in that month, was duly forwarded to Mauritius. The Curator of Vacant Estates had in the meanwhile written to the Protector in 1899 and mentioned that Goordin had:

claimed the estate immediately after the death of Chakkan. In the month of February 1900 he again applied to me for a settlement of his claim and would not wait any longer. I paid Goordin upon production of (1) an affidavit by himself and (2) another affidavit by another Indian immigrant, both to the effect that Goordin is *the sole* heir of Chakkan. As Goordin left Mauritius for India in 1884 and returned to Mauritius in 1890 it could be supposed that he was aware whether Chakkan had any other heir, than himself, in India.[33]

The Curator suggested that the heir traced in India might claim his share from Goordin, No. 385,806. The Protector at Mauritius accordingly informed the Emigration Agent at Calcutta:

> all that I can now do is to endeavour to find Goordin and prosecute him for the fraud of which he has been guilty. Should Goordin be in possession of any property either moveable or immoveable I may be able to obtain Karia's share, if he has no property nothing more can be done to secure Karia's share.

Such correspondence reveals the slow working of the emigration bureaucracy in such cases, but also highlights the family character of migration, Chakkan having followed his brother Goordin to Mauritius. It seems likely that Chakkan had come to the island as a result of his brother's migration, but evidently, assuming that Karia's claim was not a fraudulent one, Goordin felt no sense of responsibility towards his surviving family in India.[34] Goordin is pictured in Figure 5.4.

Other attempts to trace relatives overseas were made not to claim the earnings or estate of migrants, but rather to defend property interests in India itself. Bhyro Roy, the brother of Hanooman and Matadeen Roy who had emigrated to Mauritius around 1864, wished to inform them, if still living in Mauritius, 'of the state of their private affairs in India'.[35] He therefore addressed a petition to the Magistrate of Bustee asking him to write to Mauritius and request that Hanooman and Matadeen be sent back to India:

Cherisher of the Poor,

I humbly beg to represent that Ramchurn Roy, my deceased father executed a deed of mortgage termed 11 years, in favor Ramtohul Sahoo, Bijnath Sahoo, and died after the execution of the said document, leaving four sons namely, Hunooman Roy, me, Bhyro Roy, Doorga Roy and Matadeen Roy. Hunooman and Matadeen went away to Mauritius in the year 1271 Fuslee, the former has three sons, of whom two are minors, and one has arrived of age and the latter has one son only, besides myself and Doorga Roy – are in existence. The term of the above document is about to expire, & owing to the minority of the son of Hunooman Roy the Mohajun do not wish to make out a fresh document, & thus being the case, our ancestral property will shortly be destroyed for nothing. I can not go to such a distant place in search of Hunooman & Matadeen.
I suppose that the address of the second person may be obtained through the chief officer at Mauritius. I therefore pray that a letter from your office may be forwarded to office at Mauritius requesting them to search out the above individuals and send them up here informing them of the above facts.

s. of Bhyro Roy
Proprietor share holder of
Malownee by the pen of
Samboo Persand Moollteor.[36]

His petition pointed out that Ramchurn Roy, their dead father, had mortgaged the ancestral property and Bhyro now required the presence of his brothers to renew the document. Both men evidently had families in India but had failed to maintain contact with their wives and children. Bhyro's petition indicates that the Roys in Mauritius came from a small landowning family in India; not all of the brothers had perhaps been able to sustain a livelihood from the fields they owned. Unusually, the name of the writer is appended to the petition.

Figure 5.4 Goordin arrived in Mauritius at the age of 30. He was of the Chamar caste, from Gorakhpur. He is registered as an old immigrant in 1883 and returned to India in 1884. The photograph was taken a month before his departure. Source: PE 131 and PG 29.

Money was also often claimed by migrants who had returned to India, in the form of debts which had not been recovered by them prior to their departure. In the case of Shamin, however, the Protector informed his opposite number in Calcutta that the amount due to him by M Robillard had been paid and was being forwarded, but that:

> Shamin could easily have recovered the amount previous to his leaving the island but being indebted to another man in the service of M Robillard he was apprehensive of a counter claim being made against him.[37]

It was evident that many migrants returning to India were worried about carrying their savings with them, for fear of being robbed. The authorities provided a service whereby the money could be paid into the Immigration Office, and bills given which were then drawn at the port of arrival. But the returnees were unhappy at being kept in Calcutta a day longer than necessary, and commenting on bills given to migrants by one return vessel the Protector noted:

> a much larger number would have been taken if the people had not feared detention in Calcutta, their idea in leaving this appears to be not to wait beyond a day in Calcutta and to start for the mofussil at once and in Bands; – were the agents of the Bank to discount those Bills on presentation, I have no doubt that as soon as the fact was known here, many would avail themselves of this safe mode of taking home their savings.

The return to India of emigrants with their savings, as well as the sending of remittances, must undoubtedly have had some impact on the families left behind, and indeed on those villages which sent a significant proportion of their youth to the colonies. There is however, scant evidence of the scale of this return of capital or the uses to which it was put, other than the observations of contemporary officials who tended to be proponents of emigration, such as George Grierson. Nevertheless his records of conversations with returnees in the 1880s are of some value. He notes sums spent by such individuals in order to reintegrate themselves in their villages. Thus Gobardan Pathak, a returnee from Demerara, was described as having spent Rs300 – 400 to 'get back into caste'. It had cost Nankhu Rs100 to achieve this; he had subsequently married and was running a shop in the bazaar at Baksar. Jibod Chamar, whom Grierson met in Shahabad, had apparently lent out most of his savings of Rs300 to his circle of acquaintances, but was evidently not much of a success as a money lender, as he had not been able to claim the interest and was returning to Mauritius after a five-year stay in India.[38]

New Lifestyles: Property, Landownership and Family Regroupment

It was perhaps inevitable that most migrants should ultimately forge a new life for themselves overseas. As Ram Bahadur remarked:

> After five years indenture you could go back to India at your own expense – but on 8 annas a day how could you save the fare. After five more years the government would pay your fare back; but this was cunning, they knew that after 10 years most would have settled, have a wife and family, and wouldn't want to go back.[39]

Those most likely to be able to acquire capital and settle as property owners were the sirdars, who received higher rates of pay for their supervisory functions and were sometimes given responsibility for the pay of the men under their charge. Examples abound of sirdars acting as money lenders on estates, opening shops and even gambling establishments, and playing key roles in land and property acquisitions in the various colonies. In 1877, a man called Barathsing, who had arrived in Trinidad as an indentured labourer in 1856, owned an estate and was reportedly worth £11,000.[40] Visiting the Albion Estate in the Black River district of Mauritius in 1872, the Inspector of Immigrants reported being directed by an Indian sirdar to:

> his very comfortable quarters, to which he had returned from India with two wives, and where he had cattle, fowls, and other comforts, and a donkey and cart.[41]

Having acquired capital from their work as sirdars, Indians went on to set up as independent proprietors, job contractors and shop owners. As they moved into the colonial elite, they became in their turn employers – and exploiters – of Indian labour. The Indian contractor Doolub is a case in point. Calleemootoo, who had migrated from Tranquebar as a boy in 1859, was engaged to Doolub for five years, and then went to work for Gungah, an Indian jeweller. However, he was arrested as a deserter from Doolub's employ, and to avoid imprisonment and separation from his pregnant wife he was forced to enter a new three-year engagement with Doolub. The status and position of Doolub seemed to be analagous to those of his white counterparts: at his shop and residence he frequently played host to the British magistrate of the district, and was thus hand in glove with the local judiciary. It was this same magistrate who had forced Calleemoottoo to re-engage with Doolub.[42]

The legal battles of the Ramtohul family reveal that whilst Indians could and did emerge from indenture to join the elite class of estate owners in Mauritius, this did not always guarantee trouble-free interactions with the legal profession. Ramtohul, a Rajput from Patna, had arrived on the island in 1856 as a 34-year-old indentured immigrant.[43] By 1870 he was possessed of sufficient capital to establish himself on an estate of his own, Mon Choix. Following the death of

Ramtohul, his family experienced difficulties with the legal requirements for transfer and inheritance of their estate. Corbane and Sougnia, who were the heirs of the old immigrant, found that their claim to Mon Choix was blocked by the dead man's legal representative, who was effectively reaping the proceeds of the estate himself. Ramtohul, who died in July 1871, had paid in cash one-fifth of the asking price a year earlier, and during the following year a further sum had been paid over from the produce of the estate. When he died only around one-fifth of the total amount was still outstanding, but on that day Ramtohul had appointed A. Boule to oversee his affairs. Mr Boule was now showing some reluctance to turn the estate over to Ramtohul's heirs. The whole story was related to the Protector in a petition drawn up for the heirs:

> *The humble petition of Corbane, son of Khoyrathy and his wife Sougnia both Heirs of Mon Choix Estate, of Pamplemousses.*
>
> *Respectfully Sheweth,*
> *That your Petitioners' being the Heirs of Ramtohul no. 172275, who deceased about some years ago and he was a Landowner and Planter of Mon Choix Estate.*
> *The deceased Ramtohul had bought the abovesaid of Mon Choix on the 25th June 1870 with Mr Autard de Bragard for the sum of $49000, and paid the same on that very day, the sum of $10000, and the remaining sum of $39000, due to Mr Autard de Bragard and pledged the same, with him and payable instalmently by the produces of Mon Choix Estate as mentioned terms. Ramtohul had taken Mr A. Boule son, as a Broker and mandatairy for his own affairs on the 5th July 1871 previous to his death, who still possess with the same Estate up to this day. Unfortunately the said Ramtohul having been died on the 5th July 1871 he left his legitimate wife Sougnia and his Daughter a minor girl Cadnee.*
> *That your petitioner Sougnia after her husband's death, she married with one Corbane the son of Khoyrathy on 25th May 1872 in Civil Status office of Pamplemousses.*
> *But now that the said Broker and mandatairy Mr A. Boule son who is unwilling to show the accounts and Benefits of the produces of the Estate of Mon Choix he himself enjoying the same.*
> *Therefore your petitioner's prays your Honor may be pleased to take their poor case into your favourable consideration upon reading the note which is annexed with this, and that your Honor will have the kindness to visit the Estate and to examine the accounts from her late husband's time up to this day.*
> *And your petitioner not having a proper protection in taking cares of the produces of the said Estate but Mr A. Boule son Enjoying the same.*
> *By doing this act of Benevolence your petitioner's will ever pray the almighty to give good life and prosperity for your Honor and your Honor's family.*
>
> *X Sougnia's mark	C. Khoyrathy.*[44]

The petition of Corbane and Sougnia reveals that whether indentured or free, Indians in Mauritius had to battle with a judicial system which was weighted against them. Whether issuing penal sanctions against deserters or drawing up dubious sale and transfer documents, Indians had few friends amongst the legal community. Such legal wrangles nevertheless provide an insight into the family ties of Mauritian Indians and the mores which they adopted. Sougnia's case, for example, demonstrates the ease with which Hindu widows, especially if possessed of some property, were able to remarry overseas.

Whilst few ex-indentured Indians could aspire to acquire the status of Ramtohul, many did at least seek to remove their family and kin from the work contracts which bound them. Madharee offered to pay the remaining industrial residence, which constituted the equivalent of two years' wages, of his relative who was engaged to a Mr Koenig at Black River, so that he could send him back to India. He outlined his intentions in a petition addressed to the Protector:

> *The humble petition of Madharee of the District of*
> *Plaine Wilhems, place called 'Beau Bassin', proprietor.*
>
> *Respectfully sheweth:*
>   *That your Petitioner has a parent who arrived in this colony as coolie, and who is now in the depot. That your Petitioner wishes to have his parent who is still a new immigrant. That your Petitioner's parent is now working in the employ of Mr Koenig, at Black River.*
>   *Wherefore your Petitioner come respectfully before your honor and pray that you will be pleased to tell your said Petitioner whether he can pay two years wages in advance for his said parent, and then, to send his parent in India.*
>   *Your Petitioner further saith that his said parent, was engaged in the service of Mr. Koenig for five years, and he has made three years, now.*
>
> *And as in duty bound*
> *your Petitioner will ever pray*
>
> *Madharee.*[45]

The financial sacrifice this must have entailed is a testimony to the will of old immigrants to remove relatives from indenture.

Veerapen's attempt to buy his son out of indenture provides a further insight into the processes of Indian family settlement. Veerapen and his wife were from Tiruchchirappalli in south India and established a family on the island. Veerapen's name – Maistry – indicates that he was a recruiter, and perhaps as such he had returned to India with his wife and children. They arrived back in Mauritius in March 1870: Veerapen, his wife Jholachy, a son and daughter of 6 and 10, and 12-year-old Colendaveloo.[46] His creole-born elder son was under contract to the same planter as himself, and soon after their return Veerapen sought to buy both of them out of indenture. In 1870 and 1871 he made two payments to Hirth for this purpose, but Colendaveloo was not released from his contract. Veerapen accordingly addressed the following petition to the Protector:

> *The humble Petition of Veerapen Maistry, no. 339,842,*
> *residing in Port Louis. Respectfully sheweth:*

That your Petitioner who had left Mauritius for India, came back in this island in the month of March 1870, with his family among whom was a son, native of this colony, aged twelve years, named Colendaveloo, under engagement with Mr. Hirth of the Sugar Estate Wolmar in the District of Savanne. That soon after his arrival viz: on the 8th day of August in the same year, your Petitioner obtained from Mr. Hirth, leave to purchase his industrial residence and then of his son by paying to his Employer the Expences incurred by him: That on that very day he paid to Mr Hirth the sum of $47.50 and on the 25th July 1871, another sum of $50, as the same is evidenced by two receipts signed by Mr Hirth, who on the same day, authorized his son Colendaveloo to remain with his father for a period of one year. That up to this day and notwithstanding the application of your Petitioner, Mr Hirth has not signed the necessary document for the release of Colendaveloo.

That your Petitioner whose wife died on the Estate Wolmar and one child in town, respectfully submits that he believes that the sum of ninety-seven dollars and fifty cents, paid by him to Mr Hirth is more than sufficient to meet the Expences of this latter.

Under the above circumstances, your Petitioner humbly prays, your Honor will be pleased to take his case into consideration and order the release of his son aforenamed if it is in your power, or to take some steps to have the same granted by the competent authority.

Your Petitioner has the honor to be Sir
your most obedient and humble servant. [47]

The Stipendiary Magistrate reported that Veerapen Maistry had been released from industrial residence by Hirth on 28 July 1871 and although two other children of Veerapen were mentioned on the receipt, there was nothing about Colendaveloo. The latter was engaged to Charron, probably a Franco-Mauritian colonist and sugar estate owner who required $64 to release the boy from his engagement. [48]

The compassion for relatives evinced by those who petitioned to remove them from work contracts is powerfully demonstrated by Shahaduth's attempt to rescue his aunt, Gahoree. He explained that she was very old and infirm and had been ill-treated by one Mangroo, shopkeeper, in whose house she resided:

The humble petition of Shahaduth no. 141887, old immigrant of the District of Grand Port at the place called Rose Belle, a laborer.

Respectfully sheweth:

That your Petitioner's Aunt named Gahoree is now residing in the house of Mr Mangroo of the district of Grand Port at the place called Rose Belle, a shop keeper.

That the said Gahoree is very old and unable to work. That your Petitioner having been informed that the said Gahoree was ill-treated by the said Mangroo went four days in order to see the said Gahoree and was prevented by the said Mangroo. That as your Petitioner is ready to supply for the necessary wants of life of his Aunt, humbly prays that he should be authorized to take her from the said Mangroo's house.

That your Petitioner hopes that you will take into favorable consideration this his present application in ordering that he should be authorized to see his said Aunt 'Gahoree', in order that she may come and live with your said Petitioner.
And as in duty bound your Petitioner shall ever pray.[49]

Shahaduth was a Muslim who had arrived in 1854, and having acquired the status of old immigrant was evidently determined to help his relatives in need.[50] This feature of the indenture process, entailing loss of control over the lives of family and kin, was one aspect which was keenly felt by the participants, and which their petitions and letters forcefully expressed, but which the official literature rarely documented.

By the end of the indenture era, many thousands of young, able-bodied Indians had given their working lives to the sugar plantations of Mauritius, and then either returned to India for their final years or stayed on the island with their locally born families. Mansahai was one of those who chose to return to his native land to die, but like many he had raised a family in Mauritius for whom that island was home, and back in India he found himself once again in exile, separated from his loved ones. The correspondence between Mansahai and his son and grandson, written in a working man's Hindi, underscores the sense of isolation of the old man, as he sought to persuade the younger members of the family to pay him a last visit in India before he died.

Mansahai, No. 429,838 had come to Mauritius on the steam ship *Surada* from Calcutta in August 1910. He was then aged 18 and his caste was listed as Dhuniar (that is, Bhumiya). He was from the village of Kudasu in zillah Etah. Mansahai was allotted to Antoinette estate. He remained in Mauritius for thirty-seven years and was repatriated to India per *Jehangir* in 1947, just as his country was freeing itself from the yoke of British rule. Mansahai's daughter Calawatee, now 76 years old, is still living in Mauritius, and the letters which her father wrote from India to his grandson, Premchand Bunjhoo, have been kept by the family.[51]

The letters of Mansahai are in effect fragments only. The beginning and end of the first letter are missing (Figures 5.5a and 5.5b). The letter writer refers to Bhagwat, which was the nickname of Premchand Bunjhoo, and to the daughter-in-law, Premchand's wife. Rajo and Calawatee, also mentioned, were the two daughters of Mansahai, born in Mauritius. Premchand is the son of Kalawatee. In the first letter Mansahai writes:

I have received and read your letter and I was very happy to hear your news. I have sent you two letters. I don't know whether you have received the letter I sent to you on the 16th. I have not received any reply to it. In India everybody wants you, Bhagwat, to come here with the daughter-in-law. Bhagwat, Rajo, Calawatee and Premchand, everybody should come. Come to Bombay. When you come to Bombay, I will definitely be in a position to come and collect you. My address is village Faridpur, tahsil Kayamganj, Kanasi P. O., zillah Farukabad. And when you come to Bombay you ring me. Then I will come and meet you. Give blessings to Mansahai Lankesh and Rughoobeer; I am longing to see them . . . Thank you.

The Hindi in the first letter is more standard than that of the second letter, which appears to be Bhojpuri-influenced and is correspondingly more difficult to translate today. In the second letter, in fact, the writer is attempting to convert a spoken vernacular into the written form. It is probable that neither of the letters was written by Mansahai himself, and they seem to have been written by two different people for him. The second letter contains a plea for one of his relatives to return to India. Mansahai is worried about his impending death and is perhaps concerned that the inheritance may be difficult to secure if a member of the family does not meet him first. In common with many immigrants, Mansahai makes reference to the Protector, and seeks to persuade his son to arrange for the trip through the intervention of that officer. He is willing to deposit the money for the passage:

> *Blessings to all the family . . . Blessings also to all the people in the village. My dear son, Bhagwat, Vadvat, Vanis Sookdev, Rajo, Calawatee, all five of you, by the grace of God may you all keep well. Now I cannot see well, and I can no longer work. Somebody should come . . . If I die, you will have difficulties . . . My son, inform the Protector Sahab . . . your father, Mansahai Bhawani is staying in Faridpur . . . I came to Mauritius in 1910 and left in 1947, and am staying at this address: Faridpur, Kayamganj, Farukabad . . . If our Protector Sahab agrees I will immediately deposit some money in the Post Office of Kayamganj . . . get it passed by the Sahab.*

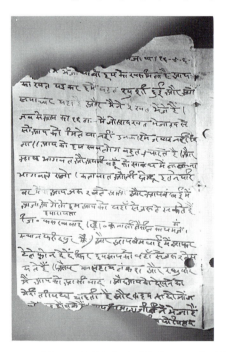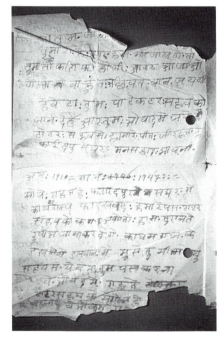

Figure 5.5(a) & 5.5(b) Letters (in Hindi) from Mansahai to his family in Mauritius. Source: Private collection of the Mansahai family, Barlow village, Mauritius.

New Diasporas: Remigrations of Overseas Indians

Migrants who had completed their terms of service overseas, returned to India, and then re-emigrated to the colonies, did so for a number of reasons. Some replicated the circumstances of the original recruitment: economic necessity, social marginalization and deception were all common reasons given. In other cases, the fact of having gone overseas prevented their reintegration into natal villages. Still others consciously endeavoured to go back to the colony where they had originally settled in order to return to employers and new families. Some of these had only been temporarily visiting India, and now saw the colony of their adoption as their real home. A further group of individuals migrated to different colonies, perhaps seeking to try their luck elsewhere, perhaps not realizing they were not returning to the same colony where they had been before. These individuals were certainly less naive than on their first egress from their native land, and some participants in these secondary migration streams were to prove active leaders in the foundation of new Indian communities, while others seemed to have got caught in a cycle of labour migration which brought them few rewards. They had in effect become the international proletariat of the British Empire's sugar capitalists.

Whatever the motives for this failure to settle back into home life, the end result was that many migrants found themselves once again on the path to the colonial emigration depot. One of the commonest causes for the involuntary re-emigration of women was spouse abandonment. Indentured labourers who married overseas could find that their wives were not accepted by their kin, or, finding their status enhanced, chose to marry a younger woman. The predicament which Gungoo described was thus not an isolated instance of a lonely return to a colony by a married woman. Gungoo, No. 97,355, came before the Protector of Immigrants in Mauritius in 1883. She produced her marriage certificate, which proved her to be the wife of Soobroydoo, formerly a peon in the Immigration Department, who had returned to live at Ellore in south India. She had a daughter aged 13 and reported that '2 or 3 years ago she went to Madras with her husband, who, shortly after his arrival there, abandoned her and married another girl'. After remaining three months at Madras, she was compelled, she said, to sell all her jewellery and to pay for her passage back to the colony. The Protector noted: 'she is now without support and is able to maintain herself and her daughter with much difficulty'. He accordingly asked the Madras Emigration Agent to enquire into the circumstances of the husband and 'try and get Soobroydoo to send something to Mauritius for the support of his wife and daughter'.[52]

On the other hand, male returnees who returned to their home village hoping to marry and resettle there could also find their expectations disappointed. In 1922 C.F. Andrews described the experiences of many Fiji Indians on their return to their native villages:

The village biraderi would not welcome them. There was no one who would give in marriage a son or daughter to them for their own children. They were not allowed (such was this piteous story) even to touch the village well for fear of pollution, or to smoke in the evening the common huqqa. Every act of their own companions of days gone by, every look, every glance now unmistakably said to them, 'Go away from us. We don't want you. Go back to Fiji'.[53]

Whilst this was certainly not the experience of all returnees, the rootlessness of some ex-migrants produced an increasing stream of individuals arriving in colonies for a second or third time (see Chapter 2).

The fact that such individuals were not strangers to indenture did not necessarily mean that they were likely to be content with the situations offered them. Each venture was for many a chance to improve their lot, and the new destination was not always better than the last. Despite the claims of the Mauritian authorities in India that most migrants preferred 'Mirich' and were often decoyed to other colonies, those indentured labourers who had gone first to the West Indies or elsewhere, and then found themselves in Mauritius, could be equally distressed. Visiting the estate of Beau Fond in the Grand Port district of Mauritius in 1872, one inspector of immigrants reported:

> On the 23rd November, 1865, Carpen hanged himself in his hut. Mr Montille [the proprietor] did not at first clearly remember the circumstance, but he subsequently recollected it, and stated that the man in question had been recruited in India under the impression that he was doing so for the West Indies, where he had previously worked under a master to whom he was much attached, and to whom he intended to return; and, that, on his finding himself at Beau Fond, in Mauritius, he lost his head, and finally destroyed himself. The Police Report on the occurrence, states that his wife had absconded.[54]

It was all too common for the police in Mauritius to attribute the suicides of new immigrants to 'jealousy' and 'disputes' over women. But it is certain that many of the numerous cases of suicide which occurred amongst overseas Indian populations resulted from disappointment with their situation, arising out of some form of treachery in the circumstances of their recruitment. The case of Jeetul was more clear cut, for he was interviewed by an Inspector of Immigrants visiting the Albion estate, who reported:

> There was a carpenter there, named Jeetul, who had been at Demerara, and had there worked as a cooper on or near the 'Ruimvedlt' estate, and who said he was going back there, but, by some treachery in the depot at Calcutta, he was sent on board a ship from Mauritius, and so came here, but that he preferred Demerara and wished to go there.[55]

Moorly's case is illuminating in so far as it recounts an individual's experience of what seems to have occurred to many returning labourers – the lack of a welcome, if not downright hostility, in the natal village. We first come across Moorly in India, when he petitioned the Protector at Mauritius for a passage back to that island. He claimed initially to have been robbed and sent away from Mauritius against his will. His story was that he had been drugged, deprived of his money and his 16-year-old daughter and, whilst in an intoxicated state, placed on a steamer which departed for Calcutta. In a petition addressed to the 'Superintendent of the Mauritius Coolys Immigration', Moorly wrote:

> *That your Petitioner most humbly begs to inform your honor that he and his daughter named Rokko that was sent from Agra to Mauritius and other Station and your Petitioner and his daughter served 13 years in the Coolys Immigration and received all his pay 140 Rs and his passage from the Manager of Mauritius Coolys Immigration, one Bhutashren or native Hotell Keeper gave him some drugs which made him intoxicated and placed him in the Steamer and sent him down at Calcutta and kept his daughter who is at present aged about 16 years and all his money.*
>
> *Therefore your Petitioner lays his deplorable and distressfull case before your worship's unbounded clemency for justice and redress merely to send him back at Mauritius and meet your Petitioner's daughter who is forcibly kept by Bhugahtenee a native Bhutashreen, or Hotell Keeper together with all his 13 years earning and if your honor may grant an order for an enquiries at Mauritius and it will find your Petitioner's statement is correct or not and after satisfied to do any justice as your honor deems fit as your Petitioner entirely depend on your honors patronage for such a Gooloomor force done on your petitioner under your honors services.*
>
> *For which act of kindness your petitioner as in duty bound will ever pray.*[56]

However, when asked to give a statement to the Agent in India, he altered his story in several material details. The second text stated that it was in India, not in Mauritius, that the theft and drugging had taken place. The woman who had been with him in Mauritius was now mentioned as his sister rather than his daughter:

> *My name is Moorly, father's name Natha, I am a native of the village Jansingkaguni, Jhanah sumsahad zillah Agra. Three years ago I returned from Mauritius and brought with me Rs140. When I returned home the zemindars of the place named Kasiram and Ramlal took by force the money I had with me after beating me severely. I therefore reported the matter to the Daroga and the tahsildar of the place. They doubted whether I had any money with me and asked me to produce documents or proof of my having brought money from Mauritius. The zemindars however managed to drug me, and the influence of the drug made me lose my sense. For the last two years I was helpless in this state of mental derangement. At last I found my way to Calcutta and it is now my prayer that a document may be given to me showing that I returned from Mauritius and brought savings to the amount of Rs140. I have my sister named Rokho at Mauritius in the Lutna Estate under Messrs Bess and Bruston – It is also my prayer that she may be brought back to me.*

The Agent at Calcutta contrived to discredit Moorly whilst forwarding details of his complaint to Mauritius. In his letter, Eales described Moorly's story as 'wholly incredible and unworthy of belief' and expressed the view that:

if not out of his mind this man is certainly labouring under some hallucination and in proof of this I may mention that the day after he presented this petition he was charged by the police with having threatened to stab some people in this neighbourhood.[57]

He added that Moorly had subsequently informed him that he had first migrated to Reunion before arriving in Mauritius in 1868 on the steamer *Ermine*.

The Immigration Department in Mauritius established that Moorly had arrived with his daughter Rocko from Reunion on 4 April 1868 and had left for Calcutta on 30 March 1875 per *Merchantman*. A few days earlier Rocko had obtained a certificate to marry Proyag. She was only 17, so the certificate must have had her father's consent. She did not go on to celebrate the marriage, however. The Mauritian enquiry concluded that the names of the estate proprietors given by Moorly in his statement were false, and it was decided that the office was 'not in a position to furnish the certificate asked for by the Petitioner, or to assist him further in the matter'.[58]

Moorly was certainly a very unhappy man whose main concern was to return to Mauritius or be reunited with his relative, and if, as with others, his garbled account of his experiences was not likely to be easily proved, his depositions demonstrate the sense of injustice felt by returnees who had laboured to little reward overseas. Such protests were dismissed by the authorities because of inconsistencies; but for the petitioners, the accuracy of the facts may have been less important than the moral conviction that some remuneration should have been made them for their labour, or some place available where they could live in peace and feel at home.

Disappointment in one migration did not prevent hope for another. Moorly had taken part in one of the smaller streams of secondary migration: that of Indians leaving Reunion for Mauritius. The complaints of south Indians who arrived to begin second indentures in Mauritius are indicative of the disappointment of such hopes. One such individual, Mootoosamy, was no stranger to the migration experience, having spent fifteen years in the neighbouring island of Reunion. He told his story to a sympathetic British official in Mauritius, Auditor General W.W. Kerr (see Chapter 3), who at that time was investigating the impending restrictions on old immigrants to be imposed by the new labour law, Ordinance 31 of 1867. Kerr assisted him in drawing up a petition and passed it to the Protector. Initially taken on as a carpenter, Mootoosamy found that when he sought to have his contractually stipulated rations upheld by the local Magistrate, far from achieving his objective he was imprisoned and demoted to the status of field hand:

> *The humble Petition of Mootoosamy, respectfully sheweth:*
>   *That your Petitioner arrived here from Reunion three months ago along with 80 other Emigrants.*
>   *That he is a carpenter by trade and had worked as such for 15 years with one and the same Master Mr Felix Piqueur (Marine Establishment) St Denis.*

That Mr Felix Piqueur having but little employment for his men, reduced his establishment and proposed to retain Petitioner at a monthly rate of wages of $7 a month.

That as your Petitioner had received $12 a month for 8 years previously, he declined the offer and determined to come to Mauritius.

That before he left his Master at Reunion he gave him a certificate of good conduct and skill in his trade.

That he went with this certificate to the British Consul and asked for a passage to Mauritius.

That the Consul told him, he could not send him to Mauritius as a carpenter, but that if he chose to go as a field laborer he would send him, and that on arriving at Mauritius, he would find no difficulty in obtaining employment as carpenter.

That on arrival at Mauritius they were taken to the Depot and after two days, he himself together with 25 men were obliged to engage themselves with Mr Garraud, planter, Moka, for five years, at a rate of wages commencing at $2 a month and rations.

That your Petitioner remonstrated against this proceeding, and stated that $2 a month were not fair wages as he had received $12 a month at Reunion.

That he was told in reply that he and all the other 25 must go to Mr Garraud, as above mentioned.

That on arrival they received as rations rice and maize in equal proportions, and that not being accustomed to maize as food the whole band went to complain to the Depot.

That from the Depot they were sent to the Police at Moka, and thence sent back to the Estate.

That your Petitioner, before the complaint was made, worked with Mr Garraud as carpenter, but since has been compelled to work in the fields as laborer as a punishment.

That whilst the other men receive their full rations, your Petitioner is only allowed dry rice (1.5 lb.) and not even salt. The rice is given to him daily.

That your Petitioner along with 4 others, went a second time to complain to the magistrate of ill-usage by the Master and were condemned to 15 days' imprisonment.

That your Petitioner instead of finding employment for his skilled labour, and commensurate wages, as he expected, finds himself now compelled to work in the fields $2 a month, that the hardship of his case is so evident, that he will now only appeal to His Excellency for release from the bondage under which he is suffering, and your Petitioner as in duty bound will ever pray.

(Signed Mootoosamy in Tamul Characters).[59]

When the Protector investigated Mootoosamy's case the latter also claimed that his employer, Garreau, 'continually beats me'. When Garreau was brought before the Protector he denied that he had taken Mootoosamy on as a carpenter, decried the latter's unruly conduct, and explained that to release the Indian from his engagement 'under the threats he utters would disorganise my whole staff of labourers'. The Protector noted that Mootoosamy's contract did not state that he was to be employed as anything other than a field labourer; he therefore advised the hapless carpenter to return to the estate and complete his engagement. Two days later Mootoosamy returned to the Immigration Office, claiming that on his arrival at the estate he had been locked up in the hospital. A trial was held; Mootoosamy was convicted of making 'a vexatious and malicious complaint against his Master' and imprisoned.[60]

No doubt the cumulative evidence of ill-treatment revealed in the petitions of Indians like Mootoosamy and Pandoo (see Chapter 3), drawn up by the British official Kerr, ultimately did help to reform the general condition of immigrants by coming to the notice of the Royal Commissioners. In the short term, the actions of Kerr brought him a reprimand from the Governor, and no relief for Mootoosamy. Enquiries made into his case from his former employer in Reunion convinced the local authorities in Mauritius that he was 'a drunkard and a bad character'.[61]

It was not unusual for returnees or remigrants to find themselves at odds with the colonial authorities. Their relative familiarity with the local labour markets gave them an edge over new immigrants, and an influence which employers might not like. The large Mauritian Indian community which arrived in Natal in the last quarter of the nineteenth century is a case in point. They prospered economically and some became important leaders, like Thambi Naidoo, who was an active participant with Gandhi in the South African Indians' struggles for recognition.[62]

Some men became habitual emigrants, like Rajoo Narayen, who made several journeys between India and Mauritius as a recruiter. Ennabie, his wife, was none the less concerned for his welfare during his long absences. On one occasion she wrote to the Protector of Immigrants at Mauritius, asking him to deliver a letter to her husband:

> *Respected Sir,*
>
> *In taking the liberty of addressing you, I respectfully beg to solicit the favor of your kindly causing the accompanying letter, to be delivered to my husband, Rajoo Narayan, who must have arrived in Mauritius, some weeks ago, having left Bombay upwards of 2 months as a Cooly passenger, per ship 'Shah Jahan'; and kindly impressing upon him the necessity of writing to me without delay, as I am very anxious to hear both of his welfare, and whereabouts;*
> *Hoping to be excused for the above presumption*
> *I am, Respected Sir*
> *your most obedient servant*
>
> *Ennabie, wife of Rajoo Narayen*
> *N.B. Please to address & oblige –*
> *No. 17 Panjarapoora*
> *2nd Lane – Bombay*[63]

Rajoo's own pleas to the Protector on behalf of himself and other old immigrants – one plea of October 1873 asking for emigration to be reopened from the port of Bombay, and one of March 1874 offering to bring recruits to the island – had obviously been answered, because according to his wife he had left for Mauritius in October or November 1874.[64]

Individuals like Rajoo Narayen were part of a growing band of migrants who made several journeys between India and the plantation colonies. Some men went not simply to one colony but to several. Cases are documented of a single individual visiting two or three of the following countries: Mauritius, Reunion, Trinidad and Fiji. As early as 1839, remigrants were reportedly arriving in Mauritius. At the establishment of Lucas & Lesieur, architects in Port Louis, magistrates found one man who had 'been for six years at Bourbon, returned to Coringhee, re-engaged for the Mauritius, and brought his wife with him'.[65] Such men were in some cases the victims of labour importers for the British sugar colonies, who preyed on the economically marginalized for over a century in the recruiting districts of India. Others seemed to be habitual migrants who were acutely aware of the varying economic opportunities on offer in the several colonies. George Grierson interviewed one man in the 1880s who was on his way to Trinidad from India. He had previously worked in Jamaica, where at one time he confided that he had been able to earn as much as Rs3 per day. He was now less happy with working conditions there, the result, he said, of too many coolies and too much cultivation, and was therefore intending to try out Trinidad.[66] Grierson also met a woman called Sukhiya, who had returned to and set up a restaurant in India after a twelve-year stay in Mauritius. She had a contract to feed migrants awaiting transfer from a Demerara sub-depot. She was reportedly scornful of Indians who were afraid to migrate, calling them cowards.[67] Major Pitcher, who authored a report on emigration in the North West Provinces and Oudh at around the same time, reported on the views of the different colonies held by return emigrants:

> Trinidad (Chinitat) has the preference ... Mauritius (Mirch) is admitted to have advantages in the shortness of the journey, the cheapness of the return passage and in the payments of monthly wages in the place of a daily task ... Rightly or wrongly Mauritius had acquired a doubtful reputation in some of the lower districts, and at Gorakhpur I was told by a recruiter that coolies would sometimes say that they were ready to go to any colony but Mauritius ... discredit attaching to it must be a reflection of the old days of vagrant hunts.[68]

The internationalization of the Indian in the nineteenth century is under-scored by the request from the Agent in British Guiana for information about one Bissoonsing. He was from Gya in Bihar and was said to have emigrated to Mauritius in 1859. The demand for information came from other members of his family who had also migrated, but to British Guiana instead! A man called Bissoonauthsing was traced in Mauritius, but he did not know whether the family in British Guiana could be among his relatives.[69] The incident may also have concealed one of the myriad family tragedies associated with indenture, where families left their homes on hearing that a relative was in a particular colony, only to be deceived into going elsewhere or unable to find the person they sought once arrived at their destination.

Because the members of one family might set out in search of each other and end up in another colony, the Protector routinely received communications from other Indian-importing territories. In 1882, the Protector acknowledged receipt of a letter asking for a search to be made for a person of the name of Amanally, son of Kassimally. However, as with many letters from India, the information was incomplete, and that official was obliged to reply:

> that the information that you have furnished, is not sufficient to enable me to trace out the man who is wanted. If you will kindly favor me with the year in which Anamally [*sic*] is supposed to have emigrated to this colony I shall have a careful search made and forward to you such information as I can obtain, with the least possible delay.[70]

Some migrants went directly from Mauritius to new destinations rather than returning to India. These offshoots from the larger diaspora tended to follow the opening up of new migration streams elsewhere. In 1883 a total of 639 Indians withdrew their savings from the bank prior to leaving the island. The majority were taking their capital back to India, but two of this number proceeded to Natal, two left for Reunion and two went to China.[71]

Where labour migrants went, merchants followed, ready to supply new overseas Indian communities with the goods and services they required. Of course, Indian mercantile families had been trading in the Indian Ocean long before the commencement of indentured migration, but there is no doubt that the influx of many thousands of Indian labourers to the Indian Ocean plantation colonies contributed to a surge in merchant immigration over the same period.[72] As labourers began to remigrate paying their own fares, the distinction between indentured and passenger Indians became increasingly blurred. If the large-scale labour migrations had created new economic opportunities for the commercial classes, the increasingly visible presence of overseas Indians produced political fears of alien populations, which resulted in repatriation schemes and restrictive immigration policies in some states.

The correspondence of the Bassa brothers illustrates the effect on one Muslim merchant family of such problems. Ally Mamode Bassa arrived in Mauritius as a passenger from Natal at the turn of the century. Five years later, following the death of his father, he received a letter from his older brother in Natal:

To Brother Ally Mamode Bassa,
Mauritius

Cassim Amod Bassa
Merchant and Importer
Commercial Road

Dear Brother,

I have received letter from Hajee Ajum Goolam Hossen of Mauritius saying that your brother was here and said if I want to go to India. I intend to go to Natal. Let me know

your decision so as to deposit the money. Now I wrote him in answer that kindly hand Rs75 to my brother. He could do what he could therefore kindly go and get it.
But brother you come here without fears but better for you to go to India and then you can come here and we will do some arrangement to land you and also suppose you come here and if the Immigration Officer refused to land them what you could do you can come to Mauritius but the steamer will proceed to England. Well you don't want to go to England therefore kindly take my advice and proceed to India and thereafter I will write you what to do and what to say and how to come.

Yours faithfully,

Cassim A Bassa.[73]

Despite the reservations of Cassim Ally Mamode wished to return to Natal, but he feared that he would not get permission to land, and therefore requested the authorities in Mauritius to ascertain what conditions he would be required to fulfil in order to be readmitted to that country.[74] He had two petitions drafted in French to this effect. The Protector in reply informed him of the conditions under which 'asiatics and others (termed undesirable)' were allowed to land at Natal:

(a) If proceeding to Natal to trade or in search of work, they must justify of their means of subsistence (I believe £20).

(b) If proceeding there to join a friend or relative, the latter must vouch for the fact, either personally or by a document to be produced by the person – He need only get an acknowledgement from his brother that he is to reside at his place. This is sufficient to ensure his being booked by one of the castle boats.[75]

The Protector was sympathetic enough to request that a letter be drafted to Cassim Amod Bassa on the boy's behalf asking him to write and say that Ally Mamode Bassa was his brother and that he was willing to receive and take care of him. The elder brother, Cassim, was described as a merchant importer residing in Durban, and a letter asking him to send the required documentation to enable him to send for his minor brother was forwarded. Evidently no reply was received for the boy, Ally, twice more visited the Immigration Department in Mauritius for news. Six months later, in mid-1906, the immigration office filed the correspondence, so that we do not know whether the young Ally was ever able to take over the family shop in Natal. The correspondence is nevertheless useful for what it reveals both of the commercial networks of Asians operating in the Indian Ocean colonies and of the increasingly restrictive measures implemented to forestall the settlement of Indians in certain of those territories.

New Communities: Experiences of Overseas-Born Indians

A not inconsiderable number of the children of migrants also found themselves undergoing further journeys when other job opportunities arose. Thus, the letters passing between migrants and relatives did not simply flow between India and the overseas destination, but enquiries also began to be made to officials by overseas migrants whose offspring had in turn undertaken journeys to new destinations.

In 1899 the Protector received, from the parents in Mauritius of one Dersady who had gone to Mombasa, an urgent request for news of his whereabouts. They were worried, not knowing whether he were alive or dead.[76] Later that year the Consul at Mombasa gave the Protector some news of the dhoby named Dersady: 'This man is in the employ of the Chief Engineer of the Uganda Railway, Mr G Whitehouse, at Nairobi'.[77] Dersady forwarded with the Consul a letter for his parents, written in Tamil. The translation reveals a typically respectful greeting to the man's parents and a great deal of information concerning his economic prospects. He ends by extending a welcome to any of his relatives who might wish to join him, with the promise of finding them work:

Protection of Lord Muruga
Mombassa

My dear parents whom I venerate as deities. I do place before your lotus feet many flowers and natural elements having perfumes. With rose water I do wash your feet, wipe them with a piece of woollen cloth, place the above mentioned flowers such as jasmine etc and show . . . as well fall to your feet for worship. I do wish long and healthy life full of prosperity. The words which both of you told me would always be considered as mantras. I join my hands, close my mouth in reverence to you. I am hereby giving you the details you need to know to the best of my ability.

Mother, my workers, and children, are fine. Yourself mother brothers and sisters, brother-in-laws are all doing fine. I am happy to learn this.

I am no more in Zanzibar. I am at present in Mombassa. The reason is that there is now work there. They are now introducing train travel for a village called Kilindini up to Uganda. There, there is a lot of work. You know there I earn for one day Rs10. I am settled at English Point and Kilindini. There is 2 miles between English Point and Kilindini. I have to travel to that place. I am going to open a workshop there on October 1st. So I have sent a fellow from Calcutta named Jothas to Zanzibar to take two or three persons to work here. Many chiefs (white men) are coming in large numbers in Kilindini and Mombassa. I feel like leaving Jothas in English Point and moving to Kilindini.

It's two months since I came here. Here only two houses (families) are friends. Including me it would make three in all. They work for 8 rupees a day. I am earning rs10 per head and 10.5 rupees for the ship. A sack of rice costs Rs18. For the time being I am working for 8 chiefs. It's just to let you know this news.

Hereafter I shall write letters every month. You also keep sending me letters.

I worship father and mother. I wish that blessings of the lord be on us and all elders. I also wish the best to all young ones.

In case there is a wish to come to Mombassa, each one can pay the ship travel fees. If once they are here I can find them a job. If not they may work for themselves.[78]

When Peria Moodally wrote from South Africa, it was primarily to secure the well-being of his elderly mother. Peria himself was born in Mauritius, but he felt justified in writing to the Protector on the grounds that his mother had come to the island 'as indenture'. It is interesting to note how Mauritian-born Indians viewed the system of labour immigration which had brought their parents to the island. In attempting to verify his mother's status he made reference to her 'free paper', presumably her ticket, as if she had been liberated from a state of servility. Peria himself is evidence of the social mobility of Indians in Mauritius; he had evidently been working as a teacher, although his mother was probably still resident on a sugar-estate camp, as her address suggests:

Sir,

I beg most respectfully to inform you that I'm a Indo-Mauritian who left Mauritius in the year of 1904.

I have left my mother at Mauritius. She has no one to look after her. The Education Department of Mauritius must give me certain amount i.e. a share in the result of the Examination of Côte D'or S.P.G Aided and Rose Hill Mahomedan Aided Schools. I wrote to the Education Dept. no answer received, then my mother wrote several times to the Director of Public Instruction unfortunately she received no answer after having sent a Power of Attorney.

As you are the protector of Indians, and my mother came to Mauritius as indenture, I hope your honour will have no objection to take this matter into your consideration and to make her get the amount which I'm entitle.

In order to get the No. of my mother, can find it easily in her free paper. If the Education Dept. does not consider that she is my mother. I can ask the Dept. to look at the Registration of Birth's Room that I have born in Mauritius in the year of 1872. On the 7th day of January where can find her name too with number.

Praying to be excused for the intrusion upon your precious and valuable time.

I remain Sir,
Your obedient servant

Peria Moodally
My mother's address:
Ammanee, c/o Saminaden Sirdar
Stanley Estate, Rose Hill.
My mother holds a receipt for the power of attorney which was sent to the Education Dept.[79]

Following the receipt of his letter, the Protector evidently did take some action on the family's behalf, for in October 1907 the Director of Public Instruction informed that officer of the result: 'Periamoodally's mother was written to from this office . . . She was asked to produce proper proof that she was authorized to draw the money'. On 15 November Peria was informed that his mother had been reimbursed the sum requested.[80]

In cases where the colonial-born offspring returned to India, information was sometimes requested from the authorities overseas as to their birth and parentage to enable them to settle inheritance and other claims. At the time the recording of births and deaths in India was limited, and inheritance claims relied more on the common recognition of established family and kin groups, but individuals who were born or had grown up abroad could not rely on such customary criteria. Fortunately, the system of registering arriving Indians provided emigrants with written evidence of their family status. Thus Vythee, whose parents had both died, requested a certificate stating when he had arrived in Mauritius, the time of his mother' death there, and his father's name, in order to settle his claims:

> *The Protector of Emigrants Office*
> *Vaupoor: Changi*
> *near Mouritious*
>
> *Honored Sir,*
>
>   *I beg to bring to your kind notice that myself and my mother by name of Aly ramy were admitted as Emigrants to Moritious in 1858 on No. 201133 and my mother died on the 4th June 1877 in the town of Vooppoor near Mouritious. I therefore beg your honor will be pleased to grant me a certificate stating the time, when we landed at Vooppoor: Changi and when my mother's death took place and including with our father's name – to produce the said certificate to the District Munsiff's court Tiroovaroor to settle my claims. I further request to send me the reply to my pleader's address as given below. I attach my petition to the collector of Madras and an order from the said court Tiroovaroor – to your honor.*
>
>   *Herewith submitted 2 eight annas stamps for the copy and one rupee for the post fee.*[81]

Vythee's petition was addressed c/o J. Krishnasamy, Pleader, Munsiff's Court, Tiroovaroor, Tanjore, indicating that he had used the services of a legal officer to draw up his appeal. His Immigration Register entry revealed that he had arrived in July 1858 aged 14, and that his father's name was Colundavaloo.[82] Again, his recollection of place names in Mauritius did not resemble any town or region on the island.

Another return migrant who sought to refer to the immigration records in Mauritius with a view to proving his identity in India was Narrainen (or Narainsamy), who wrote a Tamil letter to the Protector in 1881. The letter was deciphered by the Protector with the help of 'a Madras Indian who read the letter and told me what it contained' (Figures 5.6a and 5.6b). In the letter, Narrainen stated that he had arrived in Mauritius with his father Rungapen and mother Veeramah on 20 October 1858. He returned to India in April 1879 per *Canada*. He deposited a sum of Rs620 in the Mauritius Immigration Office to be remitted to Tanjore. The remittance was made on 2 March 1879. The writer then asked for any information that could be given from the books of the office that might lead to the affirmation of his identity in India, with a view to establishing his claim to certain landed property:

To, Honourable His Excellency Lord Bose,
serving in the place of Honourable His Excellence Lord Dalle

The Humble Petition of Narayanasamy Naikken, son of Mariamen Temple Rengappen and Viramma, From Tanjore District, Madras Presidency

May I introduce my humble self. I landed there on 20 October 1858. I may not be easily identified. I am hereby giving you particulars that may help to identify my person. I have encashed in Tanjore district, Madras presidency the sum of Rs620 being deposits made in your bank of Port Louis as follows:

20 March – Rs200   21 March – Rs200
22 March – Rs200   23 March – Rs 20
I came back to Madras in April 1879 by the ship Canada.
With the above mentioned information I beg to be issued a certificate giving the following details. I request your honour will be good enough to grant me a certificate showing

1. When I came to Mauritius
2. What was my age at that time

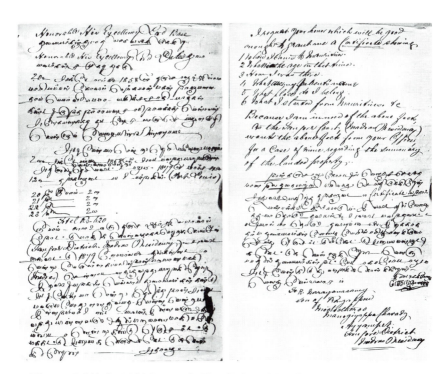

Figures 5.6(a) & 5.6(b) Letter (in Tamil) from Narrainen, written c.1881.
Source: PL 44.

3. How I was there
4. What are my parents' name
5. What place do I belong to
6. When I started from Mauritius

Because I am in need of the above facts as the Tanjore Court (Madras Presidency) wants the above facts from your office for a case of mine regarding the summary of the land property.
I have a case in the Tanjore Court regarding my land property. If I receive a certificate from you I'll have my case settled. I am very helpless since I was in that place for such a period of time. I hope that your noble person would gracefully issue me the certificate needed. Even though you do send the same through any other officer working here I may collect the same from him.

Signed, R. Narayanasamy

My address: *R. Narayanasamy*
                 Son of Rengappen
                 Mootoothevoo, Manogiyappa Chavady
                 Ayyampet, Tanjore District
                 Madras Presidency.[83]

The Protector was able to establish from his registers that Narrainen Rungapen, No. 201,058, made a remittance of Rs620 to be refunded to him at Tanjore or in the event of his death to be paid to his sister Alamayloo Rungapen at Tanjore. The shipping list described him as of malabar 'caste', aged 18 in July 1858, from the zillah of Cuddalore. He was stated to have returned to India on the ship *Canada* on 5 April 1879.

The requests of individuals like Narrainen reveal how emigration affected ascribed status in India, because individuals who emigrated as children could find on their return that they were no longer known and therefore effectively did not exist. At the same time, the letters of Narrainen and others demonstrate that those who migrated were by no means from the poorest social classes in India, but were members of landowning and property-owning families, often with some education.[84]

The channel of information could also work the other way, as when the Curator of Vacant Estates in Mauritius needed to know from the Indian authorities whether Jooree was related to Sahojee. The Calcutta Emigration Agent instituted a police enquiry, and the District Magistrate of Shahabad was able to ascertain that:

Jooree Dusadh is the son of Sahojee Dusadhin and Ganga Dusadh ... This statement is borne out by the Agency's Records, which show that Jooree's father Gangoo emigrated to the colony on 3 July 1865 by the S.S. Solway as No. 99 accompanied by his wife Sahojee (No. 315) and 4 children, among whom was Jooree, No. 100.

It had been known in Mauritius that Jooree was No. 318,674 and that Sahojee's number was 318,885. Both were listed as being of Dosaud caste, from the village of Peetaro in Arrah, and arrived in the island from Calcutta in September 1865. Sahojee was stated to be the wife of Gangoo, No. 318,693, and had come with their three children (see Figure 5.7). The Calcutta agent was able to confirm from his shipping lists the date of their departure, and the relationship between son and mother was confirmed at the village level. Two sources of information were thus used to corroborate the arrival data held at the Immigration Office in Mauritius.[85]

The continuing contacts with India of such children of indentured migrants demonstrates that colonial-born offspring did not become completely creolized. Many never returned to their parents' country of origin, and forged their lives overseas. Never the less, through their religion, culture and languages, the link with India survived. The linguistic adaptations of Bhojpuri in the overseas context are a fascinating study and can reveal much about the processes of integration and the development of syncretic beliefs.[86] The letter written by

Figure 5.7 Sahojee came to Mauritius in 1865 with her husband Gangoo and her 12-year-old son Jooree. The family were of the Dosaud caste, from Arrah, and Sahojee was 25 at that time. Both her husband and son later registered as old immigrants. Gangoo died in Mauritius in 1895. Four years after his death, this photograph was taken of Sahojee, now a widow. Source: PE 108 and PG 45.

Ramnam, or written down as a transcription of a verbal interview with him, is an interesting example of Bhojpuri/Hindi as spoken by a Mauritian-born Indian (Figure 5.8). Ramnam had come to the Immigration Office to complain about the destruction of his house by his employer. The English translation is as follows:

Sir,

I have come here because you brought my father and my brother here. I was born in Mauritius. I worked hard and built a house on a piece of land which I bought. My wife had caught a disease (the plague) and thus died. Dr Chatelier said that it was plague. The master set fire to my house and said that he would give me 10 rupees. He sent me to Beau Bassin and when I returned, I went to see Dr Chatelier. But he asked me to go from there otherwise he would kick me out. So I went to the Board of Curepipe, but noone listened to me. Then I went to see Mr Gybert an told him that my house was set on fire and I had nothing. Now I have no home and noone bothers to give us a shelter because I have caught a disease.[87]

The burning down of Ramnam's house was considered a necessary measure to isolate plague cases. But for Ramnam, who was without a home, and who seems to have been ostracized due to fears that he might have been carrying the plague, it meant a shattered life.

Betion Ramratanlal's letter to the Protector of Emigrants at Calcutta reveals a particular sad legacy of indenture. The settlement process overseas inevitably entailed some adaptation of cultural practices, and the limited number of partners available necessitated, for those who wished to marry in Mauritius, some modifications to the preferred contracting of caste-endogamous unions. Men who married women of another, usually lower, caste sometimes experienced problems when returning to India with the new family. Rejection of his wife and children by the man's relatives in India, or indeed by co-villagers, could, despite ceremonies conducted by local priests, make it impossible to remain in India, and such families often remigrated. In Betion's case his parents had returned to India, leaving him in Mauritius. When his parents asked him to join them there, he was not well received by his father's family, because the marriage had not been given their sanction and the mother was alleged to be of another caste. He therefore requested information from the Calcutta Agent as to whether his parents had really been married:

Sir,

Most respectfully I beg to inform you that I the undersigned Betion natural son of Ramrattan of the said Zillah Arrah, Pergana Behiah, thana Belannly, Garri Kanampur praying as follows:

That my father the said Ramruttun No. 130,154 and mother Beehasy No. 130,237 bis daughter of Ressawulsing both left Calcutta by or through your department as coolies for the island of Mauritius in the month of November 1853 per ship Hyderee.

That on the 17 September 1859 my father the said Ramruttun declared himself before the officer of the civil status of Mauritius that I am his natural son.

रामनाम

साहेब मैं आप केा सामने आायें हैं कयों
आप नें मेरा बाप औ मेरा माइ केा आप लाये
है देस सेा मैं मेारीस का पैदा हुं मैं काम
केा बनाया घर और एक कार जगह बनाया
ब सेा मेरा पास एक गरइता था उसका
पास एक बेमारी या सोव्ह नेंमर गया।
तेा देाक दर सासतेल्मीये नै कहा की
लाप्रेस का बेमारी हे सेा साहेब नै मेरा
तीन घर जल्वा दीया और कहा की हम
दसव्र रुपया देंगे और हमको भी बेासें
लेगया हम घुम कर आया और देाक दर
सासतेलीये नें कहा भागेा नहेातेा मैं
लात मारेंगे तब मैं कीरपीप का
बेारदु मैं गया तेाकहा मेरा कुछ दरकार
नहीहे जाव तबमें गीबेर साहेब काप्रास गयू
हेाहमें कहा हम दखें गे मेरा घर मीषूका
देाया अब हमें कुछ नहीं हैं मैं अब बाहेर
मैं रहते हैं और केाइ नहेाघर देता है की
कयेां की लाप्रेस्तेसन बेमारीकामारूषूल) पूरतापू

That my parents left the island of Mauritius per ship 'Leo' on 23 July 1880 for their native place and left me there for some time. After that they called me here by letter. I left the island accordingly. On having arrived here at Kalianpore the families of my father refusing to take me as the heir of my father because while my father was here he was a bachelor, and my mother is of another caste. Wherefore requesting you that you will kindly forward by an official letter that at the time when they were leaving the port of Calcutta for Mauritius per ship Hyderee in the month of November 1853, how they declared and registered their marriage at your record, whether my mother as married wife of my father or concubine. By your doing so I should be most obliged.

I remain
your most obedient servant

Betion Ramruttanlall
Zilla Arrah, Pergana Behiah, Mouza Kalianpore.[88]

The letter was forwarded to the Protector at Mauritius by the Calcutta Agent.[89] Because Betion knew his parents' immigrant numbers, his request was relatively easy to comply with. The Register entries at Mauritius described his parents Ramruttun and Beehasy as both being of the same caste (Koyeth) and from the same village of Kalianpore in Arrah. Beehasy was two years older than Ramruttun. Whilst there was no record to show that they were a married couple on arrival, the Department did find a subsequent marriage certificate, which was sent to Calcutta with a covering letter.[90] Perhaps Beehasy was from a sub-caste not acceptable to Ramruttun's family. More probably the young couple had left together to continue a relationship which had not been sanctioned. In returning to India, however, they had bequeathed an uncertain future to their child.

Thus the impact of indentured migration spread outwards from the lives of those in Mauritius back to India, where families and friends also experienced emotional upheaval as a result of the displacement of their kin. Some families survived on the remittances sent back by migrants; many others experienced economic disruption when male relatives left, or found that the loss of the absent person could not be compensated for by occasional bank drafts, and pleaded for the person's return at whatever cost.

Notes

1. PA 42 Walter Wells, Assistant Commissioner, Sultanpore, Oudh, to Protector of Emigrants, Calcutta, 19 July 1880.
2. PA 42 Emigration Agent, Calcutta, to Protector of Immigrants, Mauritius, 14 Aug. 1880.
3. PA 42 Letter from Ganesh Tewary, n.d. The reference to Serimal Bhagwat may refer to the writer receiving the blessings of God in some form. Ganesh comes across in this letter as an earnest and concerned patron of his extended family, involved even in complex transactions over the purchase of land.
4. PA 42 Letter from Sheoraj, Sultanpore, 15 July 1880.
5. PA 54 Letter of Kulup and Sahadewo, Rose Hill.

6. PA 54 Emigration Agent, Calcutta, to Protector of Immigrants, Mauritius, 17 Jan. 1883.
7. Immigration Department note, 9.3.83.
8. PL 46 Protector, Mauritius, to Emigration Agent, Calcutta, 9 Apr. 1883.
9. PE 131 Immigration Register of Ellora, 1878.
10. PA 54 J. Grant, Protector, Calcutta, to Emigration Agent, Calcutta, 18 Jan. 1882.
11. PA 54 Magistrate of Gopalganj, Sarun, to Agent, n.d.; Emigration Agent, Calcutta, to Protector of Immigrants, Mauritius, 2 June 1883.
12. PL 22 Memorandum of Protector, 6 Dec. 1905.
13. PL 22 Mr J. Desplaces to Protector, 15 Dec. 1905. In fact the Immigration Register of Chottee lists his caste as Thakur and his age as 20.
14. PL 22 Protector to Comptroller, India Treasuries, 8 May 1906.
15. PL 22 Chottee Lal to Protector, 9 July 1907.
16. PL 22 Chottee to Protector of Immigrants, Port Louis.
17. PL 22 Protector's note, 12/9/1907.
18. PL 22 Chottee to Protector, 9 Sep. 1907.
19. PL 22 Chottee Lal to Mr Dupre, 20 Nov 1907.
20. PA 69 Dauhoo, No. 128,188, to Protector, 10 Feb. 1885.
21. PA 203 Emigration Agent, Calcutta, to Protector of Immigrants, 19 Mar. 1901.
22. PE 108 Bhoyroo was described as of the Kahar caste, from Hazaribag. He registered as an old immigrant in 1869 and died in June 1915. He was reportedly already a returnee in 1864 on his arrival in Mauritius.
23. PA 34 Malayen to Protector of Immigrants, 10 May 1876.
24. PA 54 Nolan, Magistrate, Shahabad, to Protector, Calcutta, 16 June 1883; Emigration Agent, Calcutta, to Protector of Immigrants, Mauritius, 30 June 1883.
25. PA 42 Petition of Bishnu Upadhia, Ghazeepore, 12 Aug. 1881.
26. PA 42 Immigration Dept Note, 20.12.81.
27. PL 46 Protector, Mauritius, to Protector of Emigrants, Calcutta, 24 Feb. 1883.
28. PA 206 Daroobibi to Inspector General of Police, Panalja, 11 Aug. 1899.
29. PL 48 Immigration Office note, 27.5.1886.
30. Translated by Professor Sivarama Murthy, Mahatma Gandhi Institute, Mauritius.
31. PL 48 Protector's note, 22.6.1886.
32. PL 3 Magistrate of Benares to the Protector of Emigrants, Calcutta, 4 Sept. 1886.
33. PA 202 Curator of Vacant Estates to the Protector of Immigrants, 31 July 1901.
34. PA 202 Emigration Agent, Calcutta, to Protector, 10 May 1901.
35. PA 24 Emigration Agent to Protector, Calcutta, 11 June 75.
36. PA 24 Petition of Bhyro Roy.
37. PL 32 Protector to Protector of Emigrants, Calcutta, 11 Dec. 1849.
38. Report on Colonial Emigration from the Bengal Presidency, G. Grierson, 1883, Diary, pp. 32–9.
39. Wilson, 1987: 2.
40. Laurence, 1971: 77–8. For oral evidence of social mobility amongst Indian immigrants in Trinidad, see Seesaram, 1991: 2–3.
41. PP C 1115–1 Appendix B to Royal Commissioners' Report No. 38 Report of a Visit to Albion Estate, Black River, 16 Sep. 1872.

42. Report of Enquiry into the case of Calleemoottoo, Jenner to Protector, 25 Aug. 1872.
43. PC 922 'Atiet Rohoman', Oct. 1856.
44. PA 22 Petition of Sougnia and Corbane, 19 Aug. 1874.
45. PA 22 Petition of Madharee, Aug. 1874.
46. PE 115 'Inverdruie', Mar. 1870. Veerapen returned to India again in April 1880, perhaps on another recruiting mission.
47. PA 14 Petition of Veerapen, 10 July 1872.
48. PA 14 Stipendiary Magistrates Report, n.d.
49. PA 14 Petition of Shahaduth, n.d.
50. PE 48 'Jalanar', 30 Aug. 1854.
51. Prittiviraj Jayram, who is undertaking research on aspects of family history in some rural communities of Mauritius, interviewed Calawatee Mansahai, who related to him the story of her father and entrusted the letters to him. Mr Jayram kindly translated and passed on these letters to me, with her consent. The full family history of Mansahai and his descendants in Mauritius will be discussed by Jayram in his forthcoming work on Indian family settlements in Mauritius.
52. PL 46 Protector to Emigration Agent, 5 Sep. 1883.
53. *Indian Review*, July 1922.
54. Parliamentary Papers 1875 C 1115-1, Appendix B, Report of Visit to Beau Fond Estate in Grand Port, 3 Oct. 1872.
55. Appendix B No. 38, Report of a Visit to Albion Estate, Black River, 16 Sep. 1872.
56. PA 42 Petition of Moorly, 16 Feb. 1880
57. PA 42 Eales to Protector of Immigrants, Mauritius, 23 Feb. 1880.
58. PA 42 Immigration Department Note, 14-4-80; Grant to Eales, 27.2.80.
59. Royal Commissioner's Report, Appendix F22, Petition of Mootoosamy, 10 Nov. 1867.
60. The discussions concerning this case and the following correspondence came to light as a result of the investigations of the Royal Commissioners in Mauritius and were printed as Appendix F22 of their report.
61. Barkly to Kerr, 12 Dec. 1867.
62. Brain, 1983: 208; Ginwala, 1976: *passim*; Mesthrie, 1991: 196.
63. PA 22 Ennabie to Protector, 9 Jan. 1875.
64. PA 14 Rajoo Narayen to Protector, 20 Oct. 1873; PA 22 Rajoo Narayen to Protector, 29 Mar. 1874.
65. CO 167/210 Nicolay to Glenelg, 21 May 1839, encl. Queries and Responses Concerning the Conditions of Indian Labourers.
66. Report on Colonial Emigration from the Bengal Presidency, 1883, Diary, p. 17.
67. *Ibid.*, p. 9.
68. Pitcher Report, p. 32.
69. PE 42 Immigration Agent General, British Guiana, to Protector of Immigrants, Mauritius, 21 Dec. 1880.
70. PL 46 Protector, Mauritius, to Immigration Agent General, British Guiana, 21 Nov. 1882.
71. CO 170/123 Administration Report 1883 Report of the Government Savings Bank, Annexure 4.
72. See Kalla, 1987: 45–65, and the Z2D Series in the Mauritius Archives for details of passenger arrivals.

73. PL 19 Letter from Cassim Amod to Ally Mamode Bassa, 30 Mar. 1905.
74. PL 19 Correspondence concerning the Bassa brothers, Oct. 1905.
75. *Ibid.*, Protector's note, 6 Nov. 1905.
76. PA 206 Immigration Office note, 12 Oct. 1899.
77. 30 Nov. 1899 HM Acting Consul to Protector.
78. PA 206 Letter from Dersady to his family; translated from the Tamil by Mr Soornum, MGI.
79. PL 23 Periam Oodally to Protector, 19 Aug. 1907.
80. PL 23 Protector to Peria, 15-11-1907.
81. PA 43 Vythee to Protector, 3 Apr. 1880.
82. PE 71 'Isabella', 9 July 1858.
83. PL 44 Letter of N. Naikken, translated by Mr Soornum, MGI.
84. PL 44 Immigration Office note, 5 Apr. 1881.
85. PA 204 Emigration Agent, Calcutta to Protector of Emigrants, 8 July 1901.
86. For discussions of the use of Bhojpuri in diaspora see Mesthrie, 1991; Gambhir, 1986.
87. PA 207 Bhojpuri statement of Ramnam, n.d. The English translation is by Ms Vedidta Mayput, Eduction Officer, MGI.
88. PA 42 Betion to Emigration Agent, Calcutta, 8 Aug. 1881.
89. PA 42 Eales, Emigration Agent, Calcutta, to Protector of Immigrants, Mauritius, 20 Aug. 1881.
90. PE 42 'Hyderee', 1853. Koyeth is probably a version of the Bengali writer caste Kayasth.

Conclusion

The modes of expression of labour migrants, ill-versed in English and French (the languages of officials and courts in Mauritius), often knowing only their own vernaculars and non-literate in Hindi or Urdu, were limited. The voice of the indentured Indian was first heard in the form of depositions given before Committees of Enquiry set up in the 1830s. As translators and interpreters arrived to assist them, some from within the ranks of the ex-indentured, petitions became a common medium of the migrant. As remittances and correspondence began to flow back to India, some letters were lost within the postal system and ended up in the archives; others were retained by families in memory of their relatives, and provide another major source in the search for the 'authentic' words of migrants. Because these forms of expression developed over time, the documents themselves help to chart the changing experiences of the Indian labourers and the evolution of the community in diaspora.

The oral depositions of Indian labourers, whether given before panels of supposedly 'sympathetic' European officials or provided as evidence in courts of law, are worthy of study from a number of points of view. Indians were frequently derided as witnesses and considered to be inveterate liars because of their inability to comprehend the legal exactitude required in European courts. Attempts by Indians to fight their cases were often weakened because in-accuracies or exaggerations in their testimonies provided an easy pretext for magistrates to dismiss their plaints. Of course, their manner of recounting events was no less valuable for their purported lack (or differing notion) of 'accuracy'. Depositions in court cases are often useful not so much for the information they convey about incidents on estates as for the snippets of detail about personal relationships which are incidentally offered. Statements made by returning migrants offer appraisals of the indenture experience which are quite unique as source materials: depicting socio-economic circumstances pre-migration, reactions to the recruitment proposition, and evaluations of the attitudes of employers, police and others at Mauritius, as well as of the work regime and living standards on the island.

The petitions and depositions presented here highlight both the abuses of the system and the particular grievances of indentured labourers. They also indicate the concerns of those who had completed contracts and sought to establish themselves on the island as small entrepreneurs, cultivators, market gardeners and the like. Missives were sent to the Protector detailing the most intimate aspects of immigrants' lives: men who wanted a wife or sought revenge against an abductor, and women who wished to escape from unhappy relationships or were fighting for the return of children from estranged husbands, all had recourse to the professional writers in their search for justice. A close analysis of these petitions opens a window into the private lives of indentured Indians, and enables the historian to assess aspects of this diaspora which the official sources were unable or unwilling to confront.

As more labourers emerged from indenture to form a growing, time-expired, property-owning class, the number of individuals seeking redress for grievances increased and the content and tone of petitions shifted. The literate amongst the immigrants and those who had acquired a knowledge of English and French joined with their professional compatriots, and with the handful of young European or creole lawyers, to act as mediators between the ordinary Indian and the colonial state. By articulating the grievances of indentured labourers in the stylized written form of the petition, they created invaluable documentary expressions of the experience from the viewpoint of the migrant. Here, dissatisfactions with living and working conditions are forcefully raised, but alongside them are concerns which are not by and large duplicated in the litany of published accounts: issues, for example, of a domestic or family nature, such as concerns about child rearing and attempts to find a marriage partner. In such matters, as well as in the more narrowly defined field of employment, Indians turned to the Immigration Department, so that the office of Protector took on almost mythical significance. Appeals to him in such matters were the Indians' attempts to fulfil the need for an arbiter over their disputes and relationships in the absence of elders from their own community, and in a society where the traditional avenues of justice were heavily weighted in favour of the European creole. Petitions to the Protector and Governor, and verbal depositions before Committees of Enquiry, inevitably had a cathartic role for the Indian immigrants, in the same way that the *cahiers de doléances* (petitions sent from the regions to complain of local problems during the early days of the French Revolution) helped to crystallize grievances at the onset of the French Revolution. The study of petitions is important, because of the opportunity they offer to visualize immigrants not as objects of analysis by colonial officials but as individuals articulating fears, disappointments and expectations in their own manner and idiom.

The letters between immigrants and their relatives represent an even more tangible link to the feelings and aspirations of those participants in the indenture system. Their significance goes well beyond their prosaic, even banal contents. Karen Blixen's perceptive account of the Kikuyu's attitude to the written word has deep resonance for the world of the indentured Indian:

> As I opened and studied one letter after another, I wondered at the insignificance of the contents. It was the common mistake of a prejudiced civilised person. You might as well have set to herborize the little olive branch that Noah's dove brought home. Whatever it looked like, it carried more weight than all the ark with the animals in it; it contained a new green world.

She writes of the Kikuyu's utter faith in the power of the pen, and her depiction of Jugona carrying his worthless land claim and almost driven mad because his faith in its veracity is shaken has its parallel in the sad case of Moorly with his unverifiable land document (see p.209). If the Afro-Creoles in Mauritius failed to enter contracts because they were afraid to touch the pen and, so they thought, sign their lives away, the Indians believed that the resort to the professional letter writer was the surest way to right misdeeds. Blixen's description of the literate individuals who wrote letters for the Kikuyu and put their own idiosyncrasies into them is also clearly paralleled in the varying tone and content of the letters and petitions written for indentured Indians.[1]

The voice of the Indian was mediated by the men who transcribed depositions, by those who wrote petitions (such as Vellyvoil Rajarethnum Moodeliar), and by those who translated letters. However, those letters written between migrants and their families, particularly in the vernacular languages, are perhaps the closest the historian can approach to the world of indenture, and serve to throw light on features of indenture which are neglected in the traditional historiography. For example, the letters of the Narayens (see p.212) reveal the extent to which indentured labourers themselves harnessed the processes of migration to Mauritius for their own ends. Return migrants took on the roles of commercial recruiters and labour supervisors, but they also played a part in the dissemination of information to would-be migrants, and in the retention of links between families at home and overseas. Indentured labourers trusted returnees with remittances for their families, and in general they were involved in a wide range of activities which operated outside, or parallel to, the official functions of the Protector's office. Thus the migrants found a variety of ways to contest the hegemonic ordering of the indenture process. The fact that these contestations might be small-scale and obscure makes them no less important, as Scott, Haynes and Prakash have emphasized.[2] In order to understand the dynamics of Indian migration better, therefore, we need to find further evidence of these activities of indentured and time-expired migrants.

Letters between migrants and their families were rarely written without some discussion of money, and often came into being simply as a result of a need for funds on the part of the relative left behind, or to record a remittance made by the migrant. Nevertheless, the analysis of such letters often enables us to assess far more than the flow of capital between Mauritius and India. The social and economic background of writers and relatives is often revealed, whilst individual motives for and expectations from emigration emerge from the remarks of indentured labourers. The remittances themselves were symbolic as well, reminding relatives of links and maintaining some claim on the natal home, a function that may well have been more important than the actual sums involved. The changing pattern of knowledge about the colonies to which Indians emigrated can also be charted from the letters, providing an invaluable perspective from which to view the evolution of the diaspora, and a counter to the frequently ahistorical approach of uncritical commentaries based on more traditional sources.[3] The harshness of separation is also sharply underlined in the letters; relatives in India are not uniformly playing the role of helpless dependents, but attempt in many examples given here to secure the return of migrants by paying sums of money to the local agent sufficient to defray the return passage. However, as the cases of Peary Ghose (see p.173) and others show, migrants were in many cases unwilling or unable to return as requested.

The correspondence and oral or written depositions of individual migrants do not in themselves confirm or deny the conflicting historical appraisals of the system. However, the evidence contained within them does provide a significant contrast to previous works on indenture, which have principally utilized official records, and which therefore discuss the actions and reactions of migrants only through the medium of colonial reports or observers' accounts. Inaccuracies of representation are an ever-present danger in the use of such sources, as historians can all too easily become complicit in the discourses and epistemologies employed by the colonizers to describe the colonized. In this study, an attempt has been made to show that the documents through which recruits describe the meaning of indenture in their own terms not only make compelling reading, but provide new and important insights into the indenture experience.

This work has attempted nevertheless to reappraise the enduring stereotypes prevalent in the literature on indentured migration, through the use of 'subaltern' rather than official sources. Previous studies have rightly stressed the difficult working conditions and harsh legislation imposed on Indian migrants, producing labour-management methods and treatment little different from those endured by the slaves they followed onto the plantations. Many of the depositions and petitions presented here confirm existing appraisals of treatment meted out to indentured workers. By emphasizing the neo-slave living standards of post-abolition immigrants, however, scholars have tended to neglect other features of the indenture experience which distinguish it from the servile institution it replaced.

The historical literature has tended generally to stress the similarities rather than the differences between slavery and indenture.[4] As the preceding chapters have shown, the working conditions of Indian immigrants, and the instruments of labour coercion used by the state, certainly acted to place Indians in a servile relationship to their employers. However, the natal alienation which is a core feature of slave diasporas has not the same force in assessments of the indenture migrations. Indians were not necessarily or generally cut off from their ancestral villages or from their regional cultures, because there were better means of communication through the British postal and remittance systems, and because returnees could act as transmitters of information and money. The networks which developed through such channels were very important to the indentured Indians and their relatives at home, and reunited many families. However, if migrants failed to contact those left behind in India, or inform them of their intended destination and whereabouts, relatives could wait decades for news. Shame at their situation and the inability to send money home were factors which prevented indentured labourers from contacting their families in India. The letters which passed between diaspora Indians and their kinfolk usually concerned the overriding economic issues which had given rise to the separations in the first place, but for those desperate for news, money matters became a secondary issue – perhaps it had never been uppermost – and the urgent epistles make for emotive reading. The correspondence thus provides insights into the indenture experience and the extent of contacts with India which the official sources hardly even hint at; and by its very existence, the correspondence between overseas Indians and their relatives in India emphasizes the gulf between the slave and indenture diasporas. The maintenance of contacts with home, however limited, defined and shaped the Indian overseas experience, bringing it closer to that of the European labour migrant, since both shared a 'myth of return' and a dream of eventual reconciliation with relatives and friends. The letters cited in this volume reveal these dreams to be an important preoccupation of migrants throughout the period considered, hopes which, however unrealistic they may have been, cannot readily be dismissed.[5]

The dominant preoccupations of Indian letter writers, like their European counterparts, were with relatives, remittances and enrichment. Much of the discussion in the letters concerns money sent home, which could assist in collective debt repayments, in the organization of family functions such as weddings, or as part of a grand schema aimed at eventual family settlement overseas. The numerous examples available of letters written by European migrants have helped to enrich the relevant academic literature. It is to be hoped that by using similar sources, and by use of oral materials, students of non-European migrations may also be able to depict the participants in those diasporas as three-dimensional beings rather than as simply the passive victims of wider economic forces. An important conclusion of this study is that the analysis of the verbal and written statements of indentured Indians can help redefine the diaspora as having more than one rationale and result, depending on the participants' position and perspective. Thus for some migrants the indenture contract meant merely an unpleasant induction to a process of resettlement in the face of adverse socio-economic conditions at home, whilst for employers it could represent a successful experiment in labour coercion. Others still amongst the migrants might rationalize their experience in different ways, choosing to see something more positive in the experience, unrealistic as this may have been. Officials may also occasionally be found who were stricken with a moral or racial conscience, and considered the treatment meted out to workers in some way inappropriate or unjust. Without the evidence of subjective accounts, as found in the letters of migrants, such diversities in the representation of shared historical experiences are less easily revealed.

The documents reproduced in this volume represent only a fragment of the verbal and written output of the indentured Indians. Many letters must be in private hands, heirlooms of a migrant ancestry alongside the brass lotahs, wooden chests and religious texts which are still to be found in the homes of overseas Indians. When these sources are further tapped, more of the rich history of the Asian diaspora will be available to the student of Empire and of the revolution in human settlement which it engendered, and our search for the experience of indenture outside the official mind will be extended. The repercussions of those population transfers are still being felt today in the struggles of overseas Indians to articulate a distinctive identity within their respective communities. The recolonization of their history is an important part of this process.

Notes

1. These and related issues have been addressed in detail by European and Indian historians. See, for example, Skaria (forthcoming). Skaria has commented that 'the notion of writing as a weapon of the dominant is ... often a crucial element in the experience of subaltern groups'. As he points out, this can cause subalterns to place enormous faith in the power of words written on their behalf. At the same time the literate may be regarded with suspicion, and those in open rebellion will often burn or destroy written or printed pages, such as court records, whenever they can lay hands on them.
2. See Scott, 1985; Haynes and G. Prakash, 1991: 1–24, 290–307.
3. The official nature of some source material obviously need not necessarily render conclusions based upon it invalid (as Dharma Kumar has pointed out), although the problematics of its use have been underrated in the past. See Kumar, 1995: preface.
4. Samaroo, 1987b.
5. Breman and Daniel have suggested that hopes of returning to India were reified and employed by plantation owners and colonial officials, in a myth of the 'nostalgic peasant', to justify continuing use of the short-term indenture contract. To some extent, and in some colonies, this might be true, but the letters cited here reveal the enduring strength of such emotions. Even when, as in the Mauritian instance, the vast majority of migrants were offered inducements to stay on after the expiration of their contracts, at least one in three returned to India: the evidence suggests this

cannot solely be attributed to dissatisfaction with their conditions of work. See Daniel *et al.*, 1992.

APPENDIX A

Migration to selected colonies from Indian Presidencies, 1842–70

To	From	Men	Women	Children
Mauritius	Calcutta	148,669	35,650	24,496
	Madras	72,230	22,066	16,529
	Bombay	22,954	5,743	3,064
British Guiana	Calcutta	46,081	14,497	7,654
	Madras	7,242	2,486	1,731
Trinidad	Calcutta	25,059	8,023	4,445
	Madras	2,971	1,257	764
Jamaica	Calcutta	8,180	2,671	1,526
	Madras	1,842	562	388
Natal	Calcutta	695	194	122
	Madras	3,421	1,269	747
Reunion	Calcutta	6,076	1,359	680
	Madras	1,410	491	230
	French ports	3,265	1,089	405

Source: Geoghegan Report, p.66.

APPENDIX B

Numbers of remigrants arriving in Mauritius, 1865

Key
M = men
W = women
B = boys
G = girls

Cal = Calcutta
Mad = Madras
Bom = Bombay

No. = Number
Pres. = Presidency (India)

Ship name	Ship no.	Pres.	Previous migration	M	W	B	G
Atiet Rohoman	1102	Cal	Mauritius	7	5		
Theresa	1103	Mad	Mauritius	9	9	1	
			Reunion	3	1	2	
			Ceylon	18	1		
			Martinique		1		
Orient	1104	Cal	Mauritius	20	5	1	1
			Cachar	21			
Eranee	1105	Cal	Mauritius	4			
			Cachar	18	3		
Porchester	1106	Mad	Mauritius	7	7	3	1
			Reunion	3	2	2	2
			Penang	3			
			Singapore	2			
			Martinique	1			
Arabstan	1107	Cal	Mauritius	12	8	2	
			Cachar	7			
Shah Jehan	1108	Cal	Cachar	2			
			Demerara	2			
			Mauritius	16	3		
Ophir	1109	Cal	Mauritius	10	6		
			Cachar	6	6		
Allum Ghier	1110	Cal	Mauritius	7	4		
			Burma	2			
			Cachar	8			
Shaw Alum	1111	Cal	Mauritius	9	1		
Blackwall	1112	Mad	Mauritius	16	4		
			Reunion	3			
			Rangoon	5			
			Singapore	1			
			Ceylon	9			
Regina	1113	Bom	Mauritius	7	6	4	
			Rangoon	1			
Fathe Salam	1114	Cal	Mauritius	9	2		

Ship	No.	Depot	Place				
			Cachar	6			
			West Indies	1			
			Rangoon	1			
Colgrain	1115	Cal	Mauritius	16	5	3	1
			Cachar	10			
Nimrod	1116	Cal	Mauritius	14	2		1
			Cachar	3			
			Rangoon	2			
			China	1			
Gunga	1117	Cal	(Not stated)	18	1		
John Masterman	1118	Cal	Mauritius	9	1		
			Demerara	1			
Indomitable	1119	Cal	Mauritius	11	1		
Agra	1120	Cal	Mauritius	9	2		
Bhima	1121	Cal	Mauritius	10	8		
			Cachar	2			
Tarquin	1122	Mad	Mauritius	20	14	5	6
			Reunion	4	4	3	4
			Moulmein	1			
			Ceylon	10			
Solway	1123	Cal	Mauritius	19	2	1	
Far East	1124	Cal	Mauritius	20	5	3	
			Demerara	1			
Scindian	1125	Mad	Mauritius	15	5	2	
			Bourbon	4			
			Martinique	1			
Canning	1126	Cal	Mauritius	5	2		
			Ceylon	1			
			Cachar	1			
Matilda Atheling	1127	Cal	Mauritius	11	3		
Arabstan	1128	Cal	Mauritius	11	3		
Sebastopol	1129	?	Mauritius	15	1	1	
St Hilda	1130	Cal	Mauritius	9			
			Demerara	1			
C. Coventry	1131	Bom	Mauritius	12	8	1	
Clara	1132	Mad	Mauritius	9	1		2
			Singapore	4			
			Burma	2			
			West Indies	1			
			Reunion	3			

Source: CO 167/480–2

APPENDIX C

The petition of the old immigrants of Mauritius

Presented on the 6th June, 1871.
To his Excellency the Honourable Sir Arthur Hamilton Gordon, K.C.M.G., Governor and Commander-in-Chief in and over the Island of Mauritius and its Dependencies.

The petition of the undersigned Indian Immigrants.

Humbly Sheweth:

That your Petitioners suffer many and great grievances from the existing Laws by which they are deprived of that freedom which all other inhabitants of Mauritius enjoy.

Your Petitioners are required to have and always carry with them a ticket with their photograph and a police pass. Though these are supplied to them free of charge on the expiration to their five years' term of engaged service, yet if they are lost, as frequently happens through being obliged always to carry them about, your petitioners are required immediately to apply for others, for which they must pay five dollars for the ticket, and for the photograph two shillings, making together twenty-two shillings, a sum nearly equal to two months' wages on an estate. To procure one of these papers some of your petitioners have had to wait many days, and to walk from a hundred to hundred and fifty miles; when, at the Immigration office, they have make the slightest remonstrance, they have been beaten with rattans. If found without either of the above papers they are taken to the Police Station and locked up until they can be brought before the magistrate; if arrested on Friday in a district where the magistrates do not sit on Saturday, they are imprisoned until the following Monday morning. It may be that their wife or some friend brings them their papers which they had forgotten at home, but this will not procure their release until Monday.

Your Petitioners cannot read their papers, which are written in English, and it often happens that on account of some error which they cannot verify they are lodged in prison just the same as if they had neglected to have their papers changed in time, or had the misfortune to lose them.

Some of your Petitioners who had their papers in order for the district in which they resided, have been committed to prison with hard labour, because the police were mistaken as to the boundaries of the district in which they really lived, and supposed them to be living in another; others have been taken to prison because the estate on which they were tenants had changed hands, and a discrepancy had thus arisen in their police passes.

If one of your Petitioners loses his papers and has not sufficient money (twenty-two shillings) to pay for others, he gets a pass from the Immigration Office authorising him to

238

remain absent eight days; but he may not work as a day labourer, for which he would have to obtain a license costing five dollars, he must find some one who will employ him continuously; but unsuccessful at the expiration of the eight days, his pass may perhaps be extended, or he may be sent to work at the Vagrant Depot until an engagement is found for him; there he dare not venture to refuse to engage for whatever period and on whatever terms are proposed to him.

If one of your Petitioners leaves his employ, he must present himself at the Central Police Station of this district within eight days to have his pass put in order; he may be obliged to come two or three days in succession, and in the meantime, the eight days may be exceeded and he be afterwards arrested and sentenced to hard labour as a vagabond. A man has been lying sick with fever, and has therefore been unable to go for his pass, and in spite of evidence to this effect, when on recovery he went for his pass, has been condemned to imprisonment with hard labour as a vagabond.

When one of your Petitioners wishes to go into any other district than the one for which he has a police pass, he must get his pass endorsed, which can be done only by the Inspector of Police, who is at the Station only a small part of the day; your Petitioners have friends and relatives in the Island, and it may be that one of them hears that a brother, sister, or son is dangerously ill, and has sent for him, yet, if he goes into any other district without having his pass endorsed, he will probably be arrested and sentenced to hard labour as a vagabond.

Many of your Petitioners are sellers of vegetables and carry baskets of produce to the market every morning; they have their passes endorsed for the district of Port Louis for three months. They seldom get to town without being stopped by a policeman and having their passes examined, perhaps on an average, three times during the double journey; they must wait until the policeman chooses to give them back their pass, and frequently lose their market in consequence.

Your Petitioners are thus at the mercy of the police, and the most industrious and best-conducted man amongst them cannot stir but by their sufferance. An old immigrant may be honestly maintaining his wife and family, sending his children to school, be possessed of some little property, and carefully endeavour to observe all the laws and ordinances, yet, if by some mischance he loses his papers, he may be, and often is, condemned indiscriminately with a number of others, all charged on the same sheet, to imprisonment with hard labour as a vagabond.

The police can always arrest them; they do so by fifties at a time, and if it should prove to have been without any reason, they have no redress. They humbly beg your Excellency to consider what use a policeman, who was unscrupulous, would make of this power over them which the law gives him.

Your Petitioners implore your Excellency's humane protection, and humbly beg your Excellency to cause the laws which oppress them to be repealed; and this they ask with greater confidence, since it is shown by the instructions accompanying your Excellency's Commission, that Her Most Gracious Majesty the Queen of Great Britain and Ireland, whose subjects they are, is unwilling that assent should be given to her name to 'any Ordinance whereby persons not of European birth or descent may be subjected or made liable to any disabilities or restrictions to which persons of European birth or descent are not also subjected or made liable'.

And your Petitioners as in duty bound will ever pray.

Here follow nine thousand four hundred and one signatures.

Source: CO 167/529 Gordon to Kimberley, 17 Nov. 1871

Bibliography

PRIMARY SOURCES

Public Record Office, London, UK

CO 167 Correspondence, Government of Mauritius
CO 172 Blue Books and Administration Reports (Mauritius)

India Office Library and Records, London, UK

Manuscript Sources

Bengal Public Proceedings
Madras Public Proceedings
Bombay Public Proceedings
Indian Public Proceedings

Printed Sources

Bengal Emigration Proceedings
Indian Emigration Proceedings
G.Grierson (1883) Report on Colonial Emigration from the Bengal Presidency (1882) Report of Major Pitcher on Emigration in North West Provinces and Oudh.
Sannyasi and Chaturvedi (1931) A Report on the Emigrants Repatriated to India under the Assisted Emigration Scheme from South Africa and on the Problems of Returned Emigrants from all Colonies, Calcutta.

National Archives of Mauritius, Coromandel, Mauritius

PA Series Immigration Department Incoming Correspondence
PB Series Immigration Department Outgoing Correspondence
RA Series Secretariat Records
Z Series Departmental Records

Mahatma Gandhi Institute Immigration Archive, Moka, Mauritius

PC Series Immigrant Certificates
PE Series Immigrant Lists of Arrivals
PG Series Immigrants' Photographs
PL Series Correspondence and Departmental Records

Secondary Sources

Adamson, A.H. (1972) *Sugar Without Slaves: The Political Economy in British Guiana, 1838–1904*, Yale University Press, New Haven, NJ.

Anat, A. (1977) *Lal Pasina*, Rajkamal Prakashan Private Ltd, New Delhi.

Arya, U. (1968) *Ritual Songs and Folksongs of the Hindus of Surinam*, Leiden University, Leiden.

Baines, D. (1991) *Emigration from Europe 1815–1939*, Macmillan, London.

Bates, C. and Carter, M. (1992) 'Tribal Migration in India and Beyond', in *The World of the Rural Labourer in Colonial India*, ed. G. Prakash, Oxford University Press, Delhi.

Bates, C. and Carter, M. (1993) 'Tribal and Indentured Migrants in Colonial India: Modes of Recruitment and Forms of Incorporation', in *Dalit Movements and the Meanings of Labour in India*, ed. P. Robb, Oxford University Press, Delhi.

Beall, J. (1991) 'Women under Indenture in Natal', in Bhana, 1991b.

Bhana, S. (1991a) *Indentured Indian Emigrants to Natal, 1860–1902*, Promilla & Co., Delhi.

Bhana, S. ed. (1991b) *Essays on Indentured Indians in Natal*, Peepal Tree Press, Leeds.

Bhana, S. and Bhana, A. (1991) 'An Exploration of the Psycho-Historical Circumstances Surrounding Suicide Among Indentured Indians, 1875–1911', in Bhana, 1991b.

Bissoondoyal, U. and Servansing, S.B.C. (1986) *Indian Labour Immigration*, MGI, Moka, Mauritius.

Bolt, C. (1971) *Victorian Attitudes to Race*, Routledge & Kegan Paul, London.

Brain, J. (1983) *Christian Indians in Natal 1860–1911*, Oxford University Press, Capetown.

Breman, J. (1989) *Taming the Coolie Beast*, Oxford University Press, Delhi.

Bruce, Sir C. (1910) *The Broad Stone of Empire*, vols 1 and 2, Macmillan, London.

Callikan-Proag, A. (1984) 'La Representation des Immigrants Indiens dans Le Cerneen', in U. Bissoondoyal, *Indians Overseas: The Mauritian Experience*, MGI, Moka, Mauritius.

Carter, M. (1992a) 'Strategies of Labour Mobilisation in Colonial India: The Recruitment of Indentured Workers for Mauritius', in Daniel *et al.* 1992.

Carter, M. (1992b) 'The Family Under Indenture: A Mauritian Case Study', *Journal of Mauritian Studies*, vol. 4, no. 1.

Carter, M. (1994) *Lakshmi's Legacy: Testimonies of Indian Women in Mauritius*, EOI. Stanley, Rose-Hill, Mauritius.

Carter, M. (1995) *Servants, Sirdars and Settlers: Indians in Mauritius, 1834–1874*, Oxford University Press, Delhi.

Chakrabarty, D. (1989) *Rethinking Working Class History*, Princeton University Press.

Chandavarkar, R. (1994) *The Origins of Industrial Capitalism*, Cambridge University Press, Delhi.

Chatterjee, S. and Das Gupta, R. (1981) 'Tea Labour in Assam: Recruitment and Government Policy, 1840–80', *Economic and Political Weekly*, vol. xvi.

Clark, P. and Souden, D. eds (1987) *Migration and Society in Early Modern England*. Hutchinson Education, London.

Clarke, C. *et al.* (1990) *South Asians Overseas: Migration and Ethnicity*, Cambridge University Press, Cambridge.

Cohn, B.S. (1985) 'The Command of Language and the Language of Command', *Subaltern Studies IV: Writings on South Asian History and Society*, ed. R. Guha, Oxford University Press, Delhi.

Cooper, F. (1992) 'Colonizing time: work rhythms and labor conflict in colonial Mombasa', in *Colonialism and Culture*, by N. Dirks, The University of Michigan Press, Ann Arbor.

Crisp, J. (1984) *The Story of an African Working Class: Ghanaian Miners' Struggles 1870–1980*, Zed Books, London.

Dabydeen, D. and Samaroo B. eds (1987) *India in the Caribbean*, Hansib, London.

Daniel, V., Bernstein, H. and Brass, T. eds (1992) *Plantations, Proletarians and Peasants in Colonial Asia*, Frank Cass, London.

Eltis, D. (1983) 'Free and Coerced Transatlantic Migrations: Some Comparisons', *American Historical Review*, vol. 88.

Elwin, V. (1946) *Folksongs of Chattisgarh*, Oxford University Press, London.

Elwin, V. and Hivale, S. (1935) *Songs of the Forest: the folk poetry of the worlds*, Allen and Unwin, London.

Emmer, P.C. (1984) 'The Importation of British Indians into Surinam, 1873–1916', in Marks and Richardson, 1984.

Emmer, P.C. (1986a) 'The Great Escape: The Migration of Female Indentured Servants from British India to Surinam, 1873– 1916', in *Abolition and its Aftermath*, ed. D. Richardson, Frank Cass, London.

Emmer, P.C. (1986b) 'The Meek Hindu: The Recruitment of Indian Labourers for Service Overseas, 1870–1916', in Emmer, 1986c.

Emmer, P.C. ed. (1986c) *Colonialism and Migration; Indentured Labour before and after Slavery*, Martinus Niejhof Press, the Netherlands.

Emmer, P.C. (1993) 'Intercontinental migration as a world historical process', *European Review*.

Equiano, O. (1967) *The Interesting Narrative of Olaudah Equiano, or Gustavus Vassa the African, Written by Himself*, ed. P. Edwards, London (first edition 1769). Heinemann, London.

Erickson, C. (1972) *Invisible Immigrants: The Adaptation of English and Scottish Immigrants in 19th-century America*, London School of Economics and Political Science, Weidenfeld and Nicolson, London.

Galanter, M. (1990) *Law and Society in Modern India*, Oxford University Press, Delhi.

Gambhir, S.K. (1986) 'Mauritian Bhojpuri – An International Perspective on Historical and Sociolinguistic Processors', in Bissoondoyal and Servansing, 1986.

Gillion, K.L. (1962) *Fiji's Indian Migrants*, Oxford University Press, London.

Ginwala, F. (1976) 'Class Consciousness and Control: Indian South Africans, 1860–1946', DPhil thesis, Oxford.

Graves, A. (1984) 'The nature and origins of Pacific islands' labour migration to Queensland, 1863–1906', in Marks and Richardson, 1984.

Guha, R. ed. (1984) *Subaltern Studies I*, Oxford University Press, Delhi.

Gupta, A. ed. (1971) *Indians Abroad: Asia and Africa*, Orient Longmans, Delhi.

Haraksingh, K. (1987) 'Control and Resistance among Indian Workers: A Study of Labour on the Sugar Plantations of Trinidad 1875–1917', in Dabydeen and Samaroo, 1987.

Haynes D. and Prakash W., eds (1991) *Contesting Power*, Oxford University Press, Delhi.

Hira, S. (1987) 'The Evolution of the Social, Economic and Political Position of the East Indians in Surinam, 1873–1980', in Dabydeen and Samaroo, 1987.

Hitchens, F.H. (1931) *The Colonial Land and Emigration Commission*, University of Pennsylvania Press, Philadelphia.

Hu-De Hart, E. (1993) 'Chinese Coolie Labour in Cuba in the Nineteenth Century: Free Labour or Neoslavery?', in *The Wages of Slavery: From Chattel Slavery to Wage Labour in Africa, the Caribbean and England*, ed. M. Twaddle, Frank Cass, London.

Jain, R.K. (1993) *Indian Communities Abroad: Themes and Literature*, Manohar, Delhi.

Kalla, C. (1987) 'The Gujarati Merchants in Mauritius c. 1850–1900', *Journal of Mauritian Studies*, vol. 2, no. 1.

Kelly, J. (1991) *A Politics of Virtue*, Chicago University Press, Chicago.

Kelly, J. (1992) 'Coolie as a Labour Commodity: Race, Sex, and European Dignity in Colonial Fiji', in Daniel *et al.*, 1992.

Kumar, D. (1995) *Land and Caste in South India*, reprint, Oxford University Press, Delhi.

Lal, B.V. (1980) 'Approaches to the Study of Indian Indentured Emigration with Special Reference to Fiji', *Journal of Pacific History*, vol. xv, nos 1–2.

Lal, B.V. (1983) *Girmitiyas: The Origins of the Fiji Indians*, Journal of Pacific History, Australia National University, Canberra.

Lal, B.V. (1985a) 'Kunti's Cry: Indentured Women on Fiji Plantations', *Indian Economic and Social History Review*, no. 1.

Lal, B.V. (1985b) 'Veil of Dishonour: Sexual Jealousy and Suicide on Fiji Plantations', *Journal of Pacific History*, vol. xx, nos 3–4.

Lal, B.V. and Shineberg, B. (1991) 'The Story of the Haunted Line', *Journal of Pacific History*, vol. 26, no. 1.

Laurence, K. (1971) *Immigration into the West Indies in the 19th Century*, Caribbean Universities Press, London.

Mahabir, N. (1985) *The Still Cry: Personal Accounts of East Indians in Trinidad and Tobago during Indentureship (1845–1917)*, Calaloux Publications, Ithaca, N.Y.

Majumdar, D.N. ed. (1946) *Snowballs of Garhwal*, Lucknow University Press, Lucknow, 1946.

Mangru, B. (1987a) *Benevolent Neutrality: Indian Government Policy and Labour Migration to British Guiana 1854–1884*, Hansib, London.

Mangru, B. (1987b) 'The Sex-Ratio Disparity and its Consequences under the Indenture in British Guiana', in Dabydeen and Samaroo, 1987.

Marks, S. and Richardson, P. eds (1984) *International Labour Migration: Historical Perspectives*, Maurice Temple Smith, Hounslow.

McDonald, J. and Shlomowitz, R. (1990) 'Mortality on Immigration Voyages to Australia in the 19th Century', *Explorations in Economic History*, vol. 27.

Mesthrie, R. (1991) 'New Lights from Old Languages: Indian Languages and the Experience of Indentureship in South Africa', in Bhana, 1991b.

Mishra, V. (1979) *Rama's Banishment: A Centenary Tribute to the Fiji Indians 1879–1979*, Heinemann Educational, London.

Mohapatra, P. (1995) 'Restoring the Family: Wife Murders and the Making of a Sexual Contract for Indian Immigrant Labour in the British Caribbean Colonies, 1860–1920', *Studies in History*, New Series, Volume II, No. 2, July–December 1995, pp. 227–60. New Delhi: Sage.

Newbury, C. (1975) 'Labour Migration in the Imperial Phase: An Essay in Interpretation', *Journal of Imperial and Commonwealth History*, vol. iii.

North-Coombes, M.D. (1991) 'Indentured Labour in the Sugar Industries of Natal and Mauritius', in Bhana, 1991b.

O'Hanlon, R. (1994) *A Comparison between Women and Men: Tarabai Shinde and the Critique of Gender Relations in Colonial India*, Oxford University Press, Delhi.

Omvedt, G. (1979–80) 'Migration in Colonial India: The Articulation of Feudalism and Capitalism by the Colonial State', *Journal of Peasant Studies*, no. 7.

Pike, N. (1873) *Sub-tropical Rambles in the Land of the Ahanapteryx*, London.

Prakash, G. (1990) *Bonded Histories: Genealogies of Labor Servitude in Colonial India*, Cambridge University Press, Cambridge.

Prakash, G. (1992) *The World of the Rural Labourer in Colonial India*, Oxford University Press, London.

Ramasamy, P. (1992) 'Labour Control and Labour Resistance in the Plantations of Colonial Malaya', in Daniel *et al.*, 1992.

Ramnarine, T. (1987) 'Over a Hundred Years of East Indian Disturbances on the Sugar Estates of Guyana 1869–1978: An Historical Overview', in Dabydeen and Samaroo, 1987.

Reddi, S. (1986) 'Vellyvoil Rajarethnum Moodeliar: An Indian Nationalist in Mauritius (1865–1876)', *Journal of Mauritian Studies*, vol. 1, no. 1.

Reddock, R. (1985) 'Freedom Denied: Indian Women and Indentureship in Trinidad and Tobago, 1845–1917', *Economic and Political Weekly*, vol. xx, no. 43.

Reynolds, L. (1935) *The British Immigrant*, Oxford University Press, Oxford.

Richardson, D., ed. (1985) *Abolition and its Aftermath: The Historical Context, 1790–1916*, Frank Cass, London.

Rodney, W. (1981) 'Guyana: The Making of the Labour Force', *Race and Class*, vol. xxii, no. 4.

Saha, P. (1970) *Emigration of Indian Labour*, People's Publishing House, Delhi.

Salinger, S.V. (1987) *Labor and Indentured Servants in Pennsylvania*, Cambridge University Press, Cambridge.

Salleh, H. (1990) 'Labour Control in Colonial Plantations in Malaya', unpublished paper, Amsterdam.

Samaroo, B. (1987a) 'The Indian Connection: The Influence of Indian Thought and Ideas on East Indians in the Caribbean', in Dabydeen and Samaroo, 1987.

Samaroo, B. (1987b) 'Two Abolitions: African Slavery and East Indian Indentureship', in Dabydeen and Samaroo, 1987.

Sandesh, (1990) 'Our Surviving Indian Immigrants', *Sandesh*, 25 May.

Saunders, K. (1982) *Workers in Bondage: The Origins and Bases of Unfree Labour in Queensland 1824–1916*, University of Queensland Press, St Lucia.

Saunders, K. (1984) *Indentured Labour in the British Empire, 1834–1920*, Croom Helm, London.

Schrier, A. (1959) *Ireland and the American Emigration, 1850–1900*, University of Minnesota Press, Minneapolis.

Scott, J.C. (1985) *Weapons of the Weak: Everyday Forms of Peasant Resistance*, Yale University Press, New Haven, NJ.

Scribner, R.W. (1987) *Popular Culture and Popular Movements in Reformation Germany*, Hambledon, London.

Seesaram, R.B. (1991) 'An indentured Indian family's Experience', *Oral and Pictorial Records Programme Newsletter*.

Semmingsen, I. (1978) *Norway to America: A History of the Migration*, University of Minnesota Press, Minneapolis.

Shlomowitz, R. (1986) 'Infant mortality and Fiji's Indian Migrants, 1879–1919', *Indian Economic and Social History Review*, vol. 23, no. 3.

Shlomowitz, R. (1990) 'Differential Mortality of Asians and Pacific Islanders in the Pacific Labour Trade', *Journal of the Australian Population Association*, vol. 7, no. 2.

Shlomowitz, R. and Brennan, L. (1990) 'Mortality and Migrant Labour in Assam, 1865–1921', *Indian Economic and Social History Review*, vol. 27, no. 1.

Shlomowitz, R. and McDonald, J. (1990) 'Mortality of Indian Labour on Ocean Voyages, 1843–1917', *Studies in History*, vol. 6, no. 1.

Skaria, A. (forthcoming) 'Writing, Orality and Power in the Dangs, Western India, 1800–1920s', in *Subaltern Studies*, Oxford University Press, Delhi.

Swan, M. (1991) 'Indentured Indians: Accommodation and Resistance, 1890–1913', in Bhana, 1991b.

Thomas, W.I. and Znaniecki, F. (1920/1984) *The Polish Peasant in Europe and America*, Chicago, 2 vols; abridged edition, University of Illinois Press, Urbana.

Thompson, E.P. (1967) 'Time, Work Discipline and Industrial Capitalism' *Past and Present*, vol. 38.

Tinker, H. (1974) *A New System of Slavery*, Oxford University Press, Oxford.

Tinker, H. (1977) *The Banyan Tree: Overseas Emigrants from India, Pakistan and Bangladesh*, Oxford University Press, Delhi.

Uttar Pradesh Ke Lak Geet, (1971) Lucknow.

van Onselen, C. (1980) *Chibaro: African Mine Labour in Southern Rhodesia*, Pluto Press, London.

Vatuk, V.P. (1964) 'Protest Songs of East Indians in British Guiana', *Journal of American Folklore*, vol. LXXVII.

Washbrook, D. (1993) 'Land and Labour in Late Eighteenth Century South India: The Golden Age of the Pariah?', in Robb, ed.

Wilson, J. (1987) 'Some Glimpses of Hinduism in Fiji', unpublished conference paper, Oxford.

Yamin, G. (1989) 'The Character and Origins of Labour Migration from Ratnagiri District 1840–1920', *South Asia Research*, vol. 9, no. 1.

Index